P9-EME-584

French Taste

HarperCollinsPublishersLtd

French Taste

ELEGANT EVERYDAY EATING

Laura Calder

French Taste

Published by HarperCollins Publishers Ltd

Originally published in a hardcover edition by HarperCollins Publishers Ltd: 2009
This trade paperback edition: 2010

HarperCollins Publishers Ltd
2 Bloor Street East, 20th Floor
Toronto, Ontario, Canada
M4W 1A8

www.harpercollins.ca

Library and Archives Canada Cataloguing in Publication information is available

ISBN: 978-1-55468-102-0

PP 9 8 7 6 5 4 3 2 1

Printed and bound in China

Photographs by James Ingram
Food and props styling by Patti Hetherington
Design by Sharon Kish

I dedicate this book, with much love, to my parents,
John and Doris Calder, for giving me an appreciation
for good food from the very beginning and for
always supporting my dreams, however wild.

I also dedicate the book to my early mentors
Anne Willan and her husband, Mark Cherniavsky,
for opening the door to France for me.

Contents

Introduction

To me, the most important thing to take away from the French when it comes to food (if not everything else) is their passion for pleasure. That's why this book is more a French approach to food than it is a crash course in French cuisine. The key to what makes French food extraordinary (and arguably what enabled the cuisine to emerge and flourish in the first place) is the way the French come at it, which is from the point of view that pleasure is not merely a nicety in life but a necessity. Putting pleasure first means that we shop better, we cook better, we eat better, and, by extension, we live and love better. In France, this is fundamental, so the rest of us should feel just fine about keeping pleasure at the forefront, too, when we cook French style.

I also believe that we should borrow from French cooking only as much as we want, and not feel pressured to take on more than makes sense for where we live and for the way we live. In other words, there's no need to commit to mastering the entire canon of French cuisine just to make *mousse au chocolat* or a *steak au poivre.* We come from other proud culinary traditions, and we should be relaxed about slipping elements of French cooking into what we already know – just like making space for another welcome guest at our table. For example, French flavors work perfectly with English and Italian dishes in the same menu. I love the idea of *coq au vin* followed by my grandmother's gingerbread or by tiramisù. Why not? A French main course doesn't dictate that we must start with a foie gras terrine and end with Grand Marnier soufflé. The French aren't that purist themselves!

What they are fanatical about – and I am too – is starting with good-quality ingredients. This is fundamental no matter what kind of food you want to cook. You can't cook well if you haven't shopped well first. The good news is that if you have shopped well, you're already on the home stretch before you've even tied on an apron.

The other trick is to present everything you cook as beautifully as you can. The French are masters at creating an allure around the table, and the result is always irresistible: everyone gets excited about dinner and participates in making an event of it, even when it's just weeknight dining at home. Look after the sensuous aspects of food and, it seems, the social side happily follows.

As you can see, my love affair with French food goes beyond recipes. Delight in discovering beautiful ingredients, the joy of making a mess in the kitchen, a passion for style, and the lingering pleasures of a lively table – this is the stuff that makes great French recipes worthwhile.

A FEW THOUGHTS ABOUT RECIPES

This collection of recipes is the result of several years of gathering, testing, and tweaking. As I pulled it all together for the book, I was reminded more than ever how recipes and our way of cooking them and appreciating them constantly evolve. Recipes aren't static, and they can't be. Even when we write them down or print them out in an attempt to say, "There. Stay put!" they'll slip out of our grip and mutate into something new every time we make them. Really, a printed recipe is no different from a photograph of a person, snapped off guard at a specific moment in time. I see that as a good thing, because it means that every time I cook a dish, even if I've made it a hundred times before, it will have something new to tell me about itself, about the day I'm having, about what I'm hungry for in the broadest possible sense. Food has that way of pointing away from itself and back at us: that's why I find it interesting.

You'll notice I have a fairly minimalist recipe-writing style. Personally, when a recipe offers too much information, I find it more confusing than it needs to be and I get scared off. Besides, French cooking in particular has so often been presented in a highly detailed way that I thought a lighter approach would be refreshing. That's why this book is not made up of cooking lessons; it's more geared toward getting dinner on the table in a relaxed and cheerful way – and in a way that leaves us enthusiastic about eating it, rather than ready to fling ourselves off the nearest balcony. That's the intent of the simple recipe style, at least.

One last point I want to add is that we often have to make recipes more than once to get the hang of them. I have made all of the recipes in this book many times, trying to figure out their quirks, to make sense of the challenges they throw at me, to draw out the best in them. That process isn't going to end for me now, just because the recipes are printed and bound between covers. Next time I make my own *blanquette de veau* (p. 160), for example, I know I'll learn something new about it; just like the next time I talk to a friend I've known for twenty years, I'll learn something new about them, about me, about the goings-on in the big wide world. So, if you try a recipe for the first time but you don't quite think you've got it right, don't give up. Try it again. It's only by making dishes over and over that we learn to understand them, and they become ours.

A note about measurements and ingredients

I give a mix of both imperial and metric measurements in this book. I cook with both, depending on where I am in the world and whether I have scales or measuring cups on hand. Increasingly, I lean toward metric whenever possible, because I usually find it tidier to weigh things (fewer cups to clean) and quicker. But there are days when imperial has its merits, too.

You'll see that I don't give every single conversion for every measurement, because that's not the way people cook. I give the measurement that an average cook, working in either imperial or metric, would use. Since imperial cooks generally use cups for both dry and liquid, I almost always give the imperial volume (1 cup flour or 1 cup milk). Where I give imperial weights, it's because we're dealing with meats, cheese, or vegetables, which are sold that way. For the metric, however, I change depending on whether I'm dealing with weight or volume. Some ingredients are more commonly weighed when cooking in metric (hence, 125 g flour, but 250 mL milk, both of which equal 1 cup). The exception is anything measured in spoonfuls: then I give a volume measure, whether the ingredient is wet or dry. A spoonful is a spoonful, really.

Sometimes, just to keep us all on our toes, I say to use "a generous handful of" or to add an ingredient "to taste." What can I say? I'm not going to tell you how much salt, lemon juice, or chopped parsley you want on your fish – what do I know? So, if I don't give a specific measurement, go ahead and add enough of the ingredient to please your own palate. If it's crucial to a recipe that I be exact, don't worry, I have been.

In case there is any confusion about ingredients, in my vocabulary:

flour = all-purpose flour, unless otherwise indicated
salt = regular fine salt, unless I specify fleur de sel or coarse
pepper = black, out of a grinder, unless otherwise indicated
Parmigiano-Reggiano = not that stuff in the green canister, please
heavy cream = 35%, aka whipping; otherwise I'm specific
butter = butter, not a synthetic substitute. As for unsalted or not, personally I always use salted butter, except in most desserts. So use what you have in the fridge, and adjust the salt in the recipe accordingly.
yogurt, cream cheese, etc., are all full-fat in my world

Happy cooking!

HOW TO EAT

Before we start cooking, we should probably consider how to eat. That is, after all, the goal of all the cooking we're about to launch into. Also, it's relevant to the whole French theme, because where the French have a distinct advantage over the rest of us is not so much because of *what* they eat as *how* they eat. The social and sensuous pleasures of dining in France are inseparable from the basic act of nourishment, so the attitude is that if you haven't enjoyed eating, then you haven't really been fed.

It may be cliché to go on about pleasure, but I do feel it is the secret to living well. (And I say this fully aware that pursuing it is more easily said than done.) At its most basic, the natural human pursuit of pleasure is what makes the body prefer a ripe fruit over a rotten one (a very practical feat of genetic engineering, that). At a higher level of evolution, it's what makes a person bother to stop, sit down at a table, and enjoy a sandwich off a plate with some dignity, rather than rip at one like a bloodhound while simultaneously driving a car through a deluge and phoning the cleaners about the overcoat dropped off last Wednesday. (We all have our desperate moments, fair enough, but you'd have to be a masochist to make a habit of them.)

The trouble is, no matter how antisocial we seem determined to make it these days, eating, along with all the associated values and practices, is cultural. It's easy to eat with relish in France because "everybody's doing it" (and because the country doesn't run on the mind-boggling belief that unnecessary deprivation is somehow a virtue). French dinner parties can easily have seven courses and last five hours, and everyone at the table will eat and drink everything in sight with unbounded glee. (Even fashion types, in my experience!) Elsewhere it's not so easy to maintain a food-loving lifestyle. In North America, for instance, the number of people on special diets is staggering, to the point where it can be difficult to entertain at all because we simply can't cater to everyone's restrictions. Then there's the guilt. How often do we see a woman savor a piece of chocolate cake and say, "Mmm, fabulous!" without adding a comment about how she really shouldn't, how she's going to regret it, how "a moment on the lips . . ."? How did we let ourselves get like this?

Something I'll always be grateful to my mother for is her total lack of interest in weight watching. I grew up with a role model who could polish off ten ears of corn in one sitting and who, afterward, would sit back, smack her lips, and grin. This was apparently an effective antidote to the media messages telling girls we had to be thin to be cute, because, although I paid attention to those, too, they were never powerful enough to overthrow my mother's stance and lure me onto the bandwagon. I always enjoyed three square meals a day and ate pretty much whatever I fancied. I still do.

There are two reasons why this works for me, and I'll tell you in case it ever comes in handy. First, I was brought up with, and continue to cultivate, a taste for high-quality food of the natural variety and for dishes cooked from scratch. The result is that junk food is not temptation. Okay, so I do like the odd potato chip, and for nostalgic reasons I have a soft spot for licorice, but by and large I'm

only interested in the good stuff – a category in which I include butter, baguette, blue cheese, and blackberry tart. In other words, when I say "natural," I'm not just referring to lentils and spinach. My theory is: good food is good food no matter what it is. I don't put chocolate in one category and carrot sticks in another. (Anyway, there is such a thing as seriously bad carrot sticks.) Second, I am realistic about my body: I have a curvy one, and I figure there's no point trying to force it to be anything else. "Normal" may not sell bikinis, but I can tell you one great thing about it: "normal" is relatively easy to maintain.

Look, I don't have any delusions about being the poster girl for good eating, but since there is so much propaganda out there designed to put us off good food, I figure it can't hurt to put a word in for a more cheerful alternative. If you're looking for justification, Virginia Woolf said it: "One cannot think well, love well, sleep well, if one has not dined well." Furthermore, as many others have pointed out, "We are what we eat." Well, who wants to be a hard, dry, low-fat, salt-free biscuit?

My own personal guidelines for good eating:

- As much as possible, buy good, natural ingredients, and cook from scratch.
- Never eat alone if you can avoid it.
- The only other activities to engage in while eating are talking (between bites, that is) and drinking.
- Always eat sitting down.
- Never lay a guilt trip on your appetite.
- Relish every bite.

TIZZA SOUP

Now, after all that, a diet recipe! (Sort of.) This soup was taught to me by an excellent Moroccan cook, Mme Tizza, who serves it to her family once or twice a week for the evening meal. It is all vegetables, but the variety and balance of ingredients make the most startlingly delicious and healthful soup you can imagine. It has a warm golden color and a satisfying thickness, just the thing when your body needs a soothing break from feasting but doesn't want to go as far as fasting. If you've overindulged a bit, eat this for a meal or two and you'll be right back to your fabulous self.

Makes: about 3 quarts (3 L)

1 pound (450 g) potatoes, peeled and chopped
½ pound (225 g) zucchini, chopped
½ pound (225 g) carrots, peeled
1 turnip (not rutabaga)
2 leeks, trimmed, washed and sliced
2 artichoke hearts (not marinated), quartered
2 small tomatoes, chopped
½ celery stalk, chopped
1 cube chicken or vegetable stock
1 tablespoon (15 mL) olive oil
Salt and pepper

Put all the vegetables in a large pot. Add the stock cube, olive oil, and salt and pepper. Add enough water to just cover the vegetables. Bring to the boil, then reduce heat and simmer, uncovered, until all the vegetables are tender, about 30 minutes, depending on the size of the vegetables. Put the mixture through a food mill or blend with an immersion blender. Reheat before serving.

ON PASTRY

We've all had our run-ins with pastry making. I had as many frustrations as anyone until one day I decided to face my demons once and for all. I bought a big bag of flour, countless bricks of butter, and I started in. For days I did nothing but bake tart shells until I figured out where and why I'd been tripping up. So, lucky you, you're off the hook! Just sit back, read on, and take in the tips.

Before I reveal all, let me remind you what total bliss a well-made tart shell is: picture sweet, buttery, crumbling perfection against a creamy lemon-yellow wobble; or recall savory, buttery flakiness mingling in the mouth with caramelized onions and bacon. How far back do those memories go? If you're one of those poor, deprived souls who has succumbed to commercial pie crusts for years and come to imagine they're okay, then you honestly don't know what you're missing. Once you find out, there's no going back.

Now, I'm sure your hopes have been building that I'm going to reveal the secrets of "the best" crust recipe. Sorry. Part of what makes a tart crust perfect, I've found out, is when it's the right crust for the right filling. Therefore, you need more than one in your repertoire. Most of the tart recipes in this book use one of the following three types of dough, each of which is just right for specific uses. (A couple of other dishes require a particular kind of dough, and that is included with the recipe.) All freeze well for a few months, wrapped in plastic and sealed in a freezer bag.

PASTRY FOR GALETTES AND FLAT TARTS

This pastry, like English-style pie crust, contains no egg and is easy to maneuver. The recipe comes from Deborah Madison's *Vegetarian Cooking for Everyone* (one of the great cookbooks of our time), and I use it for any tart that I bake on a baking sheet, without using a tart mold. There are savory tarts using this pastry in the apéritif chapter and sweet versions in the dessert section, so you'll find yourself using this recipe often. For savory galettes, simply omit the sugar and vanilla. If you're using salted butter, omit the salt in the recipe. Finally, know that you can make the recipe in the food processor, if you prefer. Just mix the dry ingredients, then add the wet and pulse only as long as you must for the dough to hold together.

Makes: 2 pastry disks

2¼ cups (300 g) flour
½ teaspoon (2 mL) salt
2 tablespoons (30 mL) sugar (for sweet tarts only)
1 cup (225 g) cold unsalted butter, cut into pieces
⅓ cup (75 mL) ice-cold water
1 teaspoon (5 mL) vanilla (for sweet tarts only)

Put the flour, salt, and sugar (if using) in a large bowl. Add the butter pieces, and pinch with the fingers to create a crumb texture. Make a well in the middle, and pour in the water and vanilla (if using). Quickly work in the flour with your fingers to create a dough. Do not over-mix, as that toughens the dough. Divide into 2 disks, wrap in plastic, and chill at least 15 minutes before rolling out. (See p. 12 for baking instructions.)

PASTRY FOR SWEET AND SAVORY TARTS

This crisp and buttery pastry is perfect for all sorts, from savory quiches to fruit tarts. I got the recipe, which works like a charm, from my friend Jennifer McLagan, author of two very relevant cookbooks, *Bones* and *Fat.* I make it by hand, but Jennifer prefers the food processor. If you're like her, just put the flour, salt, and butter in the processor and pulse to crumbs. Whisk the sugar (if using for the sweet version) into the egg and add, then pulse just long enough for the dough to pull together into a ball.

Makes: 2 pastry disks

2 cups (250 g) flour
Pinch salt
½ cup + 2 tablespoons (150 g) cold unsalted butter, cut into pieces
1 egg
⅓ cup (70 g) sugar (for sweet tarts only)

Mix the flour and salt together in a large bowl. Cut in the butter, and pinch with the fingers to make fine crumbs. Make a well in the middle. Stir together the egg and sugar (if using), and pour into the well. Swiftly mix in with the fingertips until the mixture forms a dough. Do not over-mix, as it toughens the dough. Divide into 2 disks, wrap in plastic, and chill at least an hour before rolling out and lining your tart pan. Chill another 30 minutes before baking. (See p. 12 for baking instructions.)

COOKIE PASTRY

The proper term for this particular pastry is *pâte sablé* (sand pastry), so named because of its crumbly, shortbread-like texture. This is the crust I use for creamy tarts such as chocolate (p. 260), lemon (p. 254), or raspberry (p. 253). A crisp, buttery bite of it crumbling on your tongue alongside any thick, smooth, creamy filling is heaven on earth. (This is the wrong pastry for tarts with whole fruit in them, though, so don't assume it is ubiquitously ideal. For apple or plum tarts, for example, see the recipes on the previous pages.)

As you'll see in the ingredients list, you have the option here of two different amounts of butter. With the lesser quantity, you get a shortbread-like pastry that rolls out cooperatively and is smooth sided and sturdy when baked. With the greater quantity of butter, you get a pastry that falls apart when you try to pick it up, so you have to press it into place and patch it up here and there, but it has a much more delicate crumbliness when baked and tastes richer. I like both versions for their own reasons, so I thought I'd let you decide for yourself which you prefer.

Makes: 1 large pastry disk

1½ cups (185 g) flour
½ cup (110 g) OR ¾ cup (170 g) cold butter, cut into pieces (see above)
¼ cup (55 g) sugar
2 egg yolks
½ teaspoon (2 mL) vanilla (optional)

Mix the flour and butter with your fingers, or in the food processor, until it turns to fine crumbs. Mix in the sugar. Finally, add the egg yolks and vanilla (if using), and mix with the fingers just long enough for it to come together into a ball. Pat into a disk, wrap in plastic, and chill at least 30 minutes or overnight. Roll out and line your tart pan. Chill again for 30 minutes before baking. (See p. 12 for baking instructions.)

HOW TO BLIND BAKE A TART SHELL

Many recipes require that the pastry shell be cooked before the filling goes in, whether or not the tart cooks further with the filling in it. The point is to ensure a crisp crust. When you pour, say, custard into an uncooked pastry shell and bake it, the tart will end up with a soggy bottom; if you pour custard into an already baked shell, then all turns out well.

What drives novices to distraction (and what nearly put me in the loony bin for years) is that pastry shrinks if you don't bake it properly, and you end up with a pancake in the bottom of your tin instead of the perfect shell you'd dreamt of. Here is how to avoid that.

First of all, pastry must rest before you roll it out and bake it. Don't ask me the scientific reasons – just trust me. Before you roll out pastry, you must wrap it and chill it for a good 30 minutes (even safer if you can leave it in the refrigerator overnight). Personally, I also like to chill it 30 minutes more once I've got the pastry in the pan. It just seems to behave better that way. Since these timing issues can be a bit of a pain in the neck, it's nice to have a stash of pastry (already rolled out, if you can be that organized) in the freezer.

Just as crucial as the chilling trick is the dried-bean one. For years, I thought the point of dried beans in a raw shell was to keep the bottom from buckling up. I cannot be alone, because kitchen shops all over the place sell strings of metal beads or tiny boxes of terra-cotta marbles that do nothing but barely scatter themselves over a tart base – useless for blind baking, unless you own them by the thousands. For blind baking to work, you must line the pastry with parchment or foil in such a way that you can lift it out partway through cooking, and you must pour in dried beans (or similar weights) *right to the very top.* That way, the sides are given plenty of support. This requires quite a few dried beans, which is why you must have a jar of dried beans in your pantry that you can use again and again strictly for blind baking. Jennifer McLagan (she of pastry recipe #2 on p. 10) has one with all sorts of legumes in it: white and black beans, brown and red lentils, pale chickpeas – so beautiful to look at. Of course, I now have one, too!

Now, tart shells must start off hot in the oven in order to set quickly. (Some bakers also swear by setting the tart on a baking sheet, preferably one that has already got hot in the oven while it preheats.) I get the oven to 400°F (200°C), then pop in the pastry for 12 minutes. At this point, I lift out the parchment and beans (the tart will have set enough not to shrink by now), put the tart straight back in the oven, reduce the heat to 350°F (180°C), and continue baking until it is just starting to show signs of color on the base, 10 to 15 minutes more. The timing will be less for tiny tarts. And if you can't handle fiddling with oven temperature, do the whole thing at 375°F (190°C), removing the beans after 15 minutes.

A good trick when making a tart shell that you plan to fill with a liquid mixture is to brush the base with a little lightly beaten egg white, using a pastry brush, before baking. This seals the crust so it stays crisp once the filling goes in – important if you care about a cookies-and-cream textural contrast in the finished tart.

Occasionally, I make a high-sided tart in a springform pan. Depending on the size of the pan, this sometimes requires more than one disk's worth of pastry, say, one and a third. You'll have to work that out depending on your pan. Lining the pan is no different from lining a tart shell, except that I don't necessarily go all the way to the top (depends on the tart). In any case, you definitely need parchment and enough beans to go to the top of the pastry if you want it to stay up.

Sorry to be so home-economist-like about all this. It's just because I wasted so many years wondering what was wrong with me and why I could never get my tart shells perfect that I'm trying to spare you the same pain. Believe me, pastry is easy when you do it right. Thanks to my professional friends who shared their great pastry recipes here, you can know that you and your tart shells are in very good hands!

Hors d'œuvres

THREE EASY BITES

Fennel with Paprika

This is a good little trick I stole from a friend: Take a fennel bulb and use a vegetable peeler to take off a thin layer of the not-so-nice outside bit, then cut it lengthwise into slices about half as thick as your finger. Drizzle over a few thin threads of olive oil. Add a squeeze of lemon (not too much) and scatter with fleur de sel and a light snowfall of paprika. This is simple but very tasty, and I love how the salt and paprika are like fairy dust against their pale and crunchy anise canvas.

Cucumber with Salmon Roe

I am creative and dextrous when it comes to wrapping presents, but otherwise I can't handle anything finicky. Appetizers, for example, are my *bête noire*, which explains this recipe. It started off in the hands of my friend, Jennifer, who considers herself a type A of the highest order and me a type B of the lowest order. Her version had cucumber shaved into thin strips and rolled into spirals that stood on end, held with a pick, their garnishes perched glamourously on top. Stunning, and with enough time on my hands, I *can* do that. What I can't do, however, is get the platter of these pretty towers from kitchen to salon without having half of them wobble and teeter and crash to their doom. Here, then, is my crash-tested, type B version of the same recipe: Slice an English cucumber into rounds, about half a finger thick. Arrange on a platter. Season with salt and pepper. Top each round with a dollop of crème fraîche and a tiny mound of salmon or trout roe. Garnish each with a sprig of dill, and serve.

Cherry Tomatoes with Basil and Chèvre

Ahem. If you'll indulge me while I reminisce . . . I remember having these at a vineyard dinner party outside Beaune once. There were sausages spitting their fat on a grill built over a fire of twisted old grapevines; salads were being tossed in the stone-floored kitchen of the old house; rare Burgundian wines were poured as casually as Kool-Aid; and a light summer breeze ruffled the evening in a way that made you feel that this was the life. And it was! There must have been other pre-feast nibbles, but I don't remember them: these tomatoes stood out. You just slice the tops off tiny cherry tomatoes, season with salt and pepper, lay a basil leaf on each, and pin it down with a pinch of chèvre. *C'est tout, et c'est bon.*

SESAME SOY AVOCADO

A roommate of mine used to make this all the time when people dropped by our Paris apartment for drinks. It takes about 30 seconds, start to finish, and involves nothing more than a quick chop, a bit of sprinkling, and a few squirts. The result is startlingly good: a rubble heap of fleshy avocado chunks, transformed with soy sauce for depth, lemon for acidity, and sesame seeds for a teensy scattering of crunch. Serve with picks at apéritifs, keeping in mind that it is also great beside a toasted tomato sandwich for lunch.

Makes: 4 to 6 servings

2 perfectly ripe avocados
Lemon juice
Olive oil
Organic soy sauce
Fleur de sel or Maldon sea salt
Freshly ground pepper
Toasted sesame seeds

Just before serving, halve, pit, and peel the avocados. Cut into cubes onto a flattering plate. (The sauce will run to the bottom if you put them in a bowl, so avoid that.) Squeeze over lemon juice to taste, then drizzle lightly with olive oil and a thread of soy sauce. Sprinkle with salt, and grind over some pepper. Scatter over the sesame seeds. Taste and see if the avocado needs more lemon or soy. Correct the seasonings, and nibble away to your heart's content.

SPICY BEET BITES

In France, beets are usually sold cooked, which is convenient as they do take a long time to prepare otherwise. (A baseball-sized beet, for example, would have to be boiled, or roasted at 400°F/200°C, for about an hour, but then you could always buy smaller beets to speed things up.) This is an original way to treat cooked beets. I love the crunch of the spices with the freshness of the coriander, rubbing up against the natural ruby sweetness of oil-glistened beet. By the way, ras el hanout means "head of the shop," and the spice mixture is so named because it refers to the spice-shop proprietor's own mix. In other words, the mixture varies slightly by brand, but it will always have the fragrance of Middle Eastern cooking. I serve these beets when Moroccan tagine (p. 129) is next on the menu. They look great in candlelight, as do people.

Makes: about 4 servings

1 large beet, cooked and peeled
¼ cup (60 mL) olive oil
1 teaspoon (5 mL) coriander seeds
1 teaspoon (5 mL) cumin seeds
½ teaspoon (2 mL) ground cumin
½ teaspoon (2 mL) ras el hanout (optional)
¼ teaspoon (1 mL) cayenne pepper
½ teaspoon (2 mL) fleur de sel
Black pepper
A handful of fresh coriander, chopped

Cut the beet into ¾-inch (2 cm) cubes, and toss with the oil in a bowl. Gently toast the coriander seeds and cumin seeds in a dry frying pan over medium heat to release their aromas, 30 to 60 seconds. Tilt into a mortar and pestle, and crush the seeds slightly to release their flavor (not to turn them into powder, however). Add the ground cumin, ras el hanout (if using), cayenne, and salt and pepper, and toss with the beets to coat evenly. Cover and leave to marinate several hours in the fridge. Before serving (with picks, so you don't get pink fingers!), bring to room temperature and toss with the chopped coriander.

For a more formal presentation, as in the photograph, simply dip one side of the beet cubes into the spice mixture and chopped coriander, add picks and serve.

ARTICHOKES WITH ROASTED GARLIC AÏOLI

For this to be the sublime appetizer it is, you need the tiny *poivrade* artichokes with the long stems that are sold in bouquets. If you can only find globe artichokes, then the right approach is simply to boil them until tender, cut off about a third of the tops, hollow them out to remove the choke, and pour the aïoli right inside. You need a roasted head of garlic for the aïoli, and to get that, lop the top off a head of unpeeled garlic, wrap it in foil, and bake for an hour at 350°F (180°C). When it's ready, it will be soft and sweet.

Makes: 4 servings

For the aïoli

1 egg yolk
1 teaspoon (5 mL) white wine vinegar
1 teaspoon (5 mL) Dijon mustard
1 cup (250 mL) grapeseed oil
1 head garlic, roasted (see above)
Salt and pepper
Lemon juice

For the artichokes

12 baby artichokes (*poivrade* variety, which are the tiny ones)
1 or 2 lemons
2 to 3 tablespoons (30 to 45 mL) olive oil

For the aïoli, beat the yolk with the vinegar and mustard. Whisk in the oil, drop by drop, to make a thick mayonnaise. Squeeze the garlic out of the roasted cloves into the mayonnaise, and whisk smooth. Season with salt, pepper, and lemon juice.

For the artichokes, bring a pot of water to the boil with the juice of a lemon in it. Trim the artichokes (rubbing them with lemon as you go to prevent browning) until you are down to the core with a bit of stem attached. Halve. Salt the boiling water, and drop in the artichokes. Gently boil until tender, about 10 minutes, depending on their size. Drain, and pat dry.

Heat the olive oil in a frying pan, and brown the artichokes on all sides until the edges are golden. Transfer to paper towels to drain. Serve hot and crisp with aïoli for dipping.

CHÈVRE DIPPING SAUCE FOR CRUDITÉS

This is a variation on a recipe from chef Michel Roux's handy book *Sauces,* in which he infuses milk with rosemary before whisking it into the cheese. Sometimes I infuse the milk with rosemary or thyme, but sometimes I don't bother and just whisk it in as is. Either way, the sauce is easy and fast and lends itself well to experimentation, so feel free to explore other flavor options, too. This makes a wonderful pool for a platter of crudités to dip their feet in.

Makes: about 1½ cups (375 mL)

¾ cup (175 mL) milk, more if needed
1 tablespoon (15 mL) fresh thyme leaves
12 ounces (375 g) fresh chèvre
Zest of 1 orange
Zest of 1 lemon, and juice to taste
Freshly ground black pepper and salt, if needed

Put the milk with the thyme in a saucepan. Bring to the boil, remove from the heat, cover, and set aside to infuse until cool.

Beat the cheese to soften. Gradually whisk the cool milk into the cheese. Add the orange zest, lemon zest, lemon juice, and pepper. Taste, and add salt if needed (it will depend on how salty the cheese is to begin with). Serve with raw vegetables, for dipping.

CERVELLE DE CANUT

The name of this Lyonnais recipe translates, for reasons beyond me, as "silk weaver's brain." Don't let that put you off, however, because it is only fresh cheese with garlic and herbs. It has a creamy yogurt texture, only it's savory and garlicky tasting, and in Lyon everyone eats it from a bowl with a spoon at the end of a meal (a replacement for the cheese or dessert course). I find it's also good as a spread or dip, or, to be Germanic, dolloped alongside boiled potatoes. Depending on how you want to eat it, you can vary the thickness with the amount of cream you add.

Makes: about 1½ cups (375 mL)

1 cup (250 mL) fromage blanc or puréed cottage cheese
¼ cup (60 mL) heavy cream or crème fraîche
1 tablespoon (15 mL) white wine
A spoonful of olive oil
1 to 2 garlic cloves, minced
1 small shallot, minced (optional)
1 to 2 tablespoons (15 to 30 mL) chopped fresh parsley
1 to 2 tablespoons (15 to 30 mL) chopped fresh chives
Salt and pepper

Cream the cheese, then stir in enough cream to give a yogurt consistency. Stir in the wine, olive oil, garlic, shallot (if using), parsley, chives, and salt and pepper. Eat with a spoon (if you're feeling adventurous) or use as a dip or spread.

BLUE CHEESE AND DRIED FRUIT TERRINE

To call this a terrine is a bit of a cheat, because it's really more like "cheese log," which sounds very much like something from a dubious 1960s church-basement cookbook. I think I actually apologized to my guests the first time I served it, but then the whole thing disappeared in the wink of an eye. I suppose that means I really owe the apology to the recipe. (Sorry!) If you love blue cheese, you'll love this terrine. The fruit and nuts make it very festive, wonderful in winter with a glass of port, which the French, for some reason, consider an apéritif.

Makes: 1 small terrine, serving 10 as an appetizer

1 pound (450 g) blue cheese (such as Roquefort or Gorgonzola), at room temperature
8 ounces (225 g) mascarpone cheese
1 tablespoon (15 mL) honey (optional)
Freshly ground pepper
A handful of chopped toasted walnuts
A handful of chopped green pistachios
A handful of chopped dried apricots
A handful of chopped dried figs
A handful of currants

Mash the blue cheese and mascarpone together with the honey (if using) and some pepper using a fork. (You can do this in the food processor, too, but it will cream the blue cheese so much that you get a greenish terrine. Not the end of the world, but just warning you.) Stir in the nuts and dried fruits to distribute evenly. Season with some pepper. Wrap in plastic, and shape into a terrine, by which I mean a low-lying rectangular log. Refrigerate for several hours until firm. Serve with an assortment of rustic country breads or crackers, and deck it out with some whole dried fruits and nuts if you like.

TUNA MINT DIP

I had this dip at a dinner party in Paris once, then I set it in motion at one of my own parties, and soon it was showing up at every party I went to all over the city. It's not usually my kind of thing, because it involves commercial ingredients, but it does come in handy in a pinch and is quite marvelous for plunging carrot sticks into. I also think it's nice to know that French home cooks sometimes resort to these magaziney sorts of recipes, too. Hors d'oeuvres in France don't *always* mean foie gras on toast points.

Makes: about 2 cups (500 mL)

8 ounces (225 g) cream cheese (St. Moret in France)
A spoonful of sour cream or crème fraîche
1 tin (6½ ounces/185 g) tuna, drained and flaked with a fork
Freshly ground pepper
Lemon juice
Leaves from a very large bunch of mint, chopped

Cream the cheese. Stir in the sour cream until smooth and thinned to the consistency you're looking for (thin for dip, thicker for spread). Mix in the tuna with a fork to blend. Grind in some pepper, squirt in lemon to taste, and stir in the mint. Serve.

SHRIMP WITH GRAINY MUSTARD MAYONNAISE

Shrimp are not the delicate creatures their name suggests. In fact, they are quite strong tasting and have firm texture, which is why they have no trouble standing up to a punchy grainy mustard mayonnaise as a dipping sauce. My friend Ivan, who is the source of this idea, also likes to toss the shrimp right in the mayonnaise to coat and serve piles of them on beds of arugula as a first course. In either case, restrained portions are key: you can't eat too many or you won't have room for the main course.

Makes: 24 bites with about 1 cup (250 mL) sauce

1 egg yolk, at room temperature
Pinch salt
2 teaspoons (10 mL) grainy Dijon mustard
1 teaspoon (5 mL) white wine vinegar
About 1 cup (250 mL) grapeseed oil (or vegetable, canola, or peanut)
Lemon juice
Salt and pinch white pepper
1 tablespoon (15 mL) olive oil
24 shrimp, peeled, but with tails intact

Whisk together the egg yolk, salt, mustard, and vinegar in a roomy bowl. Start whisking the yolk mixture, and whisk in the oil, drop by drop, until you have achieved a thick, velvety mayonnaise. Taste it. Add lemon juice, salt and white pepper until the balance is to your liking.

Heat the olive oil in a sauté pan over high heat. Fry the shrimp until just cooked through and still juicy, about 5 minutes. Arrange on a platter, with the mayonnaise in a dish alongside for dipping.

IVAN'S OYSTERS

One of the best cooks I know, my friend Ivan, lives in a gorgeous country house in Normandy, where he has a yard with pecking chickens, a sprawling apple orchard, a vegetable garden, and enviably convenient access to a coastful of seafood. No wonder his cooking is so inspired. Every dish he serves has a nifty twist. This is his dressing for oysters. It's the same idea as the typical French accompaniment of red wine vinegar and shallot, but ever so much better.

Makes: 24 oysters

24 oysters
3 tablespoons (45 mL) rice vinegar
1 tablespoon (15 mL) soy sauce
2 teaspoons (10 mL) mirin
2 tablespoons (30 mL) minced leek (preferably the pale green bit)

Keep the oysters refrigerated until ready to open. Make the sauce by stirring together the vinegar, soy sauce, mirin, and leek. Open the oysters, and arrange them on a platter. Spoon ¼ to ½ teaspoon (1 to 2 mL) of the sauce onto each oyster, and serve immediately.

PERNOD MUSSELS ON THE HALF SHELL

This is another recipe that has evolved since its early days and has now, I think, reached its peak. The anise scent imparted by the Pernod is delicious with mussels, and it's a wonderful surprise because you don't expect it to be there. I also love the textural contrast of the crunchy crumbs on top. I'll take these delectable little bites over plain old *moules marinières* any day. A bonus is that you can get them ready in advance and just blast them under the broiler at the last minute.

Makes: 4 servings

1 pound (450 g) mussels
½ cup (125 mL) Pernod
3 tablespoons (45 mL) salted butter, softened
1 teaspoon (5 mL) chopped fresh chives
1 teaspoon (5 mL) chopped fresh tarragon
3 tablespoons (45 mL) fresh bread crumbs
Freshly ground pepper
4 lemon wedges

Heat the oven to broil with the rack near the top. Clean the mussels, discarding any that are open. Bring the Pernod to the boil in a large pot, add the mussels, cover, and cook for 3 minutes or until they've opened. Drain the mussels, and discard any that have remained closed.

Pull the mussels apart, discarding half the shell and leaving the mussels sitting on their remaining half shell. Arrange on a baking sheet.

Mash the butter with the chives and tarragon. Sprinkle the bread crumbs over the mussels, top with a pinch of herb butter, grind over some pepper, and broil until the crumbs are golden, about 2 minutes. Serve with lemon wedges for squeezing.

SAUSAGE, APPLE, AND SAGE BITES

My French cooking friends Camille and Ivan have both served me divine apple-and-blood-pudding tarts over the years. In France, I would definitely use blood sausage in this recipe. Elsewhere, I let plain pork sausage take its place. Either way, very edible indeed.

Makes: 24 pieces

2 pork sausages, cooked
1 Granny Smith apple
2 tablespoons (30 mL) olive oil, more as needed
2 tablespoons (30 mL) butter
A few pinches of sugar
24 small fresh sage leaves

Cut the sausage diagonally into 24 slices ¼ inch (5 mm) thick. Peel the apple, and cut it into 24 cubes. Heat the oil in a sauté pan over medium-high heat, and fry the sausage slices on both sides until golden brown, a matter of seconds. Remove to a platter.

Wipe out the pan, and return it to the heat. Melt the butter in it. Add the sugar, and fry the apple cubes, tossing occasionally, until tender and golden on all sides, about 5 minutes. Remove. Add a little oil to the pan, if needed, and fry the sage leaves until crisp, 30 seconds to 1 minute.

Lay a sage leaf on each sausage slice, top with a cube of sautéed apple, pierce with a pick, arrange on a nice dish, and dash into the salon to serve.

TARTINES

No hors d'oeuvres are more ubiquitous and well loved in France than tartines, those wonderfully crisp rounds of baguette with their endless variety of delectable toppings. What we're really talking about here is toast, of course, so that should be a comfort to anyone who's worried they're not up to the challenge. Here's what you do: buy a baguette; slice it into pinky-width slices; brush with olive oil and set on a baking sheet; then toast in a 400°F (200°C) oven, turning once, for just a few minutes, until they're golden but still easy to get your teeth through.

My typical modus operandi is to root around in the refrigerator while the toast is in the oven and see what leftover bits of this and that I can cleverly mash into an appealing topping. Less typical is that I actually have a plan before I set out, but when that does happen, it's along the lines of the recipes that follow.

BLACK OLIVE AND PISTACHIO TARTINES

These sound boring on paper, but they are smashing to look at (think crushed jade against glistening black onyx), they taste fabulous, and they are dead easy to assemble. (Thank you, Patti Hetherington, the food stylist on my TV series, *French Food at Home,* and on this book, for the idea!) I'm equally fond of a green olive and toasted almond variation, despite its more military hue.

Makes: about ⅔ cup (150 mL) olive paste, enough for 12 tartines

1 cup (165 g) black olives, pitted
3 to 4 tablespoons (45 to 60 mL) olive oil
Black pepper
3 tablespoons (45 mL) pistachios, toasted and chopped

Chop the olives quite fine, and stir in the oil. Season with pepper. (You could add a bit of lemon zest if you like, too.) Top croûtes with a spoonful of the olives, then top with a sprinkling of toasted nuts.

WARM CRUSHED TOMATO AND PARMESAN TARTINES

The amounts of vinegar and sugar in this recipe depend very much on the quality of your tomatoes. If you have very sweet summer tomatoes, you may not need either; if you have acidic tomatoes, you may need only the sugar; and if you have grocery tomatoes in the dead of winter, you may need both. Taste, then make a decision based on what you feel is right. That's the only real way to cook anything anyway.

Makes: about 1 cup (250 mL), enough for 16 to 20 tartines

1 pound (450 g) tomatoes
1 tablespoon (15 mL) olive oil
1 shallot, minced
2 teaspoons (10 mL) red wine vinegar
2 garlic cloves, peeled
1 bay leaf
1 teaspoon (5 mL) sugar
Salt and pepper
Parmesan cheese, for garnish

Plunge the tomatoes into boiling water for 10 seconds. Remove, and rinse immediately under ice-cold water. Peel, seed, and chop. Heat the oil in a sauté pan over medium heat, and gently sauté the shallot until soft. Add the tomatoes, vinegar, garlic, bay leaf, sugar, and salt and pepper. Cover, lower the heat, and cook gently for 15 minutes. Remove the garlic and bay leaf. Correct the seasonings. Spoon onto croûtes, and garnish with shavings of Parmesan cheese.

CRUSHED FAVA BEAN AND CHÈVRE TARTINES

These are wonderfully bright and springtimey. You can use fresh peas or edamame instead of fava beans if you like.

Makes: enough for about 16 tartines

1 cup (250 mL) shelled fresh or frozen fava beans
Extra virgin olive oil
Salt and pepper
Lemon juice
A handful of chopped fresh mint
About ¼ cup (60 mL) fresh chèvre

Bring a pot of salted water to the boil, and blanch the fava beans about a minute, to loosen the skins and soften. Drain, then run under ice-cold water. Remove the skins by opening the top with your thumbnail and squeezing out the bean. Discard the skin, keeping only the soft, bright jade-green insides. Mash the beans in a bowl with a fork, adding a drizzle of extra virgin olive oil, and salt and pepper. Add lemon juice to taste. Stir in the mint. Spread croûtes with chèvre, and top with the minty crush of favas.

MUSHROOM TARTINES

I used to involve cream in this recipe, but one day I got nibbling away at my mushrooms while they were cooking and I thought, "Who needs cream? It will only dilute the flavor."

Makes: enough for about 16 tartines

2 tablespoons (30 mL) butter
1 pound (450 g) button mushrooms, quartered
2 garlic cloves, minced
Salt and pepper
½ cup (125 mL) white wine
A generous handful of chopped fresh parsley
Lemon juice

Melt the butter in a sauté pan over medium-high heat until it foams. Sauté the mushrooms until golden, adding the garlic for 1 minute at the end. Season with salt and pepper. Deglaze with the white wine, and boil to evaporate. Remove from the heat, and stir in the parsley. Add a squirt of lemon juice, and salt and pepper. Pile onto croûtes, and serve.

AUBERGINE CAVIAR TARTINES

I used to make this as just garlicky mashed eggplant, but I got bored with that and had to embellish. The addition of some very finely cut red pepper provides a pretty confetti effect and color, while the mint adds brightness and freshness to the deep-tasting purée of cumin-scented eggplant.

Makes: about 1½ cups (375 mL), enough for 24 tartines

1 medium eggplant
2 tablespoons (30 mL) olive oil, plus more if needed
1 garlic clove, minced
1 teaspoon (5 mL) ground cumin, more to taste
Salt and pepper
About ½ red pepper, very finely diced
About 10 fresh mint leaves, shredded
A squeeze of lemon (if needed)

Heat the oven to 400°F (200°C). Halve the eggplant lengthwise, lightly brush the cut sides with some of the olive oil, and lay cut side down on a baking sheet. Bake until completely soft, about 40 minutes.

When the eggplant is done, scoop the flesh out into a bowl, and beat smooth with a fork. Add the garlic and cumin. Season with salt and pepper, then stir through the confetti of red pepper and shredded mint. Mix in the remaining olive oil, adding more to reach the right consistency if needed. Taste, and adjust the seasonings, adding a squeeze of lemon if you think it's needed. Serve on croûtes.

CHRIS MOONEY'S SARDINE TARTINES PLATTER

My friend Chris is the ringleader of several expat gourmet-wining-and-dining gangs in Paris, and he is a born bon vivant. So when I was last at his place for dinner and he dared to serve tinned sardines as a first course, I thought, "You brave man." Actually, what I really thought was, "You trendsetter, you! Why, you culinary Kate Moss!" because he had gone so far as to serve the sardines right in their tins, displayed on a massive platter and surrounded by barquette toasts, lemon wedges, pots of cold unpasteurized butter, and fleur de sel. Mind you, the sardines he was using were fancy French sardines from a specialty shop, where you can get dozens of varieties, some of which even have the vintage on the label and are meant to be eaten a number of years after being canned. Anyway, *of course* I nicked his idea, what do you think? I just hope he appreciates the hero worship inherent in this imitation.

Makes: 4 to 6 servings

2 tins best-quality sardines packed in olive oil
1 baguette
1 lemon
Cold butter
Pepper
Fleur de sel

Open the tins of sardines, drain off the oil, and set the tins in the middle of a lovely enormous platter (never mind if it has a chip in it). Halve the baguette lengthwise, cut into pieces, toast the slices, and arrange them around the sardines. Cut the lemon into wedges, and arrange on the platter as well. Serve with a pot of cold (preferably unpasteurized) butter, a pepper mill for grinding over top, a dish of fleur de sel, and lots of knives so everyone can dive in and assemble their own sardine tartines.

SALMON RILLETTES

Cold-smoked salmon is what's popular in France, whereas where I come from it's rustic fillets of hot-smoked salmon, often served with cream cheese and crackers. I like both, but sometimes I'm not in the mood for smokiness at all (it can be overpowering), which is why this recipe is a welcome alternative. Here, the salmon is fresh, so the taste is light, and because the fish is cooked, it's neither slithery nor dry. It's just tasty salmon, beaten to a creamy paste with crème fraîche and lots of tarragon. What a good way to use up leftover fish of any kind, really.

Makes: 1 cup (250 mL), enough for 16 to 20 tartines

1 tablespoon (15 mL) olive oil
6 ounces (175 g) salmon, cut into large cubes
⅓ cup (70 g) butter, softened
1 tablespoon (15 mL) crème fraîche
1 tablespoon (15 mL) finely chopped shallot
1 tablespoon (15 mL) chopped fresh tarragon
Lemon juice
Salt and pepper

Heat the oil in a sauté pan over medium heat, and gently cook the salmon, until cooked through but still tender and pink in the middle, a matter of minutes. Remove to a bowl, and shred the salmon with two forks (or pulse in the food processor). Mix in the butter, crème fraîche, shallot, and tarragon. Season with lemon juice and salt and pepper. Pack into a ramekin (glass ones let you see in). Refrigerate until about half an hour before serving, at which point you take them out so they can soften to spreadable consistency. Serve with crusty bread or crackers. (Oh, I should mention that you can decorate the tops with tarragon leaves and a chive bud, say, to look like a flower. You can also melt butter and pour it over top so that when it hardens it seals the pot.)

SPINACH WHEEL WITH ZA'ATAR

I went through a two-year love affair with this tart and made it practically every time anyone came for drinks. To be honest, it was close to the point where if I didn't find an alternative hors d'oeuvre I was going to have to find new friends. You'll see why I was so enamored: the crust is so buttery it flakes on the tongue, and the spinach is just a thin, smooth layer of wintery green, brightened with Parmesan and that marvelous Middle Eastern spice mix za'atar (which I like especially when it contains some orange zest). If you can't find it in a specialty shop, just as tasty is to make a homemade version by mixing together 1 tablespoon (15 mL) sesame seeds, 1 teaspoon (5 mL) dried oregano, 1 tablespoon (15 mL) chopped fresh thyme, and the zest of one lemon or orange.

Makes: 1 tart, about 8 appetizer servings

1 disk savory galette pastry (p. 9)
2 teaspoons (10 mL) olive oil
1 garlic clove, halved
1 pound (450 g) trimmed spinach, chopped
½ cup (125 mL) grated Parmigiano-Reggiano cheese
1 egg, lightly beaten
Salt and pepper
About 1 tablespoon (15 mL) za'atar

Heat the oven to 425°F (220°C). Roll out the pastry on a lightly floured surface into a rectangle about ⅛ inch (3 mm) thick. Place on a baking sheet, prick with a fork, and bake until lightly golden, about 15 minutes. Remove the tart base from the oven, but do not turn off the oven.

Heat the oil over medium heat in a large frying pan. Add the garlic, and cook, stirring, for 1 minute. Add the spinach, cover, and cook until soft, about 5 minutes, turning occasionally. If there is a lot of liquid, cook uncovered until it evaporates. Remove from the heat, and stir in the cheese. Now stir in the egg with a fork, working quickly so it doesn't clump. Season with salt and pepper. Spread the mixture over the tart base, right to the very edge. Scatter the za'atar evenly over top. Bake until the crust is crisp and the top very hot, about 20 minutes.

Slide the tart onto a large cutting board, cut into diamonds, and serve straight from the board.

ONION AND BACON TART

My longtime mentor in the ways of French food, Anne Willan, served this tart once for apéritifs at her Burgundian château, and I loved it so much that it immediately replaced my onion tart of the era, which involved a lot of butter and a long, slow cooking time for the onions (better for pizza, I've decided). This tart is "a wink," as my father would describe it, and it is dangerously delicious: a perfect snack as you sit before a crackling fire on a dark and stormy night, in the wilds of . . . who knows?

Makes: 1 tart, about 8 appetizer servings

1 round (or square, depending on your bent) savory galette pastry (p. 9)
½ cup (125 mL) crème fraîche or sour cream
1 small onion, very thinly sliced
3 to 4 slices bacon, cut into lardons
Freshly ground black pepper
Fleur de sel

Heat the oven to 400°F (200°C). Roll out the pastry on a lightly floured surface into a rectangle about ⅛ inch (3 mm) thick. Lay on a baking sheet, and bake until lightly golden, about 15 minutes. Remove the tart base from the oven, but do not turn off the oven.

Spread the crème fraîche over the tart base, going all the way out to the edges. Scatter over the onion slices and the bacon. Grind over pepper and sprinkle over fleur de sel. Bake until the crème fraîche is bubbling, the bacon cooked, and the onions curled and starting to brown, about 20 minutes. You don't have to race into the dining room at top speed, but it's always nicest still warm.

TOMATO AND GRAINY MUSTARD TART

The mustard, however peculiar sounding, is what makes this tart. (I left it out once and sorely regretted the move.) Its sharp acidity, foiled with a little crème fraîche, is a perfect match for the dense, soft sweetness of tomato.

Makes: 1 tart, about 8 appetizer servings

1 disk savory galette pastry (p. 9)
2 tablespoons (30 mL) crème fraîche (optional)
2 tablespoons (30 mL) grainy mustard
A few handfuls of grated Gruyère cheese
About 3 tomatoes, cored and thinly sliced
Salt and pepper
A handful of chopped fresh thyme or dried herbes de Provence
Olive oil or melted butter, for drizzling

Heat the oven to 400°F (200°C). Roll out the pastry on a lightly floured surface into a rectangle about ⅛ inch (3 mm) thick. Lay on a baking sheet, and bake until lightly golden, about 15 minutes. Remove the tart base from the oven, but do not turn off the oven.

Stir together the crème fraîche (if using) and mustard, and smear over the tart base, right to the very edge. Scatter over the cheese. Arrange the tomato slices just touching each other on top (in such a way that, when you cut the tart later, each piece will have a tomato slice on it). Sprinkle with salt and pepper, scatter over the herbs, and drizzle with a thread of olive oil. Bake until the cheese has melted and the tomatoes are hot and soft. Serve warm, *si c'est possible.*

PISSALADIÈRE

One day last winter, I was at home writing television scripts and I made a *pissaladière* at about ten in the morning. By late afternoon, I had polished off the entire thing. So, just warning you, there's that danger. This is a Provençal rendition of pizza, as the name (pissa . . .) suggests when you give it a long, hard look. Evidently, it is good for breakfast, lunch, dinner, and snacks at all hours . . . all on the same day.

Makes: 1 tart, about 8 first-course servings

For the dough

1⅓ cups (165 g) flour
1½ teaspoons (7 mL) active dry yeast
1 egg
¾ teaspoon (4 mL) salt
A grinding of pepper

For the topping

¼ cup (60 mL) olive oil
1½ pounds (675 g) onions, thinly sliced
1 bay leaf
2 teaspoons (10 mL) herbes de Provence
Salt and pepper
1 tomato, thinly sliced
12 to 16 anchovy fillets, rinsed and drained, then halved lengthwise
About ¼ cup (40 g) niçoise olives, pitted

For the dough, put the flour in a large bowl and make a well in it. In a small bowl, sprinkle the yeast over ⅓ cup (75 mL) warm water, and set aside until dissolved and slightly foamy, about 5 minutes. Beat the egg with the salt and pepper, then pour it into the well in the flour along with the yeast mixture. Gradually mix with your fingers, drawing the flour in to make a dough. Knead on a lightly floured surface until smooth and elastic, adding more flour if needed. Cover, and set in a warm place to double in bulk, about an hour.

Meanwhile, for the topping, heat the oil in a sauté pan and add the onions, bay leaf, herbes de Provence, and salt and pepper. Cover, and cook, stirring occasionally, until very soft, about half an hour. Remove the bay leaf.

Heat the oven to 400°F (200°C). Lightly oil or sprinkle with flour a baking sheet. When the dough is ready, punch it down, and roll it out into a thin circle like a pizza crust. Lay on the baking sheet. Top with the onions, going right to the edge. Lay on the tomato slices in rows. Arrange on top a lattice of anchovies, and fill in the spaces with olives. Let sit 15 minutes for the dough to rise up again a bit. Bake until the crust is cooked through and the bottom is golden and crisp, about half an hour. Serve immediately or at room temperature.

SAVORY CRACKERS

Not all that different from pastry, these crackers can act as the base for no end of toppings, although they're equally lovely all on their own. The only trick is to be sure to roll them quite thin; that way they snap so nicely in the mouth. Here are some toppings you might like:

Crushed dill seed;
Crushed fennel seed and crushed coriander seed with five-spice powder;
Paprika;
Poppy seeds;
Sesame seeds;
Parmesan cheese and herbes de Provence.

Makes: about 30 crackers

⅔ cup (140 g) butter
1 teaspoon (5 mL) sugar
½ teaspoon (2 mL) salt
1 egg
2 cups (250 g) flour
Fleur de sel

Heat the oven to 400°F (200°C). Put the butter, sugar, salt, and egg in a bowl with 2 tablespoons (30 mL) water, and mix well. Add the flour and mix quickly just until the dough holds together. Do not overwork.

On a lightly floured surface, roll out the dough into a rough square 1/16 inch (2 mm) thick. Sprinkle with the toppings of your choice and the salt. Cut into squares, and arrange on a baking sheet. (If you want to have a variety of toppings, cut the dough into squares first, then put the toppings on.) Bake until puffed, crisp, and golden, about 10 minutes. Cool slightly before serving.

L'APÉRITIF

At the risk of coming off like a complete party pooper, I cast my vote for mingy apéritifs. Perhaps it's a cook's inclination, but when you've gone to the trouble of making dinner for people, you want them to have some room left in their stomachs by the time they get to the table. Furthermore, you want your guests upright at the table when they get there. I am using the word "apéritif" here to encompass both drinks and the nibbly bits that go with them, because in my mind (and in the French psyche, too) apéritif is a whole package: you simply can't serve drink without food, or you're asking for it.

By mingy, however, I'm not suggesting parsimony. Just because I think it's smart to avoid a full-blown cocktail party as a launching pad for dinner doesn't mean I'm calling instead for glasses of tap water and bay leaves to suck on. I'm simply saying that, as with Baby Bear's porridge, there is such a thing as "just right." It comes down to understanding what apéritifs are meant to do: whet appetites for a delicious dinner and slightly loosen joints for comfort and tongues for conversation.

This requires a certain discipline. For a start, the "apéritif hour" should really be that: one hour, not three. This can only work if dinner is more or less ready by the time people arrive. I do mean "more or less," because one of the nicest moments for home cooks is when we can enjoy a drink with people in the kitchen while putting the last touches on our *boeuf bourguignon.* (Speaking of which, p. 162.) But it's also important to have enough time to sit down with our guests (indeed, to transform ourselves into one of them), catch up a bit, and settle in for a good time. That's impossible if we're still scrambling in the kitchen all by ourselves, stuffing fish and peeling potatoes.

In addition to keeping the apéritif hour to a reasonable time frame, it's also paramount to restrain ourselves from going overboard, from striving frantically to offer five different platters of tartlets, cheese balls, dips, skewered meats, stuffed mini vegetables . . . I always wonder why so many veer off in that direction whenever they plan a dinner party. (Not to mention *how,* because if I tried to do that, I'd be a sobbing mess on the pantry floor hours before anyone even showed up.) Perhaps people view it as a show of generosity and abundance, and maybe they're afraid of being viewed as cheap and lazy if they narrow hors d'oeuvres down to hors d'oeuvre. Personally, I think the singular is more elegant and convivial. (Okay, I'll allow two or three, depending on the size of the party and the size of the appetizers.) But the bottom line, as far as I'm concerned, is less is more. It's not only a question of leaving room for dinner but of leaving palates sharp so that people can actually taste. If, at appetizers, everyone is jumping around from one flavor to another like seagulls, their palates will be made as dull as doorstops. (How's that for a leap from one metaphor to another?)

So, if ever there was a time to follow a French example, the apéritif hour is it. Too often the French are accused of complicating matters of food, but if you take a look at their predinner drinks ritual, you see that, in fact, simplicity is one of their fortes. For proof, the most common apéritif food in France is very thinly sliced dried sausage, and/or a bowl of pistachios, and/or a bowl of olives. That's it. For actual drinks, what's most common is a bottle of white or sparkling wine. I have never been offered a cocktail in a French home, although occasionally some have a local specialty to show off, such as RinQuinQuin from Provence (a peach-flavored apéritif to which I was only recently introduced and discovered I adore) or Pinot de Charentes (a sweetish drink made from unfermented grape must *and* Cognac, which I adore less). This is not to say the French don't splash out on special occasions, because they do. They'll make *tartines de foie gras* or *gougères* or some other treat, but even then, at home, it's usually just one, done well.

Anyway, ultimately I have a very selfish motive here (the truth comes out): I wish everyone would stop trying to turn themselves into tapas bars before dinner at home, because I don't have it in me to reciprocate! I am a one-drink, three-bite hors d'oeuvres kind of girl, and I think that should be okay when we're just at home, craving some happy time with people we like. That's what I always say about dinner itself, too: this is home cooking, folks, not a restaurant, and we are all going to eat and drink the same thing, together. True togetherness is rare enough in the modern world. I figure the apéritif hour is as good a time as any to rekindle it.

A GOOD KIR

This is right up there with a recipe for buttered toast, and I'd apologize for what I'm sure sounds patronizing, except that it is so difficult to get a good kir or kir royale, even in French establishments, that I think someone has to pipe up and call for improvements. *(Clears throat and leaps onto soap box . . .)* Just as a matter of interest, Kir was the name of a mayor of Dijon in the last century who, partly as a means of promoting regional products, used to serve visiting dignitaries a glass of the region's crème de cassis (blackcurrant liqueur) topped up with a regional white wine (Bourgogne Aligoté or Chablis, for example). And so, the drink took his name.

Because of its origins, therefore, I feel the first step to a proper kir is to use a white wine that is not too heavy. It doesn't necessarily have to be a Burgundian white, but some authenticity (and taste) is lost when a heavy, oaky wine from a sunny climate gets splashed in. A kir royale is the same as kir, only made with Champagne, and it's served in a flute rather than a wineglass. This may all be obvious, but here's where people trip up: way too much cassis! A friend of mine who is a kir connoisseur insists on just a coin-sized puddle of cassis, a mere teaspoon, in the bottom of the glass so that once the wine goes in you get a pretty, pale drink with a bit of mystery in the mouth. Too much cassis and you have something obnoxiously sweet and jammy. (You'd never get anyone to sign a treaty after a kir like that!) So, that's my last word: in a drink designed as a gesture of good diplomacy, subtlety is the key ingredient. *(Steps down from soap box. Takes perfect kir royale in hand. Raises it to all mankind, and then . . . sippity sip!)*

First Courses

SUMMER TOMATO SOUP WITH BASIL AND CROUTONS

Gazpacho may not be French, but everybody in France eats it, mostly in puréed form rather than chunky. What makes this rendition especially delicious is that it marinates a day, so the flavors really have time to meld. I made this for a food show once and handed it out in clear tasting cups. It may not have been the most original-*sounding* bite going round, but it got rave reviews! For the butter-fried croutons, simply cut crustless white bread into very tiny cubes and fry in sizzling butter until golden and crisp.

Makes: 4 servings

2 pounds (900 g) very ripe tomatoes, quartered, seeded, and chopped
½ English cucumber, peeled, seeded, and diced
½ red pepper, cored and diced
½ small onion
1 garlic clove, crushed
¼ cup (20 g) fresh brown bread crumbs
2 tablespoons (30 mL) red wine vinegar, more to taste
1 cup (250 mL) vegetable stock or tomato juice
Leaves from 2 thyme sprigs
16 fresh basil leaves
Salt and pepper
Pinch cayenne pepper
Honey (optional)
¼ cup (60 mL) tiny butter-fried croutons (see above)

Put the tomatoes, cucumber, red pepper, onion, garlic, and bread crumbs in a large glass bowl. Toss with the vinegar, stock, thyme, and 12 of the basil leaves. Cover and refrigerate overnight.

The next day, purée the mixture, and season to taste with salt, pepper, and cayenne. If too acidic (and this will depend on the tomatoes you've used), add a little honey. Serve cold with the remaining basil leaves shredded and scattered over top along with a spoonful of tiny croutons.

VICHYSSOISE

It's possible that no one in Vichy has ever actually heard of this leek and potato soup because, according to reliable sources, it was invented in America by a French chef who was homesick for his town. Well, what a fine tribute to a place! It is so much more than the sum of its parts, and it is soothing and satisfying whether you serve it hot or, as it's meant to be, cold. I can't understand why this soup is not more popular, especially when the price is so right.

Makes: 6 servings, easily

4 all-purpose potatoes, peeled and sliced (or chopped)
4 leeks, trimmed, sliced and washed
2 celery stalks, thinly sliced
1 onion, sliced
Vichy mineral water (or tap water, obviously)
Salt and pepper
¼ cup (60 mL) heavy cream or milk
Chopped fresh chives, for garnish

Put the vegetables in a pot. Add enough mineral water to cover. Season with salt and pepper. Cover, bring to the boil, then reduce heat, and simmer until very tender. Purée, and strain into a glass bowl. Thin with the cream, adding more liquid if needed. Cool, and chill.

Before serving, thin the soup, if needed, to your desired consistency with more water or milk. Check the seasonings. Serve sprinkled with chives.

PISTOU

There are countless variations on this vegetable soup from Provence, which is so wonderful in summer when vegetables peak. It's light yet substantial, with bright, confident flavors, and it looks positively glamorous with its emerald pool of pesto splashed through the confetti of vegetable colors. One optional ingredient is "vegetable water." My mother, who is a superb soup maker, always saved the water that she boiled vegetables in to use as stock. I love the frugality of that concept, and I love the flavor those waters add.

If you're cooking your own white beans, first soak them in plenty of cold water overnight. Drain and rinse them, then put them in a pot, cover with fresh water (don't add salt), and simmer until tender, about an hour. Drain well and proceed. To make your own pesto, put 2 garlic cloves, 1 cup (250 mL) loosely packed basil leaves, ¼ cup (60 mL) olive oil, and a pinch of salt in the food processor. Whiz into sauce, *et voilà.*

Makes: 6 servings

1 tablespoon (15 mL) olive oil
1 onion, chopped
1 potato, peeled and diced
1 cup (110 g) green beans cut into ½-inch (1 cm) pieces
1 cup (110 g) diced carrots
4 cups (1 L) vegetable stock or vegetable water
Salt and pepper
1 bay leaf
1 thyme sprig
1 cup (about 200 g) cooked white kidney beans (see above)
1 cup (110 g) diced zucchini
2 tomatoes, seeded and diced
Pesto (see above), for garnish
Grated Parmesan cheese, for garnish

Heat the oil in a sauté pan over medium heat, and gently cook the onion until translucent, about 5 minutes. Add the potato, green beans, and carrots. Add the vegetable stock. Season with salt and pepper, and add the bay leaf and the thyme. Bring to the boil, reduce the heat, and simmer 10 minutes. Add the kidney beans and the zucchini, and continue cooking until all the vegetables are tender, about 10 minutes longer. Remove the bay leaf and thyme sprig. Stir through the tomato.

Ladle the soup into bowls, and serve topped with a spoonful of pesto. Pass the grated cheese for garnish.

VÂCHE QUI RIT SOUP

Every French mummy has this one up her sleeve, as does every French playschool. I'd never heard of it until my friends started having babies, and then, suddenly, there it was in every lunch bowl. It's zucchini soup, thickened with commercial cheese (*vâche qui rit* means "laughing cow") instead of cream. Normally I am too much of a purist to use packaged ingredients, but here's one case where I've been suckered in. For some reason, I find the whole idea of it funny. Must be the cow.

Makes: 4 servings

1 onion, thinly sliced
2 pounds (900 g) zucchini, chopped
About 2 cups (500 mL) chicken stock or water
Salt and pepper
Pinch cumin (optional)
3 or 4 triangles La Vâche Qui Rit or 3 to 4 tablespoons (45 to 60 mL) Boursin or cream cheese
A small handful of fresh herbs, such as mint, chervil, or dill (optional)

Put the onion and zucchini in a pot and pour over the stock. Season with salt and pepper, and add the cumin (if using). Cover and simmer until soft, about 15 minutes. Add the cheese and herbs (if using), and purée. Gently reheat before serving.

SMOKY SQUASH SOUP

Soupe au potiron is one of the top autumn starters in France. It's smooth and rich with gorgeous color, and it loves all sorts of garnishes on top, including scallops, shrimp, croutons, or fried sausage slices, to name a few. Bacon and chives are my favorite, and also the favorite of everyone who comes to dinner at my house between October and March.

Makes: 8 servings

4 pounds (1.8 kg) squash or pumpkin, peeled, seeded, and cut into 1-inch (2.5 cm) chunks
1 tablespoon (15 mL) olive oil
6 slices smoky bacon, chopped
1 medium onion, chopped
1 cup (250 mL) heavy cream or milk
Salt and pepper
Pinch nutmeg
2 to 4 tablespoons (30 to 60 mL) crème fraîche or sour cream (optional)
About 2 tablespoons (30 mL) chopped fresh chives (optional)

Heat the oven to 400°F (200°C). Toss the squash chunks with the oil in a roasting pan, and bake until very soft, about an hour. Meanwhile, fry the bacon in a large saucepan until it's crisp, remove to paper towel to drain, then crumble and set aside. In the same pot, with a spoonful of the bacon fat left in, gently sauté the onion until translucent.

When the squash chunks are cooked, purée in a blender with the onion, adding a splash or two of water if needed to get it whirring. Return the blended mixture to the saucepan. Stir in the cream, heat gently, taste, and season with salt, pepper, and nutmeg. Thin the soup with a little more stock or water if needed. Ladle the soup into bowls. Put a dollop of crème fraîche in each, sprinkle with the bacon and chives, grind over a little black pepper, and serve.

CHICKPEA SOUP

Thick and earthy soup like this is very tasty with a swirl of olive oil on top. I prefer to start with dried chickpeas because they taste best, but you can use tinned if you're in a rush. This is very good food and as cheap as anything.

Makes: 4 servings

2 cups (300 g) dried chickpeas
1 medium onion, chopped
1 garlic clove, chopped
1 bay leaf
1 thyme sprig
Pinch cumin and paprika (optional)
Chicken stock or water
Salt and pepper
Excellent olive oil, for garnish

A day ahead, spill the chickpeas into a large bowl, cover generously with cold water, and soak overnight.

Drain the chickpeas. Put them in a large saucepan with the onion, garlic, bay leaf, thyme, and cumin and paprika (if using). Do not add salt. Add enough chicken stock to cover. Bring to the boil, cover, reduce heat, and simmer gently until very tender, about 40 minutes.

Pluck out the herbs. Blend the chickpeas until smooth. Strain (or put through a food mill) into the saucepan. Reheat, taste, and adjust the seasonings. Ladle into bowls, and garnish with a swirl of olive oil.

LENTIL SOUP WITH CHORIZO CROÛTES

This satisfying, rib-sticking winter soup was served to me at a Paris restaurant in a white bean incarnation. Really any beany thing will work as a base, so you can launch into it no matter what's in the cupboard: lentils, chickpeas, white beans. The chorizo adds heat and turns the frying oil an irresistible rusty color that looks perfect drizzled over the finished soup. If you want some fresh leafiness in the soup, garnish with chopped parsley – or simply wait for the green salad you'll serve afterward.

Makes: 4 servings

1 cup (200 g) du Puy lentils
1 carrot, chopped
1 onion, sliced
1 bay leaf
1 thyme sprig
4 cups (1 L) chicken stock or water
Salt and pepper
Lemon juice (optional)
About 3 tablespoons (45 mL) olive oil
1 small cured chorizo sausage, thinly sliced

Soak the lentils in cold water for 2 hours. Drain. Put them in a large saucepan with the carrot, onion, bay leaf, thyme, and stock. Cover, and simmer until the lentils are very tender, about 30 minutes.

Discard the herbs. Let the lentils cool somewhat, then purée the mixture in a blender, working in two batches to avoid an explosive mess. (Remember that if you put something too hot into a blender, you might crack it.) For a very smooth soup, strain it, although it's not necessary. Return the soup to the pot, and add salt and pepper, along with a squeeze of lemon if you like. Gently reheat.

Heat the olive oil in a small frying pan and sauté the chorizo slices until they curl, about 30 seconds. Turn and fry another 15 seconds. Serve the soup with chorizo rounds on top and with some of their fire-colored frying oil drizzled over top.

SPLIT PEA SOUP

An Acadian friend of my parents' told me that in her village, back in the day, families were so poor they used to "share the bone," which meant that after one household had made their split pea soup, they'd fish the bone out and pass it along to the neighbors so they could make their soup, too. Around the village the bone would go until it had nothing left on it. How's that for the sad and the beautiful wrapped up in one? These days, people often use ham hock instead of a bone because you can buy them separately and don't have to eat an entire ham to be able to make split pea soup. This dish is extremely popular in French Canada, and I, despite my Anglo roots, grew up on it as well. Serve small quantities for a first course and larger for a main.

Makes: 8 to 10 servings

2 cups (400 g) split peas
2 to 3 onions, chopped
½ pound (225 g) ham hock
10 cups (2.5 L) water
2 bay leaves
6 medium carrots, cut into small dice
Salt and pepper

Put the split peas, onions, ham hock, water, and bay leaves in a large pot. Bring slowly to the boil, skimming any foam that rises to the surface, then simmer until the peas are tender, about 1½ hours. Remove the ham hock, cut off the meat, and dice small. Put the meat back in the soup, adding the carrots at the same time, and continue cooking until the carrots are tender, about 20 minutes. Remove the bay leaves, season the soup with salt and pepper, and serve.

PARSLEY AND PARMESAN SALAD

I don't know how French parsley salad is, really. In France, they're fonder of salads made from a mixture of very delicate herbs, and frankly those are rather restauranty. Parsley, on the other hand, is crude, ubiquitous, strong tasting, banal . . . until you get shallots, garlic, lemon zest, and Parmesan cheese in there with it. Then it turns into the most delightful salad you can imagine! I don't serve this on its own; I serve it alongside other starters, such as Parmesan Flan (p. 82). It would also be good with poached fish.

Makes: 1 to 2 servings

1 pink shallot
1 garlic clove
3 large handfuls flat-leaf parsley leaves
Parmesan cheese
Lemon zest and juice
Olive oil
Salt and pepper

Mince the shallot and garlic, and put in a large bowl. Add the parsley. Shave over Parmesan using a vegetable peeler. Grate over a little lemon zest, and add a squeeze of juice. Drizzle over olive oil. Season with salt and pepper, and taste. Correct the seasonings, and serve.

CHÈVRE SALAD

I can't say I've ever been served this in a French home, but bistros in France always have it on the menu. Leafy greens such as arugula (rocket), oakleaf lettuce, or butter lettuce make the nicest base, rather than anything too coarse. I also love a delicate mesclun mix. The pine nuts give buttery crunch, and the hot chèvre wrapped in crisp bacon is like a little present on top. Looks very enticing and delivers on taste every time.

Makes: 2 to 4 servings

1 log chèvre, about 4 ounces (110 g)
4 slices bacon, cut in half crosswise
2 tablespoons (30 mL) pine nuts
4 handfuls of mixed light greens
A few spoonfuls of My House Vinaigrette (p. 229)

Heat the oven to 450°F (230°C). Slice the chèvre into four disks. Lay two half-slices of bacon in a cross, and set a chèvre disk at the center. Fold the ends of the bacon up over the chèvre, and lay seam side down on a baking sheet. Continue with the remaining bacon and chèvre. Bake for about 5 minutes, until the bacon is crisp and the cheese very hot.

Meanwhile, toast the pine nuts in a dry pan on the stovetop until golden. Put the salad together just before serving: toss the greens with some dressing, arrange on plates, scatter over the nuts, and lay the bacon-wrapped cheese packages on top.

BACON AND EGG SALAD

This is a first course in France, but I love it for lunch. You need frisée, which is a type of chicory, rather than lettuce, because the greens get tossed in a hot dressing and they need to be sturdy enough to stand the heat. When you're shopping for frisée, keep in mind that, like endive, the whiter the better, because it is less bitter. In France the heads are sold mostly white, but with some inevitable green leaves on the outside, which are always discarded. Here, growers tend to let the heads grow green, so there is only the slightest amount of white. This, fortunately, will change once we all start making a fuss about it. (Hint, hint.)

Makes: 2 generous servings

A splash of white wine vinegar
2 eggs
3 generous handfuls of frisée
4 slices bacon, cut into small pieces
About 3 tablespoons (45 mL) red wine or balsamic vinegar
1 to 2 tablespoons (15 to 30 mL) olive oil
Fleur de sel and freshly ground pepper

Bring a shallow pan of water to the boil. Add white wine vinegar. Reduce the heat to a simmer, and break in the eggs, one at a time. Poach until the white is set but the yolk is still runny inside, 2 to 3 minutes. Lift them out with a slotted spoon, and set them on paper towel to drain. (You can trim the edges a little if you want to.) Turn off the heat, and cover the pan to keep the water warm for reheating the eggs.

Wash the greens, and spin them dry. Fry the bacon in a sauté pan until crisp, about 5 minutes. Deglaze the pan with the red wine vinegar, and boil to reduce to about 2 teaspoons (10 mL). Whisk in enough oil to make a dressing. Toss the greens in the pan for a few seconds just to coat (don't let them wilt). Divide between two plates. Reheat the eggs in the water for a second or two, lift out, drain, and set alongside each salad. Season the salad and eggs with fleur de sel and pepper, and serve.

CELERIAC RÉMOULADE

This is a first course in France, and that's why I've put it here, but I also like it as a side dish for room-temperature meats, such as Pork Florentine (p. 145). The apple is a nice surprise in this version, and the fennel seed makes it far more interesting than the rémoulades you find in an average French bistro. Celeriac is also sold as celery root.

Makes: 4 servings

1 pound (450 g) celeriac (1 medium)
1 Granny Smith apple
1 egg yolk
1 tablespoon (15 mL) grainy Dijon mustard
1 teaspoon (5 mL) white wine vinegar
1 cup (250 mL) grapeseed oil
Salt and pepper
Lemon juice
2 teaspoons (10 mL) crushed fennel seeds

Peel the celeriac, halve the bulb, and slice into very thin julienne slices. Julienne the apple, and toss with the celeriac. In a small bowl, whisk the yolk with the mustard and vinegar. Whisk the grapeseed oil, drop by drop, to make a thick mayonnaise. Season with salt, pepper, and lemon juice. Stir in the fennel seeds, then toss with the celeriac to coat. Cover, and refrigerate until serving (several hours is fine; some would even argue it's *de rigueur*).

CAULIFLOWER SALAD

Here, cauliflower provides a mild, crunchy canvas for the punchier flavors of sun-dried tomatoes, black olives, lemon, and tarragon. The salad was served to me in France alongside grilled fish for lunch. In my house, it has garnished Roasted Red Pepper Mousse (p. 79) for an entrée (which, in France, means a first course, by the way, not a main).

Makes: 4 to 6 servings

1 small cauliflower or half a large one
1 garlic clove, minced
2 generous handfuls of oil-packed sun-dried tomatoes, thinly sliced
2 generous handfuls of black olives, pitted and sliced
2 handfuls of fresh tarragon or basil leaves, chopped
Zest of 1 lemon and juice to taste
Extra virgin olive oil, for drizzling
Salt and pepper

Break the cauliflower into florets, discarding the central stem. Slice thinly, and put in a bowl. Toss with the garlic, tomatoes, olives, tarragon, zest, juice, olive oil, and salt and pepper. Have a bite, then adjust the seasonings to please yourself. Serve, or cover and keep in the fridge until you're ready to eat it (after all, there is nothing here that will wilt).

MARINATED MUSHROOM SALAD

Picnics require food that can travel without going soggy, which is how I came to try this dish originally. To be honest, I think I first ate it in Germany, but really it says Mediterranean to me. I imagine roasted lamb on a long table outdoors, surrounded by all sorts of grilled and oil-slicked vegetables at room temperature, including these mushrooms. Peperoncini are dried Italian chili peppers the size of Thai bird chilies. Make this a day in advance.

Makes: 4 to 6 servings

1 pound (450 g) large button or cremini mushrooms
2 lemons
4 garlic cloves
⅔ cup (150 mL) olive oil
2 bay leaves
1 thyme sprig
4 whole peperoncini or a few pinches of crushed chili pepper
Fleur de sel
A handful of chopped fresh parsley

Heat the oven to 425°F (220°C). Clean the mushrooms with a damp cloth and discard the stems (or use them to make stock). Put the caps on a baking sheet, stem side down, and bake for 5 to 6 minutes to dry them out a bit and intensify their taste. Remove to a glass bowl.

While the mushrooms cook, zest and juice 1 lemon into a saucepan. Mince 3 garlic cloves and add them along with the olive oil, bay leaves, thyme, and peperoncini. Heat, but do not boil, then pour over the mushrooms and set aside to cool. Cover and refrigerate overnight, turning once.

To serve, grate over the zest of the remaining lemon. Mince and add the remaining garlic clove. Season with salt, and toss with the parsley.

FENNEL AND MUSHROOM SALAD

It was a weekend gathering at my friend Camille's in Normandy, and David Tanis, author of *A Platter of Figs and Other Recipes* and a chef from Chez Panisse restaurant in Berkeley, was cooking us all dinner. When the mention of this salad came up, I thought, "Oh, that sounds awfully . . . white, doesn't it?" So, yes, this is a little story about my having to eat my words, because the salad isn't at all bland looking (the parsley and lemon add lots of color), and neither is it remotely bland tasting. Somehow mild soft mushrooms, crisp licoricey fennel, and fresh leaves of parsley bring out the best in one another. So, this is David's recipe, mentally jotted down while I watched him prepare it in his usual effortless way. It has become one of my top salads.

Makes: 4 servings

1 shallot, minced
2 tablespoons (30 mL) white wine vinegar
1 fennel bulb
½ pound (225 g) button or cremini mushrooms, sliced
Leaves from a large bouquet of parsley
A handful of chopped fresh chives
Olive oil
Salt and pepper
Lemon juice
Parmesan curls

Put the shallot and vinegar in a ramekin, and set aside to macerate. Cut the stalks off the fennel bulb and discard, then use a vegetable peeler to peel any discolored parts off the bulb. Cut the bulb in half lengthwise, and cut out the core if it's large. Slice the bulb crosswise very thinly, and put in a large bowl. Toss with the mushroom slices and parsley leaves. Drain the shallot, discarding the vinegar, and add to bowl along with chives. Dress with olive oil, and season with salt, pepper, and lemon juice. Serve with Parmesan curls on top.

FENNEL AND PINE NUT SALAD WITH CITRUS ZESTS

This is simple and quick to prepare, and I have not served it once without being asked for the recipe. It's perfect as a first course before something substantial like Beef and Carrot Stew (p. 158).

Makes: 4 servings

1 large fennel bulb
Zest and juice of 1 lemon
Zest of 1 orange
3 tablespoons (45 mL) toasted pine nuts
Olive oil
Fleur de sel and freshly ground pepper

Cut the stalks from the fennel, and discard, reserving a good handful of the green fronds. Chop the fronds, and toss into a bowl. Use a vegetable peeler to peel any discolored bits off the bulb, then halve, core, and slice paper-thin crosswise, using a mandoline (or a very sharp knife if mandolines scare you, as they do me). Add to the bowl. Grate over the citrus zests. Squeeze over lemon juice to taste. Add the pine nuts, drizzle over oil, and season with salt and pepper. Toss, taste, adjust the seasonings, and serve immediately.

LEEKS VINAIGRETTE

Shut your eyes for a second and think about it: a boiled leek all alone on a plate. Right, so it does sound pretty dismal. But that's why I love this recipe: the idea of it is completely misleading! The fact is that boiled leeks have a mild, sweet flavor and a delicate, silky texture. And, anyway, they're not really alone. There's dressing: a light vinaigrette with lemon zest and peelings of Parmesan cheese that make the leeks utterly elegant.

Makes: 6 servings

6 slender leeks
Salt and pepper
1 shallot, minced
About 3 tablespoons (45 mL) white wine vinegar
1 teaspoon (5 mL) Dijon mustard
About ½ cup (125 mL) olive oil
1 lemon
Parmesan cheese, for serving

Trim the root ends of the leeks, and cut the tops off just above where the dark green starts. Cut a slit lengthwise down the leek, going about halfway into it, and rinse thoroughly in cold water to remove any grit. Bring a pan of water to boil. Salt it. Tie the leeks in bundles so they don't fall apart, and gently boil, covered, until tender, about 10 minutes, depending on their size. Drain and rinse under ice-cold water to preserve their color. Drain thoroughly, pat dry with a towel, and refrigerate until about an hour before serving.

For the vinaigrette, macerate the shallot in enough vinegar to cover for 10 minutes. Drain off the vinegar. Stir the mustard and oil into the shallots, and season well. Taste, adding more oil or vinegar to balance as needed.

Arrange the leeks on a serving platter. Spoon over the vinaigrette. Shave over lemon zest and Parmesan cheese, then finish with a grinding of pepper.

COURGETTE RÖSTI

Courgette is the French word for zucchini (Both mean "small squash," as a regular squash is *courge* in French and *zucca* in Italian). Anyway, we had an absolute glut of them in the garden one year (or is that every year?), but once I found this recipe, I didn't mind. Fresh herbs would be a more French flavoring, but I prefer spices here because zucchini are so notoriously bland. These cute grated cakes are excellent with thick homemade mayonnaise (and see p. 20 for Roasted Garlic Aïoli) – a nice light start to a summer dinner.

Makes: 4 servings

2 pounds (900 g) zucchini
Salt and pepper
1 egg, lightly beaten
1 bunch green onions, thinly sliced
1 cup (80 g) dry bread crumbs
2 garlic cloves, finely chopped
½ cup (125 mL) chopped fresh parsley
1 teaspoon (5 mL) chili powder
½ teaspoon (2 mL) paprika
Pinch cayenne pepper
Olive oil, for frying

Grate the zucchini into a large colander, sprinkle generously with salt, and set in the sink to drain for 30 minutes. A good deal of water will come off. Drain, turn onto a clean tea towel, and squeeze over the sink to remove the excess water. (This is a necessary step to avoid soggy cakes.) Heat the oven to 200°F (100°C), and put an oven-safe platter in it.

In a bowl, combine the zucchini with the egg, green onions, bread crumbs, garlic, parsley, chili powder, paprika, cayenne, and black pepper; mix thoroughly. Taste, and adjust the seasonings. Shape into small fritters. Cover the bottom of a sauté pan with olive oil (or other oil, frankly), and heat over medium-high heat. When it is very hot, fry the fritters in batches. Turn the fritters when they are golden on the underside, and cook until golden all over and tender. Transfer the cooked fritters to the platter in the oven so they stay warm while you finish the others. Serve hot.

TOMATO-STUFFED PEPPERS

You can stuff a pepper with lots of things – for example, rice, cheese, and sautéed vegetables for a main course – but for a first course it's nice to keep things light. These are cheerful and flavorful, with a little chèvre sneaked in or not, and they do wonders to brighten a buffet table. This recipe is easily multiplied.

Makes: 2 servings

1 orange pepper
2 tablespoons (30 mL) tapenade
4 fresh basil leaves
1 ripe tomato, quartered
2 garlic cloves, thinly sliced
Extra virgin olive oil, for drizzling
Salt and pepper

Heat the oven to 375°F (190°C). Cut the pepper in half lengthwise, leaving the stems intact. Remove the seeds, and place the pepper halves in a small baking dish. Spread a spoonful of tapenade on the bottom of each pepper half. Lay two basil leaves in each, then place two tomato quarters in each pepper half, seed side up. Scatter over the sliced garlic. Drizzle with olive oil, and season with salt and pepper. Bake until the pepper is completely soft and getting dark around the edges, about an hour. Serve with crusty bread.

ASPARAGUS WITH ORANGE SAUCE

I have a recipe for this in my book *French Food at Home,* but I have to give it to you again here because I have improved and simplified it since the old days. This is one of those dishes that people eat at my house and then go home and immediately add to their repertoires, which is the greatest compliment any cook can hope for. That's why it baffles me that anyone would ever be stingy about sharing recipes.

Makes: 4 servings

1 pink shallot
3 tablespoons (45 mL) white wine vinegar
2 oranges
½ teaspoon (2 mL) Dijon mustard
3 to 4 tablespoons (45 to 60 mL) olive oil
Salt and pepper
20 spears green asparagus, trimmed
Parmesan cheese, for shaving

Mince the shallot, put it in a ramekin, and pour the vinegar over it. Set aside for 5 minutes. Zest 1 orange into a bowl, and set aside. Juice both oranges into a small saucepan, and boil the juice down to about 3 tablespoons (45 mL).

Strain the reduced juice over the zest, and whisk in the mustard. Drain the shallot, discarding the vinegar, and add. Whisk all together, then slowly whisk in the oil. Taste, and season with salt and pepper. Set aside.

Bring a sauté pan of water to the boil. Salt it, then add the asparagus and cook until tender. Drain, and immediately rinse under ice-cold water to set the color. Pat dry with paper towels, and transfer to a serving platter. Spoon over the dressing. Shave over Parmesan cheese. Grind over some pepper. Serve.

STUFFED MUSHROOM CAPS

I like a first course to tease the appetite, never spoil it, which explains my penchant for vegetable starters. I came up with this mushroom dish to begin a dinner with a woodland theme. They fit the bill perfectly because they're elegant to look at and there's a lot going on to amuse the mouth: the soft density of the mushrooms, the heat of the chili peppers, the crunch of the herb-flecked crumbs, the freshness of chèvre, and the rich sweet-acidity of the balsamic vinegar glaze. You wouldn't think you could get so much into a little mushroom cap, would you? (If you are using portobellos, scrape out the black gills so there's room for the stuffing.) I buy balsamic glaze in specialty shops. If you can't find it, a bit of vinegar boiled down will do the trick, although it will be thinner.

Makes: 6 servings

6 puck-sized button mushrooms or small portobellos (about 1 pound/450 g total)
Olive oil
2 tablespoons (30 mL) butter
1 shallot, minced
1 garlic clove, minced
¼ teaspoon (1 mL) crushed chili pepper
2 teaspoons (10 mL) chopped fresh thyme
3 to 4 tablespoons (45 to 60 mL) fresh bread crumbs
A handful of chopped fresh parsley
Salt and pepper
4 ounces (110 g) fresh chèvre
Watercress or pea sprouts, for serving
Balsamic glaze, for serving

Heat the oven to 375°F (190°C). Finely chop the mushroom stems, and set them aside. Set the caps, holes downwards, on a baking sheet, rub with a little olive oil, and bake 10 minutes to shrink slightly.

Meanwhile, melt the butter in a sauté pan over medium heat, and gently fry the shallot until slightly soft, about 3 minutes. Add the mushroom stems, and cook until soft, about 5 more minutes. Add the garlic, chili pepper, and thyme; sauté 1 minute. Stir through all but a spoonful of the bread crumbs. Remove from the heat, taste, and season the mixture. In a small bowl, stir together the parsley and remaining bread crumbs.

Pull the mushrooms from the oven, and turn them holes skywards. Season with salt and pepper. Divide the cheese evenly among them, pile on the filling, then scatter the parsley mixture evenly over top. Drizzle with olive oil, and bake until the tops are golden and the filling very hot, about 20 minutes. Serve with watercress or sprouts on the side and a generous swirl of balsamic glaze.

AUBERGINE CHARLOTTES WITH TOMATO SALAD

Individually portioned food is something I do only when it makes sense, and here it does because it gives every serving just the right proportion of puréed eggplant flan to cooked slices of eggplant. You can serve each little round on individual plates with the tomato salad spooned onto the side, or, for a more convivial presentation, unmold all the charlottes onto one big platter and pass a bowl of tomato salad around after it. Thinking of further possibilities, you could always serve the charlottes without the salad as a side dish for lamb, although that's getting pretty fancy.

Makes: 6 servings

For the aubergine charlottes

2 medium eggplants
¼ cup (60 mL) olive oil
Salt and pepper
1 tablespoon (15 mL) cumin seeds, toasted and ground
3 eggs, lightly beaten
¼ cup (60 mL) milk
4 ounces (110 g) fresh chèvre, crumbled

For the tomato salad

12 small tomatoes on the vine
A handful of fresh coriander leaves
2 tablespoons (30 mL) olive oil
2 teaspoons (10 mL) white wine vinegar, more to taste
Salt and pepper

For the charlottes, heat the oven to broil. Slice 1 eggplant lengthwise into ¼-inch (5 mm) slices. Arrange on a baking sheet, brush both sides with olive oil, and season lightly with salt and pepper. Broil until soft and golden on each side, 10 to 15 minutes (they should not get crisp). Remove, and set aside.

Turn the oven down to 375°F (190°C). Cut the other eggplant in half lengthwise. Brush the cut sides with oil and lay cut side down on a baking sheet. Bake until very soft, about 40 minutes. Scrape the soft flesh into a bowl. Mix in the ground cumin, eggs, and milk. Season with salt and pepper.

Line six ½-cup (125 mL) ramekins with the 2 or 3 eggplant slices each, leaving an overhang all around so that you can fold them in to cover the top at the end. Spoon half the creamed eggplant mixture into the ramekins. Scatter over the chèvre. Top with the rest of the eggplant mixture. Fold the slices in over the top. Set on a baking sheet. Bake until set, about 20 minutes. Cool at least 10 minutes before turning out.

For the salad, quarter the tomatoes, and put them in a bowl. Add the coriander, oil, and vinegar, and season with salt and pepper. Toss gently, taste, and adjust the seasonings. Turn the charlottes out onto plates, and spoon some tomato salad alongside. Serve.

ROASTED RED PEPPER MOUSSE

I resisted this recipe for a long time because I had a gelatin phobia and because the whole idea of a savory mousse was reminding me of jellied salads and flouncy wallpaper from the 1940s. There. I'm glad I got that off my chest. The thing I've learned about gelatin, however, is that when you use the right amount, it's as though it's not even there. And the thing I've learned about retro 1940s-style food is that some of it is actually good. I serve this mousse on arugula as a first course when I've got a crowd coming. It's practical, because you can make it a day ahead. The only exotic ingredient is Espelette pepper (piment d'Espelette), which is ground hot pepper from Basque country, but feel free to use paprika and a pinch of cayenne instead.

If you're roasting the peppers yourself, put them on a baking sheet and broil, turning once or twice, until the skins are blackened, about 20 minutes. As soon as they're out of the oven, put them in a bowl, cover with plastic wrap, and set aside 10 minutes to steam the skins loose. Pull the skins off the peppers and discard along with the seeds.

Makes: 6 servings

2 tablespoons (30 mL) olive oil
2 onions, diced
2 garlic cloves, minced
4 roasted red peppers, peeled, seeded, and finely chopped
2 cups (500 mL) chicken or vegetable stock
2 tablespoons (30 mL) tomato paste
Salt and pepper
Pinch Espelette pepper
4 teaspoons (20 mL) gelatin
A squirt of lemon juice (optional)
1 cup (250 mL) heavy cream

Heat the oil in a sauté pan over medium heat, and gently cook the onions and garlic until soft. Add the red peppers, ⅔ cup (150 mL) of the stock, and the tomato paste. Season with salt, pepper, and Espelette pepper, and simmer until the vegetables are tender and the liquid completely evaporated. Purée with an immersion blender, and transfer to a metal or glass bowl.

Stir the gelatin into the remaining stock in a small saucepan, and heat, stirring to dissolve. Stir it into the purée. Set over a bed of ice until the mixture is cool and mounds when dropped from a spoon. Check the seasonings, adding lemon juice if needed. (The mixture should be highly seasoned because the cream will dilute the taste a bit.) Whip the cream, and gently fold it in. Pour into a mold, cover, and chill at least 4 hours.

COCOTTE EGGS

I've always been served these as a first course in France, but I feel that anything eggish can easily sashay into main-course position for lunch. My only warning is that you should watch that they not overcook, because you want them creamy enough to dip toast fingers into.

Makes: 2 servings

2 teaspoons (10 mL) "surprise" (e.g., crumbled blue cheese or smoked fish, or a few truffle shavings or leaves of tarragon)
2 eggs
2 teaspoons (10 mL) crème fraîche
Salt and pepper
A scattering of chopped fresh chives

Heat the oven to 375°F (190°C). Into the bottom of each of two buttered ½-cup (125 mL) ramekins, put a spoonful of "surprise." Gently crack an egg on top. Top with a spoonful of crème fraîche. Season with salt and pepper. Sprinkle with the chives.

Set the ramekins in a baking dish, and pour in hot water to come halfway up the sides of the ramekins. Bake until the egg is cooked but still jiggling, 5 to 7 minutes. Serve with buttered toast fingers for dipping.

PARMESAN FLAN

Parmesan makes this more Italian, I know, but the idea of savory custard as a first course is terribly French. (Anyway, you could use Roquefort cheese instead of Parmesan if you feel disloyal.) I usually bake this mixture in one large dish, but if you lean toward individual servings, by all means use ramekins. In either case, the flan has to cool slightly before you unmold it so that it holds shape. These need a few salad leaves on the side and perhaps a cracker, and they're just right.

Makes: 6 to 8 servings

1½ cups (375 mL) milk
1½ cups (375 mL) heavy cream
1 bay leaf
1 garlic clove, halved
4 whole eggs + 2 yolks
About 1½ cups (200 g) finely grated Parmigiano-Reggiano
Salt and white pepper

Heat the oven to 325°F (160°C). Butter six to eight ½-cup (125 mL) ramekins. Bring the milk, cream, bay leaf, and garlic to the boiling point in a saucepan. Turn off the heat, cover, and leave to infuse for 15 minutes. Beat the eggs, yolks, and cheese together in a bowl. Whisk in the milk mixture. Taste, and season with salt and pepper. Pull out the garlic and bay leaf, and pour the custard into the ramekins. Set in a baking dish, pour in hot water to come halfway up the sides of the ramekins, and bake until just set, 30 to 40 minutes. Serve slightly warm or at room temperature, unmolded onto plates.

VEGETABLE TERRINE

This is not difficult to do, but it takes a bit of time preparing the vegetables, unless you have a baby in the house and can nick some of his purées. There is no rule about the type of vegetable purées you can use (anything from roasted peppers to boiled beets is fair game), only that you want three that taste good together and have different colors so that the terrine has beautiful stripes to admire. Just so you know, for 1 cup (250 mL) vegetable purée, you need about 8 ounces (250 g) of raw vegetable to start with. Simply boil the vegetables separately in salted water until soft; drain, shock in ice-cold water, drain again, and purée in the blender until very smooth. Then you're ready to go.

Makes: 8 servings

8 large beet leaves or ruby Swiss chard leaves
1 cup (250 mL) cauliflower purée
1 cup (250 mL) pea purée
1 cup (250 mL) carrot purée
1½ ounces (40 g) grated Parmesan cheese
6 eggs
1½ cups (375 mL) heavy cream
Salt and pepper

Heat the oven to 350°F (180°C). Bring a large pot of water to the boil. Salt it and blanch the beet greens for 1 minute. Remove the leaves and immediately rinse under ice-cold water to set their color. Gently lay on tea towels, and pat dry with another tea towel. They should not have any water on them for the next step.

Line the bottom of a buttered 4-cup (1 L) terrine mold with a piece of parchment. Neatly lay in the beet leaves to cover the bottom and sides completely. Leave a generous overhang so the leaves can be folded over the completed terrine later.

Into each purée, beat ⅓ of the grated Parmesan, 2 eggs, and ½ cup (125 mL) cream. Season each with salt and pepper. Pour the heaviest of the three purées into the bottom of the mold. Pour the second evenly over top, and finish with the lightest. Fold the overhanging beet leaves over top to cover. Set the terrine in a baking dish, pour in hot water to come halfway up the sides of the terrine, and bake until set, about an hour.

Remove the terrine from the water bath, and cool completely on a wire rack. If possible, chill overnight so it sets. At least half an hour before serving, turn the terrine out onto a cutting board or platter for serving in slices.

CHEESE AND HERB SOUFFLÉ

My mother often used to make cheese soufflé for dinner when we were growing up, so I never had the sense that it was something fancy. And it isn't! The only reason it has the reputation of being tricky is that you have to eat it immediately after it comes out of the oven, before it falls. Well, that's no different from pasta – you have to eat that as soon as it's out of the pot, too, and nobody seems to find that traumatic. So it's time we all started seeing soufflés for what they really are: a simple solution to supper or a classic first course.

Makes: 8 first-course servings or 4 main-course servings

1 cup (250 mL) milk
1 bay leaf
½ small onion, peeled
Pinch paprika
Finely grated Parmesan, for dusting the dish
1½ tablespoons (25 mL) butter
1½ tablespoons (25 mL) flour
3 eggs, separated + 1 egg white
3 ounces (90 g) cheese of your choice, grated or mashed
A handful of chopped fresh herbs
Salt and pepper

Put the milk with the bay leaf, onion, and a pinch of paprika in a small saucepan, and bring just to the boil. Turn off the heat, cover, and set aside to infuse for 10 minutes. Heat the oven to 400°F (200°C). Butter eight ½-cup (125 mL) ramekins or one 4-cup (1 L) soufflé dish or casserole, and dust with the grated Parmesan.

Remove the bay leaf and onion from the milk. Melt the butter in a large saucepan over medium heat. Whisk in the flour and cook, whisking, 1 minute. Gradually add the hot milk, whisking, and cook, stirring, until thick, about 5 minutes. Remove from the heat, and beat in the egg yolks. Stir through the cheese and herbs. Season well with salt and pepper.

Beat the whites to stiff peaks with a pinch of salt. Stir about a quarter of the egg whites into the yolk mixture to lighten it, then pour the yolk mixture onto the remaining whites and gently fold together. Pour into the soufflé dish, and bake until risen and set but still slightly creamy in the center, about 30 minutes, depending on the size of the soufflé dishes (ramekins don't take as long as a big dish). Serve immediately, before it slumps.

LOBSTER AND GRAPEFRUIT SALAD

Lobster is too often smothered in mayonnaise, melted butter, or buttery sauce, but it doesn't really need any of those toppings because it's rich in its own right. Combining lobster with grapefruit and avocado makes for a fresh salad classic that's nonetheless a little out of the ordinary. It's filling, so serve small portions, or serve it as lunch.

Makes: 4 servings

2 live lobsters, about 1½ pounds (675 g) each
2 large grapefruit
1 avocado
A squeeze of lemon
2 to 3 green onions
2 handfuls of flat-leaf parsley leaves
2 tablespoons (30 mL) almond, hazelnut, or walnut oil
1 tablespoon (15 mL) olive oil
Salt and pepper

Bring a very large pot of water to the boil. Salt it and add the lobsters, head first. Put the lid on the pot and boil until the lobsters are bright red and cooked, about 10 minutes. Drain, and rinse under cold water.

While the lobster is cooking, peel the grapefruit, taking care to remove all the bitter white pith. Remove the grapefruit sections with a small knife, cutting between the membranes and working over a large bowl to catch the juice. Add the grapefruit to the juice.

To remove the lobster meat, twist off the claws and crack them using the back of a chef's knife. Pull out the meat. (You may need a pick for the tube-like limbs attached.) Now twist the tails off the bodies. Lay them flat on their sides and press down to crack the center. Pull out the meat. Discard the bodies and shells (or use them to make bisque or sauce). Chop the lobster meat into large chunks and add it to the grapefruit.

Cut the avocado into chunks and add it to the bowl along with a generous squeeze of lemon. Chop the green onions, including the green part, and add along with the parsley leaves, almond oil, olive oil, and salt and pepper. Toss. Taste, adjusting the seasonings (adding a little lemon zest if you like), and serve.

SHRIMP WITH GARLIC AND BASIL OIL

This dish is so fast and lip-smacking, you can't go wrong. I learned it using unpeeled langoustines, but shrimp work if you prefer, as long as they start out raw. Usually, I serve sautéed fennel on the side (p. 206), which signals "knife and fork," but the truth is I always end up diving into the shrimp with my fingers. There are times when bad manners just seem so . . . right.

Makes: 4 servings

24 jumbo tiger shrimp or langoustine tails, unpeeled
2 garlic cloves, minced
2 generous handfuls of shredded basil leaves
¼ cup (60 mL) olive oil
Salt

Cut the shrimp in half lengthwise. Toss together with the garlic, basil, and olive oil. Cover, and let sit in the fridge for about an hour (or longer) to marinate. Remove half an hour before cooking.

Heat the oven to broil. Spread the tails over a baking sheet, cut side up, dribbling over any basil oil that stays behind in the bowl. Sprinkle over some salt, and broil 5 minutes or until the flesh is cooked. Serve.

FRIED TUNA AND EGG IN PASTRY

Brik is a North African pastry that is thin like phyllo, only made more like a crêpe so it's sturdier. look for it in Middle Eastern shops to make these divinely tasty filled and fried purses. Or make a variation with phyllo dough that gets baked in the oven. Both are great as a first course or for lunch.

Makes: 4 to 6 servings

1 tin (6½ ounces/185 g) tuna, drained
A generous handful of chopped fresh parsley and/or coriander
A few handfuls of grated Emmental or Gruyère cheese
Salt and pepper
4 to 6 sheets brik pastry (if frying) or phyllo pastry (if baking)
Cooking oil (if frying) or melted butter (if baking)
4 to 6 eggs

Mix together the tuna, herbs, and cheese in a bowl. Season with salt and pepper. Set aside.

For the fried version using brik pastry: Here's how you work with the rounds of brik: Imagine there is a square sitting right inside the circle of pastry. (If you can't picture this, draw a circle on paper, then draw a square in it with the corners all touching the circle. Get it?) Fold the parts of the circle outside the square in over the square. Now you have a square instead of a circle. In the center of that square, make a doughnut of tuna filling. Repeat with the remaining brik and filling.

Heat an inch of oil in a wok over high heat. Working with one pastry square at a time, crack an egg into the ring of filling. Fold one corner of the square over to the one kitty-corner to it, to make a triangle. Lay this in the hot oil. (This sounds risky, but don't worry: with this much spitting-hot oil, the purses seal instantly and nothing has a chance to run out.) Cook until crisp and golden on the underside, about 3 minutes. Flip, and cook until golden on the other. Lift out onto a plate (or set on paper towel to drain for a minute or two if needed). Continue with the remaining pastries, but these are best eaten more or less right away.

For the baked version using phyllo dough: Heat the oven to 425°F (220°C). Working with one sheet of phyllo at a time, and keeping the remaining sheets covered with a damp towel, cut the sheet in three horizontally. Lightly brush each third with melted butter. Arrange them on top of each other in a star shape. In the center of that star, make a doughnut of tuna filling. Crack the egg into the ring. Season. Pull the phyllo edges into a bundle, twist the top, and set on a baking sheet. Make the remaining bundles.

Brush the bundles with melted butter. Bake for 5 minutes for a runny egg inside and 10 minutes for a firm egg.

BRANDADE CAKES

Brandade is essentially salt cod puréed, sometimes with potato, served as a first course or main course in French bistros, usually in a flat terra-cotta dish. This recipe is pretty much the same thing, just fried in tiny cakes. You can make them small for a first course or larger for a main, and serve a nice arugula salad on the side. I also like a confit of red peppers and tomato to serve on top (p. 222).

Now, in case salt cod is new to you, know that you have to desalt it before you can use it. All you do is soak it in a lot of cold water for 24 to 48 hours, changing the water about three times. I use a large glass bowl and just keep it in the fridge, but any coolish place will do. This step pulls the salt out of the fish and softens it, so it's all ready to use.

Makes: about 20 cod cakes

1¼ pounds (525 g) salt cod, desalted (see above) and cut into large pieces
2 large potatoes, sliced
6 garlic cloves, halved
1 bay leaf
1 thyme sprig
3 parsley stems
¼ cup (60 mL) milk
½ teaspoon (2 mL) Espelette pepper or hot paprika
A generous handful of chopped fresh parsley leaves
A generous handful of chopped fresh chives
Salt
Peanut or grapeseed oil, for frying
Flour, for dredging

Put the cod, potatoes, and garlic in a large saucepan. Tie the bay leaf, thyme sprig, and parsley stems with string and add. Add enough cold water to cover, and bring to a bare simmer. Poach until the potatoes and cod are tender, about 15 minutes. Drain.

Discard the herb bundle. Separate the cod from the potatoes. Mash the potatoes with the milk. Shred the cod finely. Then combine the two again, mixing until creamy. Stir in the Espelette pepper, parsley, chives, and salt. Check the seasonings.

Pour an inch of oil into a frying pan, and heat to sizzling. Shape the cod mixture into small cakes. Just before frying, dip them in flour to coat. Fry in batches, without crowding the pan, until very brown and crisp on both sides, about 5 minutes per side. Drain on paper towels. Serve.

MUSHROOM VOL-AU-VENTS

Perhaps these should be a main course, but I tend to appreciate richer dishes like this in smaller portions. (Unlike when I was seven and thought these were the height of sophistication made big and with lots of green peas in the mix.) Recently, I made bite-sized vol-au-vents for a cocktail party and they disappeared very swiftly, so I know there's a market for them. You know what we're talking about, of course: chicken à la king, flaky puff pastry shells filled with chicken and mushrooms in a light creamy sauce. Oh come on, you *do so* want one!

Makes: 6 servings

For the pastry

2 (7-ounce/200 g) squares puff pastry
1 egg whisked with 1 tablespoon (15 mL) water, for egg wash

For the filling

1 cup (250 mL) chicken stock
1 bay leaf
3 tablespoons (45 mL) butter
1 onion or large shallot, minced
4 ounces (110 g) mushrooms, chopped
1 garlic clove, minced
1 tablespoon (15 mL) flour
2 tablespoons (30 mL) white wine
2 cooked chicken breasts, finely diced
¼ cup (60 mL) crème fraîche
1 to 2 teaspoons (5 to 10 mL) Dijon mustard
Salt and pepper
A few handfuls of chopped fresh parsley

First, prepare the vol-au-vent pastry shells. Heat the oven to 425°F (220°C). On a lightly floured surface, roll out the puff pastry ⅛ inch (3 mm) thick. Using a large cookie cutter, cut 6 rounds from each sheet of puff pastry so you have 12 pieces. Using a smaller cutter, cut the center out of 6 rounds, leaving a ½-inch (1 cm) margin. Lay the 6 full rounds on a damp baking sheet and brush with egg wash. Lay the 6 rings on top of each round without pressing down. Dip a finger in egg wash and run it around the top. Scallop the edges with the tip of a knife. Prick the bottoms with a fork. Bake for 10 minutes. Press down the centers. Continue baking until golden, about 10 minutes longer.

For the filling, put the stock and bay leaf in a small saucepan. Bring to the boil, and turn off the heat. Melt the butter in a sauté pan over medium-high heat, and fry the onion for 2 minutes. Add the mushrooms, and cook until shrunken and dark.

Add the garlic, and sauté for 1 minute. Sprinkle over the flour, and cook, stirring, 1 minute. Add the wine, and cook, stirring, until it disappears. Pour over the stock, add the chicken, and cook, stirring, until the sauce thickens, about 3 minutes. Stir in the crème fraîche and mustard. Season. Stir through the parsley. Remove the bay leaf. Spoon the filling into the vol-au-vent shells, and serve.

BABY ENDIVE TARTES TATIN

It's not that I'm lazy; it's that I hate to fuss, which explains everything about these cute tarts. I figure, why struggle to keep caramelizing endives intact when it's their natural instinct to fall apart? Let them fall apart! Then poke the silky bittersweet strands of leaves into muffin tins, top with rounds of pastry, and pop them in the oven. Once turned out, they are as adorable as they were painless. I serve them with a little salad on the side.

Makes: 6 baby tarts

2 tablespoons (30 mL) sugar
3 tablespoons (45 mL) red wine vinegar
1 tablespoon (15 mL) olive oil
2 tablespoons (30 mL) butter
A handful of chopped fresh rosemary
6 heads endive, halved lengthwise (quartered if huge)
Salt and pepper
A good splash of red wine, about 3 tablespoons (45 mL)
1 (7-ounce/200 g) square puff pastry

In a large sauté pan over medium heat, heat the sugar until it has melted, about 5 minutes. Stir in the vinegar, then the olive oil, butter, and rosemary. Lay the endive on top, cut side down. Sprinkle with salt and pepper, cover with foil, and cook over medium-low heat, turning a few times, until very soft and darkly caramelized, about 45 minutes. Uncover, pour over the wine, and continue cooking to reduce the pan juices to a glaze, about 15 minutes. The endives will be caramelized and soft by now, and slightly falling apart. Perfect.

Heat the oven to 400°F (200°C). Divide the endives among 6 nonstick muffin tins. On a lightly floured surface, roll out the pastry ⅛ inch (3 mm) thick. Cut out 6 rounds to fit the tops. Cover each muffin cup of endive with a pastry round, tucking it down around the endives like a blanket. Bake until the pastry is golden and puffed up, about 20 minutes.

Flip out the baby tarts onto a cutting board. Serve straight from the board at the table, along with an arugula or frisée salad.

FIG, CHÈVRE, AND WALNUT TARTLETS

These sound and look quite fancy, but nothing could be easier to throw together, especially with the puff pastry bases. The neat trick with the pastry is that when cooked between two baking sheets, it gets nice and crisp and golden, making a decadent base for the port-poached figs with fresh chèvre softly spread beneath them.

Makes: 4 servings

1 cup (250 mL) ruby port
1 cup (200 g) sugar
12 small fresh figs
1 (7-ounce/200 g) square puff pastry
1 log fresh chèvre, about 4 ounces (110 g)
¼ cup (60 mL) heavy cream
A small handful of chopped fresh rosemary
Freshly ground pepper
¼ cup (60 mL) chopped toasted walnuts (optional)
Arugula, to serve

Heat the oven to 400°F (200°C). Heat the port and sugar in a saucepan to dissolve the sugar. Lay in the figs, cover with a round of parchment, and simmer 10 minutes. Remove the figs, and boil the port down to sauce consistency. Set aside.

On a lightly floured surface, roll out the pastry ⅛ inch (3 mm) thick. Using a 4-inch (10 cm) cookie cutter, cut 4 rounds from the pastry. Lay them on a parchment-lined baking sheet. Lay a second baking sheet on top, and bake until lightly golden, 15 to 20 minutes. Remove from the oven, but do not turn off the oven.

Cream the chèvre with a spoon, then stir in the cream until smooth. Stir in the rosemary, and season with pepper. Spread the cheese mixture over the pastry rounds. Halve the figs, and arrange over the cheese, then scatter over the nuts (if using). Bake until the cheese is hot, about 5 minutes. Serve with arugula and a swirl of port syrup on the side.

SAVORY SWISS CHARD TART

This is positively magnificent, especially when you make it in a springform pan with high-sided pastry (see p. 10), and it is truly one of the most delicious things I have ever eaten. In the south of France, you see sweet versions of this tart, but I prefer savory. Serve small slices for a first course, or bring it on a picnic and help yourself to enormous wedges.

Makes: 6 to 8 servings

1½ pounds (675 g) Swiss chard (about 2 bunches)
1 tablespoon (15 mL) olive oil
2 shallots, minced
1 garlic clove, minced
4 slices bacon, cut into lardons
3 eggs
1 cup (250 mL) crème fraîche, or heavy cream and sour cream combined
Salt and pepper
4 ounces (110 g) Gruyère cheese, grated
A handful of raisins
A handful of toasted pine nuts
1 deep savory tart shell (p. 10), baked in a 9-inch (22 cm) springform pan

Heat the oven to 375°F (190°C). Cut the chard leaves from the thick ribs. Chop the ribs and stems quite small, and shred the leaves. Set aside separately.

Heat the oil in a sauté pan over medium heat, and fry the shallots until soft and translucent. Add the garlic, and fry for 1 minute. Remove to a large bowl. In the same pan, fry the bacon until cooked but not crisp. Add it to the shallots. Fry the chard ribs in the bacon fat until tender, 7 to 10 minutes. (You may want to cover the pan for a few minutes to speed this up.) Stir in the chard leaves, cover, and cook until wilted, about 3 minutes.

Beat the eggs together with the crème fraîche. Season with salt and pepper. To the shallots, add the chard, cheese, raisins, and pine nuts; toss to combine evenly. Taste, and season. Fill the tart shell with the vegetable mixture, and pour over the cream mixture. Bake until the tart has set, about 30 minutes. Cool on a wire rack. Serve at room temperature.

NUTTY PASTA

Everyone sees the word *pasta* and automatically assumes "Italy!" But that's not the only country where "noodles" are eaten. The Germans have their *Spaetzle,* after all, and the French have egg noodles and ultra tiny *ravioles* – and, especially in the Riviera, a few interesting sauces for whatever Italianate pasta is going. The best-known Provençal one is a type of walnut and garlic pesto, and I think of this recipe, which has pistachios, almonds, and mint, as a more sophisticated variation on that theme. It comes out beautifully bright green, it tastes positively thrilling, and it is full of very healthy things. Vegetarians, rejoice!

Makes: 6 servings

2 ounces (55 g) almonds
2 ounces (55 g) pine nuts
2 ounces (55 g) pistachios
Leaves from a bunch of parsley
Leaves from a bunch of mint
12 ounces (375 g) spaghetti
Olive oil
Parmesan cheese, for grating
Orange zest (optional)

Put the nuts and herbs in the food processor and whiz up. The mixture should be fine but not completely pulverized – it should still have a bit of texture. Cook the spaghetti in boiling salted water until al dente. Drain. Toss with the nut paste, olive oil, cheese, and zest (if using). Serve immediately.

HOW TO COOK

There is no one way to cook, obviously, but we do all have a way that's best for us, and life is so much easier once we know what that is. For example, I don't cook well in chaos. It stresses me out, I get flustered, then I fly into a rage and start banging pots and dropping spoons on the floor. (Not a very flattering image, but what can I say? The truth isn't always pretty.) Now that I've got that figured out about myself, I don't even so much as peel an onion unless I've got the kitchen tidy first. I hate to cook under time pressure, too. I am a putterer of the highest order.

Yet another trait I've recognized is that my cooking suffers dreadfully when I'm in unfamiliar surroundings. As it happens, that has been the case for most of my adult life. I can count at least eighteen kitchens I've called "mine" over the past ten years, and of course none of them really was, so I predict that when the day comes that I finally have a kitchen that's 100 per cent mine, with everything I want in it organized my way, then my cooking will flourish! Meanwhile, I make do with what I've got, but I suppose there's really no such thing as a perfect kitchen anyway. Even those who've spent fortunes trying to achieve one inevitably discover some unforeseen flaw they must adapt to (no shelf deep enough for the jumbo roasting pan, a fridge door that opens the wrong way). The reality is that we and our kitchens all have our quirks. The trick, therefore, is to befriend them so that we can arrange, as much as possible, always to cook in circumstances that bring out the best in us and, by extension, in our cooking. Beyond that, happy cooking is largely a state of mind.

My father is just about the best role model I can think of when it comes to an admirable cooking attitude. He's one of those carefree wing-it types who laughs at himself easily, so he's never afraid to launch into dishes that the rest of us might find fussy, tiring, too risky, or, worst of all, potentially ego-crushing. For example, with a four-course dinner already in the works, he considers adding stuffed olives in cheese pastry for drinks "a wink" (his expression), whereas I call it a pain in the neck. He's the type who wakes up in the morning and, in the time it takes for his coffee to drip through the machine, has bread rising and is cookie-cutting his third sheet of gingersnaps. *That* type. His fearlessness astounds me, and – alas! – I can't say I share it, but I do know his secret: he treats cooking like play. It's all *la-di-da* and *dum-di-dum-dum* in his kitchen world, so, as with a game of blocks, if he builds something he doesn't like, he simply piles more blocks on top, or he knocks down the "masterpiece" and starts again, humming as he goes. Partly, that approach has to do with cooking to please yourself, instead of striving, martyr-like, to do whatever it is you've decided will please the rest of the world. Partly, it comes down to not taking yourself or your food too seriously.

My mother is an equally good cook, but a cook of a different kind. I think of her cooking not so much as "making" food but as "tending" to it, "doting" over it, just as she does her houseplants.

She'll start a soup in the morning, and then spend hours coaxing it along: stirring and tasting, adding a dash of this or that, going away to water her orchids, coming back, stirring and tasting some more, adjusting the heat, leaving it alone again to simmer . . . She is so patient, in fact, that she can spend *all day* on one pot of soup! You think, "She's nuts!" But when she pronounces it done, it's always the most sophisticated and satisfying soup you've ever tasted. You realize that her way of cooking has its own particular magic.

The moral of the story is: don't let anyone bully you into cooking "their" way. After all, one of the joys of cooking at home is that we're king of our own castle. We get to be entirely ourselves and take full charge of our creations.

Now, you'll think I am utterly incapable of practical advice, what with all this "find your inner cook" kind of talk, but I do have some: the way to become a skilled and happy home cook is to cook. Wait, let me finish. Take the case of coordination. One of the greatest challenges for the novice cook is figuring out how to have five dishes all on the bubble at once, then to get them to the table, hot and at their juiciest, at the same time. I used to marvel at this ability, and I thought I would never be able to achieve it. Well, not to brag, but I finally have. It's one of those knacks you acquire over time, and, no great mystery, you arrive at it simply by cooking dinner night after night. People talk about "instinct" in cooking, but that's nonsense. What they really mean is experience, and that you get from repeating things again and again. My mother always used to advise me that bread was done when you tapped the bottom of the loaf and it sounded hollow. Well, great, but what the heck does hollow sound like? The only road to that enlightenment is to make one loaf of bread, then another and another, tapping their bottoms as you go, until you recognize the sound of "done." The same is true of every aspect of cooking. We learn by doing, and doing.

Here's the good news: apart from brushing our teeth, there's probably no other activity we have a better chance of perfecting over the course of our lives than cooking. What other skill do we have the luxury of practicing several times a day? I've often considered how good I'd be at drawing or classical guitar if I'd spent a fraction as much time at those pursuits as I do at fixing things to eat. Not to turn cooking into an extracurricular activity, because for the most part it's not. But one of the nice things about getting to a place where you can cook without really "thinking" (and, more important, without being handcuffed to a recipe) is that cooking becomes relaxing fun, rather than a chore or goal. So, no matter what our level of cooking, we should just keep at it. That's my practical advice. The more we cook, the more natural and satisfying it becomes – and the more adventurous and confident *we* become.

LE PAIN

There is a certain romance to French bread because it has so short a life (a bit like a Night-blooming Cereus, stealthily blossoming in the dark, filling the air with its magic perfume, then abruptly curling in on itself and dropping silently to the ground. *Adieu!*) A baguette, for example, lasts a matter of hours, which explains why the French devotedly queue up outside their bakeries to buy fresh bread several times a day.

These bakery lineups are important clues, should you ever happen to be bread shopping in France. It's folly to assume that every bakery should make a great baguette, but usually at least one in every neighborhood (in Paris at least) will be quite good, even outstanding. There is an annual competition in Paris for the best baguette (the winner gets to supply the French president for a year), and any bakery that wins will display that honor on its shop window for years to come. But "best" is a tricky word, because there is never any single standard when you get into the realm of *la crème de la crème* of anything. Each "best baguette," therefore, is slightly different, and some people will prefer one over another. For example, some like their baguettes to taste quite "white" (for lack of a better word), whereas I personally prefer them a little earthier.

In any case, the place to find very good bread will be, as I said, at the bakery with the longest queue outside. I do admire this trait in the French, that they don't mind waiting for something good, no matter how long it takes. For them, pleasure wins hands down over convenience every time. Failing a telling queue to guide your search for wonderful bread in France, what you're looking for is true artisan creations, not the mass-produced factory fluff that gets delivered to supermarkets and low-grade bakeries in dough form and simply baked on site (often deceptively labeled "artisanal," by the way, so watch out). Taste will always reveal the truth, however: a good baguette has a crunchy crust and a soft but chewy inside (the "crumb") full of irregular holes. Meanwhile, a fine, tight, even crumb with blanched cottony texture wrapped in a sharp, roof-of-the-mouth-peeling crust is just the pits. You may have to eat a lot of baguettes before you can learn the difference between a bad one and a good one, so chalk up every bite, pleasant or painful, to education.

There is more to French bread than just baguettes, of course. Increasingly, you see bakers experimenting with different grains (and I like where this trend is going); however, for the most part French breads still tend to be variations on a white theme. For example, a *boule* is a round white loaf, and a *pain de campagne* is an oblong white loaf (with a few other grains, such as rye), but they all start out as pretty much the same dough. The chief difference is in the ratio of crust to crumb. In France, you see a greater variety of breads in restaurants, when the cheese trolley rolls through. What a treat to pair cheeses with variously grained breads filled with olives, walnuts, or apricots.

Still, at every French table, the baguette reigns supreme, morning, noon, and night. It doesn't matter what the meal. (Even if you're serving pasta, it would be unthinkable not to have baguette, too.) I remember once having some French people to dinner and forgetting the bread (easy to do, because Anglo-Saxons rarely bother unless they're having soup). Well, nobody would start eating! I was wondering if I was expected to say grace or something, when suddenly one guest gave me an incredulous look and yelped, "You forgot the bread!" So I learned that lesson. (Another thing I found out the hard way is that it is very bad luck to lay a baguette upside down on the table. I had one roll over on me once by accident, and you should have heard the gasps.)

When in France, I tend to follow the rules, but at home my bread habits revert to "normal" (such as, I don't eat bread with every meal and, in fact, I usually avoid white altogether). Still, if I'm entertaining French style, and certainly if I'm planning a cheese course, it's nice to revive tradition. Most recipes for "French bread" don't taste anything like French bread at all (which doesn't mean they're bad – they're just different), but here is one that comes quite close.

THE MIRACLE *BOULE*

Sometime toward the end of 2006, an article was published in the *New York Times* about a new way to make French bread, devised by New York baker Jim Lahey. It caused such a sensation that I doubt the world of bread will ever be the same again. Here was a bread with a shaggy, wet dough containing almost no yeast, which you let rise for up to two days and then baked, weirdly, in a Dutch oven. There's no denying it's a project, but this bread has the most amazingly mature flavor, with an incredibly chewy, airy lightness and an unsurpassed crisp crust. Don't worry, the first time I made it, I also thought, "Groan. All this waiting!" Mind you, I was asleep through most of it, since I let much of the rising happen through the night. As with childbirth, I suppose (not that I'd know), you soon forget the pains, because the rewards of the first bite are so otherworldly it's practically a spiritual experience. I got my version of the recipe from a chef friend who, eccentric as he is, recommended I make a double batch and bake two loaves at a time in a fish poacher. I have made the bread many times but not tried that method yet, although it's not a bad idea, considering, as we all know, that no one ever uses a fish poacher for anything else, except, perhaps, geraniums.

Makes: 1 *boule*

3 cups (375 g) flour
¼ teaspoon (1 mL) instant yeast
1¼ teaspoons (6 mL) salt
1½ cups (375 mL) water
Extra flour, wheat bran, or cornmeal, as needed

Mix the flour, yeast, and salt in a bowl. Stir in the water to blend. What you'll have is wet, shaggy, sticky dough, but not so wet as to be batter. Cover the bowl with a tea towel, and let it rest in a warm place for at least 12 and up to 24 hours. It's ready for the next step when the surface is dotted with bubbles.

Flour a work surface and dump the bread out onto it. Sprinkle over a little more flour and fold it once or twice. No need to knead. Cover with the tea towel, and let rest 15 minutes.

Using only enough flour to keep the dough from sticking to your fingers, shape the dough into a ball. Coat a cotton towel with flour, wheat bran, or cornmeal and lay the dough on it, seam side down, and dust with more flour, bran, or cornmeal. (You need quite a lot of flour because you want to be sure the dough doesn't stick to the towel.) Cover and let rise about 2 hours. When ready, the dough will be more than double in size.

Half an hour before the dough is ready, heat the oven to 450°F (230°C). Put an 8-quart (2 L) lidded cast-iron pot or Dutch oven (*cocotte*) inside to heat. When the dough is ready, remove the pot from the oven, and turn the dough into it, seam side up. (It will look messy, but this is okay.) Give the pan a gentle shake to settle the bread evenly. Cover with the lid and bake for 30 minutes. Remove the lid, and bake another 15 to 30 minutes, until the loaf is nicely browned. Cool on a rack.

Just as an aside, a good thing to read before becoming a bread maker, if you aren't one already, is Laurie Colwin's essay "Bread Baking Without Agony" in her classic collection *Home Cooking*. One of her main points is that you should not organize your life around a loaf of bread, but rather time things so that the bread adapts itself to your schedule. Nonchalantly slow-rising bread makes this quite easy. Interestingly, Colwin's recipe is much like the one here, only without the Dutch oven: she simply bakes the loaf on a cookie sheet with a few slashes on the top (450°F/230°C for the first half hour, then 425°F/220°C for a final 20 minutes). Well, actually, her recipe has ¾ cup (95 g) more flour, too, and she uses half milk/half water for the liquid, plus she kneads hers a little. Still, the bread seems to follow the same principle as this one: high water content and low yeast content, with a long, slow rise. The results of hers, for the record, sound equally life altering.

BREAD SOUP

Once, a long time ago, when I was sick and living in Germany, a very nice woman fed me *Haferflockensuppe,* which is a soup of toasted oatmeal and parsley in chicken broth. Sounds ghastly, I know, but it tasted divine, and this bread soup reminds me of it a bit – a rich and soothing savory broth with toast in it and melting cheese on top. Are you kidding me? Of course I want that on a cold winter's night when I'm all alone. I'd practically be willing to catch a cold just to deserve it.

Makes: 2 servings

2 heaping spoonfuls of goose fat or duck fat
6 garlic cloves, minced
1 bay leaf
A handful of chopped fresh thyme
3 cups (750 mL) chicken stock
Salt and pepper
2 thick slices of day-old baguette or other bread, toasted
Grated Comté or Gruyère cheese, for serving
Chopped fresh parsley, for serving

Melt the goose or duck fat in a soup pot over medium heat. Add the garlic, and cook it, stirring frequently, for 2 minutes. Add the bay leaf, thyme, and stock. Simmer for 30 minutes. Remove the bay leaf, and season with salt and pepper. Lay the toasted bread in the bottom of two soup plates. Ladle over the soup. Sprinkle with the cheese and parsley, and serve hot.

PAN BAGNAT

I remember seeing pictures of this oddball sandwich in magazines when I was a child, and it was always a whole round loaf of bread hollowed out and stuffed with tomatoes, eggs, onions, olives. Impressive, but I would love to know how anyone managed to get their mouth around it. Do yourself a favor and use a baguette – that way it's easy to slice and not too big to eat. *Bagnat* means "bathed," by the way, and refers to the fact that the sandwich is wet with tomato drippings and olive oil. It's very fresh tasting, I must say – perfect poolside fare.

Makes: 4 servings

2 very ripe tomatoes, sliced
1 small red onion, thinly sliced
Fresh basil leaves
Red wine vinegar
Salt and pepper
1 baguette
2 garlic cloves, halved
Extra virgin olive oil, for drizzling
A handful of black olives, pitted and sliced
2 hard-cooked eggs, sliced

Gently mix the tomatoes, onion, and basil leaves in a bowl. Season with red wine vinegar, and salt and pepper. Set aside to marinate for 5 minutes.

Cut the baguette in half lengthwise, and pull out about two-thirds of the middle from both the bottom and top, leaving a crusty bread shell. Rub the insides with the garlic halves, and drizzle generously with olive oil.

Fill the cavity with the tomato mixture. Spoon any remaining juice over the top of the baguette, and the rest over the tomato mixture. Make a layer of sliced olives. Lay the sliced egg over top, season with salt and pepper, and put the top of the bread back on, pressing down well. Wrap in parchment until serving. The longer it sits, the more the flavors will soak into the bread.

Main Courses

BASQUE EGGS MY WAY

I'll tell you something about authentic *oeufs basquaises:* they are ugly as all get out, a dreadful scramble with too many colors for comfort. However, they do taste great, what with the garlic, tomatoes, and the characteristic hot peppers. A dilemma! Well, I can't stand ugly food, so I had to compromise, and here is the result: Basque eggs meets *huevos rancheros* in a nest of cured ham, if you can get your head around that. Don't forget lightly toasted baguette to go on the side.

Makes: 4 servings

2 tablespoons (30 mL) olive oil
2 onions, sliced
2 garlic cloves, minced
1 red pepper, cut into thin julienne
1 green pepper, cut into thin julienne
2 hot chili peppers, minced, or piment d'Espelette
1 pound (450 g) tomatoes, seeded, and quartered or chopped
Salt and pepper
4 eggs
8 slices Bayonne ham or prosciutto (optional)

Heat the olive oil in a sauté pan over medium heat. Cook the onions, stirring occasionally, until soft. Add the garlic and the red, green, and hot peppers, and cook until tender. Finally, stir in the tomatoes, season with salt and pepper, cover, and simmer 10 minutes. Remove the lid, and continue cooking until the juices have evaporated and everything is soft and melded.

Crack the eggs onto the surface of the vegetables, spaced evenly apart. Season with salt and pepper. Cover, and cook until the egg whites are just done and the yolks still a little runny. Meanwhile, make four "nests" of ham on serving plates. When the eggs are done, use a spatula to lift them, along with their peppery mattresses, into the nests. Serve very hot.

FRENCH-STYLE OMELETTE

Do you really need a recipe for this? Perhaps not, but I'll bet at the very least you need reminding to make it ("it" being the simplest, most elegant solo supper known to man). There is no cheese in this omelette, but a sprinkling of grated Comté along with the herbs, when you're in the mood for it, is good.

Makes: 1 omelette

Butter
Eggs
Salt and pepper
Chopped fresh herbs, such as basil, dill, thyme, chervil, or parsley (optional)

Melt a knob of butter in an omelette or crêpe pan over medium-high heat. (I am not generally a fan of nonstick cookware, but used here it will produce a perfect omelette and make you look like a genius.) Lightly whisk 2 or 3 eggs with salt and pepper, and pour them into the hot pan. When the bottom has just set enough to be lifted, gently lift up the edges here and there and, tilting the pan, let some of the runny part from the top spill underneath. Do this until the top is set but still a little slithery. Sprinkle with chopped fresh herbs if you like. Then roll the omelette into a log, and slip it onto a plate. Brush the top with butter to make it nice and glossy, and eat!

SOUFFLÉED SPINACH OMELETTE

My dear friend Camille has always rattled on about souffléed jam omelettes being one of the world's greatest desserts. I have yet to make one, but one dreary evening a few autumns ago, when the spinach at my Paris market happened to be particularly awe-inspiring, I decided to test her hypothesis with a savory variation. The result? Well, the recipe does use far more pots and pans than reason can bear without a groan, but it's worth it. When this thick, cloudy concoction flops onto my plate for dinner, it's all I can do not to back-flip my entire body on top of it.

Makes: 2 to 3 servings

1 pound (450 g) fresh spinach
1 tablespoon (15 mL) butter
1 shallot, minced
Salt and pepper
Pinch nutmeg
4 eggs, separated
2 tablespoons (30 mL) finely grated Parmesan or Gruyère cheese

Wash the spinach, and pull off the stems. Spin out the excess water. Drop the spinach into a large pot set over medium-high heat, and let it wilt, turning it a few times with tongs, about 3 minutes. (There will be enough water still clinging to the leaves to steam it.) When the spinach is cooked, drain it and plunge it into an ice bath to preserve the color. Drain it again, and squeeze it dry, first with your hands and then in a tea towel. Chop.

Heat half the butter in a frying pan over medium heat, and gently sauté the shallot. Stir in the spinach, and season with salt, pepper, and nutmeg. When hot, transfer to a bowl, and wipe out the pan.

Put the yolks in a large metal bowl, and set over a pot of gently simmering water (without letting the bottom of the bowl touch the water). Season with salt and pepper, and whisk until thick and frothy. Remove from the heat. Beat the whites to stiff peaks, and fold them into the yolk mixture.

Put the frying pan over medium-high heat, and melt the remaining butter for the omelette. Pour in the egg mixture, and cook until the bottom is set and golden and the top still fluffy and soft, 3 to 5 minutes. Scatter the spinach all over the omelette, then the cheese. Cover for a few minutes to soften the cheese. Fold the omelette in half. Slide it onto a plate. Serve in all its glory.

MUSHROOM RAVIOLES

Like us, the French tend to think of pasta as a main course, rather than an entrée in the Italian manner. I saw a dish like this in a Provençal restaurant (only it had squid something-or-other in the middle), and I decided to make a mushroom version, because so often I am looking for vegetarian dishes with a bit of class that fit nicely into a French menu. This may be basic, but it is beautiful: tasty, elegant, and especially practical if you have just a few people to feed, because it plates so nicely.

Makes: 4 servings

1½ pounds (675 g) mushrooms
¼ cup (55 g) butter
A splash of olive oil
2 garlic cloves, minced
Salt and pepper
½ cup (125 mL) stock
A generous handful of finely grated Parmigiano-Reggiano, more for garnish
Fresh lemon juice (optional)
3 to 4 tablespoons (45 to 60 mL) chopped fresh dill or sage
8 (3- x 4-inch/8 x 10 cm) sheets dried pasta
Dill sprigs, for garnish

Cut the mushrooms into quarters or eighths, depending on their size, and set aside. Melt the butter in a small saucepan over medium-high heat. Pour a tablespoon of the butter into a sauté pan. Continue heating the remaining butter in the saucepan until it turns light brown. Set aside. Bring a large pot of water to the boil for the pasta.

Add a splash of olive oil to the butter in the sauté pan. Set the pan on high heat, and when the oil is hot, add the mushrooms, sautéing until slightly colored, about 4 minutes. Add the garlic, season with salt and pepper, and continue cooking until the mushrooms are soft, about 4 minutes more. Pour over the stock, and boil to reduce to a couple of tablespoons, a matter of minutes. Stir in the cheese. Taste, check the seasonings, and add a squirt of lemon juice if you think it needs it. Stir in the dill, and keep the mixture warm while you cook the pasta.

Generously salt the boiling pasta water. Add the pasta and cook until al dente. Drain the pasta, and return it to the pan, tossing with the reserved brown butter. Lay a sheet of pasta on each of four serving plates. Spoon the mushrooms onto the pasta. Top with a second pasta sheet. Drizzle over some brown butter from the pasta pan. Garnish with a dill sprig, and serve immediately.

MUSHROOM PARMENTIER

It's not easy to find vegetarian recipes in the French repertoire, but I have a handful in my mental file because I have many friends (and a mother) who won't eat meat. *Hachis Parmentier* is the French version of shepherd's pie, and that's what this is, only with mushrooms replacing lamb or beef and with cheese in the potato topping for extra oomph.

Makes: 6 servings

For the mushrooms

3 tablespoons (45 mL) butter
2 tablespoons (30 mL) olive oil, more as needed
2 pounds (900 g) mushrooms, quartered
1 large red onion, chopped
3 garlic cloves
½ cup (125 mL) red wine
½ cup (125 mL) vegetable stock or water
A handful of chopped fresh thyme leaves
Salt and pepper
1 tablespoon (15 mL) flour
A handful of chopped fresh parsley

For the topping

6 medium potatoes, such as Yukon Gold, peeled and cut into chunks
2 to 4 tablespoons (30 to 60 mL) butter
¼ cup (60 mL) milk, more if needed
Salt and pepper
4 ounces (110 g) Comté or Gruyère cheese, finely diced
2 tablespoons (30 mL) finely grated Parmesan cheese

Start with the mushrooms. In a sauté pan over medium-high heat, melt 2 tablespoons (30 mL) of the butter with 1 tablespoon (15 mL) of the olive oil. Sauté the mushrooms until cooked through and golden. Remove. Heat the other spoonful of olive oil and sauté the onion until soft. Add the garlic, and sauté for 1 minute. Deglaze with the wine, and reduce to no more than a spoonful. Add the stock, thyme, and mushrooms, season with salt and pepper, and simmer until the stock has reduced by half. Knead together the flour with the last tablespoon of butter. Stir it in. Cook until the liquid has thickened to sauce, a matter of minutes. Stir through the parsley. Spoon the mixture into a gratin dish.

Heat the oven to 425°F (220°C). For the topping, steam the potatoes until very tender. Drain. Mash with the butter and milk until very smooth, adding more milk if needed. Season with salt and pepper. Stir through the diced cheese. Distribute evenly over the mushroom mixture, and smooth with the back of the spoon. (If you want to be very retro-housewife, make patterns with the tines of a fork, or make waves with a spoon.) Sprinkle with the Parmesan. Bake the gratin until bubbling hot and golden on top, about 15 minutes. Serve.

SOLE WITH TOMATOES AND GREEN OLIVE TAPENADE

What I tasted in Provence one summer was fish topped with black olive tapenade and wrapped in brik pastry, which is that wonderfully crisp, crêpe-like North African pastry reminiscent of phyllo. I made the dish several times, improvising if I didn't have exactly the right ingredients, and in the end I decided that I actually prefer green olive tapenade to black, because it's lighter and fruitier, and, frankly, I find the whole thing tastier and prettier without the pastry. Simpler wins again.

Makes: 4 servings

For the tapenade

2 garlic cloves, roughly chopped
½ cup (85 g) green olives, pitted
2 anchovy fillets, rinsed and patted dry
2 tablespoons (30 mL) capers
3 to 4 tablespoons (45 to 60 mL) olive oil
Lemon juice and pepper

For the fish

4 white fish fillets, such as sole or halibut, about ¼ pound (125 g) each
2 small tomatoes, thinly sliced
Olive oil
Salt and pepper
Herbes de Provence

Heat the oven to 400°F (200°C). For the tapenade, pulse the garlic, olives, anchovies, and capers to a purée in a small food processor. Gradually add the olive oil. Season with lemon juice and pepper. (You won't need salt because there is enough from the olives and anchovies.) You should have about ⅔ cup (150 mL), which is more than you need for this recipe, but you'll thank me for the leftovers when you're craving a tartine tomorrow afternoon.

Pat the fish dry with paper towel. Rub a baking sheet with a bit of olive oil, and place the fish on it. Smear each fillet with a spoonful of the tapenade. Arrange a few slices of tomato on top of each, and drizzle with olive oil. Season with salt, pepper, and herbes de Provence. Bake until the fish is cooked, 6 to 8 minutes.

HALIBUT WITH BROWN BUTTER

This is not really a recipe, just a nice way to fry a piece of fish and give it a little extra richness and flavor. It's ideal if your side dishes have strong personalities; for example, I have served this on Crushed Chickpeas with Olives and Lemon (p. 187), with Roasted Cumin Carrots (p. 215) on the side, and suddenly the fish seemed quite exotic.

Makes: 4 servings

½ cup (110 g) unsalted butter
Lemon juice
2 tablespoons (30 mL) olive oil
4 halibut fillets, about 4 ounces (110 g) each
Salt and pepper

Melt the butter in a small saucepan over medium-high heat, and cook, swirling the pan occasionally, until lightly browned and foaming. Add a squeeze of lemon juice, and set aside.

Heat the oil in a frying pan over medium-high heat. Season the fish on both sides, lay in the pan and fry for 4 minutes. Flip, cover, and cook until the fish is ready, another 4 to 6 minutes. Serve dribbled with the brown butter.

MONKFISH WITH RED PEPPER SAUCE

Sauces sometimes require such patience and skill that they can be quite frightening to attempt, unless of course they're as easy as this one. I used to roast the peppers for this sauce, but in the end I found the resulting intensity a bit cloying. Cooking them on the stovetop instead makes the sauce taste lighter, and it's actually faster. What you get is a mild, fire-colored peppery pool to put beneath firm white fish – sea bass or halibut, for example. The dish is very handsome, versatile, and tasty. If you are barbecuing, you may want to make a marinade for the fish, with olive oil, herbes de Provence, and a splash of white wine, instead of just sprinkling the herbs on the fish as I do below.

Makes: 4 servings

For the sauce

2 red peppers
2 tablespoons (30 mL) olive oil
1 shallot, minced
3 tablespoons (45 mL) white wine
6 tablespoons (90 mL) chicken stock
Salt and pepper
Pinch cayenne pepper
Lemon juice

For the fish

1 tablespoon (15 mL) butter
1 tablespoon (15 mL) olive oil
4 monkfish fillets (or other firm white fish), about 5 ounces (140 g) each
Salt and pepper
About 2 tablespoons (30 mL) herbes de Provence

For the sauce, seed the peppers, and dice. Heat the oil in a sauté pan over medium-high heat. Add the shallot, and cook until soft. Deglaze with the wine, and cook for 1 minute. Add the stock and the red peppers. Cook until very soft, about 10 minutes. Purée in the blender. Season with salt, pepper, cayenne, and lemon juice. Transfer to a small saucepan. Gently reheat.

Wipe the sauté pan with paper towel. Melt the butter with the oil in the pan over medium-high heat. Season the fish with salt and pepper. Generously scatter over the herbes de Provence on both sides. Fry the fish on both sides until golden and cooked through, about 4 minutes per side. (They may want a squirt of lemon juice, too.) Serve on the red pepper sauce.

SALMON EN PAPILLOTE

Fish baked in parchment paper steams, so it's delicately tender. And since you've got the packages going in the first place, it's nice to add a few extra contents. I like sliced cucumber as a base, and I also like a haystack of colorful julienned vegetables, as I've done here. A whole course, gift wrapped on a plate!

Makes: 2 servings

1 tablespoon (15 mL) olive oil
1 carrot, peeled and cut into julienne
1 small leek, cut into julienne
1 small zucchini, peeled and cut into julienne
Salt and pepper
A squeeze of lemon juice
2 salmon or halibut fillets, about 5 ounces (150 g) each
1 teaspoon (5 mL) quatre-épices (p. 152)
1 teaspoon (5 mL) fennel seeds

Heat the oven to 375°F (190°C). Heat the oil in a frying pan over medium heat, and gently fry the vegetables together until al dente (erring on the slightly undercooked side). Season with salt, pepper, and a squirt of lemon.

Cut two pieces of parchment roughly the size of a placemat. Fold each in half to form a wide rectangle, then cut half a heart shape from the top and around the open edge, so that when you open it out, the parchment will be shaped like a heart.

Arrange half the vegetables in the center of one side of the heart. Set a fish fillet on top, scatter over half the quatre-épices and fennel seeds, and season with salt, pepper, and a squirt of lemon. Fold over the other half of the paper. Working from the top edge, make small, tight folds all the way around the package to seal it, leaving plenty of room for the papillote to puff up with steam during baking. Set on a baking sheet, and repeat with the other papillote.

Bake for 8 to 10 minutes. Let sit for 2 minutes before transferring the packages to plates, cutting through the paper, and eating the contents.

SQUID STEWED WITH TOMATOES, WHITE WINE, AND BLACK OLIVES

Squid can be tricky to cook properly, judging by the number of restaurants serving rubber rings of it the world over. This recipe is a good place to start if you're worried about getting it wrong, because the squid is stewed and so it will be tender, guaranteed. This is a dish with punchy Mediterranean flavors that I like to serve rustically, straight out of the sauté pan.

Makes: 6 servings

2 pounds (900 g) small squid, cleaned and rinsed
3 tablespoons (45 mL) olive oil
1 large onion, minced
4 to 6 tomatoes, roughly chopped
2 garlic cloves, minced
1 small dried peperoncino or a pinch crushed chili pepper
1 cup (250 mL) dry white wine
1 bay leaf
A handful of fresh thyme leaves
Pinch saffron (optional)
Salt and pepper
½ cup (85 g) niçoise or other small black olives
Zest and juice of ½ lemon
A generous handful of chopped fresh flat-leaf parsley leaves, for garnish

Slice the squid crosswise into rings, like onion rings. Heat 2 tablespoons (30 mL) olive oil in a sauté pan over high heat, and fry the squid, tossing occasionally, for about 5 minutes. Remove the squid, and set aside. Add the remaining tablespoon (15 mL) of oil to the pan, and sauté the onion until soft but not colored. Add the tomatoes, garlic, and peperoncino, and cook for 10 minutes. Return the squid to the pan, and add the wine, bay leaf, thyme, and saffron (if using). Season with salt and pepper. Cover, and simmer until the squid is tender, about 30 minutes.

Remove the hot pepper (if you can find it!) and the bay leaf. Stir in the olives and lemon zest, and continue cooking, uncovered, to reduce the juices, about 10 minutes. The dish should be quite sloppy but not like a soup. Squirt in some lemon juice. Taste, and adjust the seasonings. Scatter over the parsley, and serve with crusty bread.

SALMON AND ASPARAGUS IN PUFF PASTRY

Lighter and prettier than a traditional coulibiac, this "pie" (just to bring it down to earth) is a perfect springtime dish. The pastry is golden and crisp, and inside you have a thick, pink slab of salmon with a creamy pale green sauce and tender fingers of asparagus. Very pretty.

Makes: 6 servings

1 salmon fillet, about 1½ pounds (675 g)
1 pound (450 g) asparagus, trimmed
¼ cup (60 mL) crème fraîche
A handful of chopped fresh dill
Zest of 1 lemon
Salt and pepper
2 (7-ounce/200 g) squares puff pastry
1 egg, lightly beaten with 1 tablespoon (15 mL) water, for egg wash

Skin the salmon, remove any pin bones, and set aside. Heat the oven to 450°F (230°C).

Cut the tips off the asparagus, reserving the stems, and poach the tips in boiling salted water until tender, 3 to 5 minutes. Drain well, refresh in ice-cold water, then drain again, leaving to sit so that all the water comes off. Purée, then stir in the crème fraîche, dill, and lemon zest. Season with salt and pepper. Set aside.

On a lightly floured surface, roll out one piece of puff pastry until it's large enough to hold the salmon with a generous margin. Lay the pastry on a damp baking sheet with the long edge facing you. Lay the salmon on the pastry, like a picture in its frame. Season with salt and pepper. Lay the raw stems of asparagus lengthwise along the top of the salmon, like pencils. Spread the purée mixture over top.

Roll out the second piece of puff pastry so it's large enough to cover the salmon and the margins. Brush the margins of the bottom pastry with some of the egg wash. Lay the top pastry over the salmon, and press the edges to seal, like a giant ravioli. Trim the edges, leaving a 1-inch (2.5 cm) border. Press with the tines of a fork, and then, with the dull edge of a knife, scallop the edges. Make 2 or 3 slits in the top to allow steam to escape. Brush all over with the egg wash, and bake until puffed up and golden brown, about 20 minutes.

Let cool 5 minutes before slicing to serve. This dish is also good at room temperature.

LETTUCE-WRAPPED HALIBUT WITH DILL CREAM SAUCE

One spring, I became fixated on perfecting a recipe for lettuce-wrapped fish. Don't ask me why, but that sort of drive overtakes me sometimes: I make something, and it's a complete disaster, but I know it has potential, so then I make it again (and again and again) until the recipe finally reveals to me its inner splendor. That was the case with the lettuce-wrapped fish. The reason for lettuce instead of chard leaves or spinach (which you could also use) is that lettuce has that wonderfully promising color of early spring buds, and it wraps itself lightly around the fish like a pretty silk shawl rather than like a wool blanket. Meanwhile, the sauce (which I found in an excellent book by Anthony Worrall-Thompson, called *The Elegant Chef's Guide to Hors d'Oeuvres and Appetizers*) is as simple as boiling water but tastes as sophisticated as something straight out of a Swiss finishing school. Please, please, please serve it with Radishes and Peas (p. 210) on the side. It's so beautiful that way, and the dishes belong together like violets and dew.

Makes: 4 servings

8 large Boston lettuce leaves
4 halibut or sea bass fillets, about 4 ounces (110 g) each
Salt and pepper
3 chopped dill stalks
1 shallot
½ garlic clove
1¼ cups (300 mL) chicken stock
½ cup (125 mL) white wine
1¼ cups (300 mL) heavy cream
2 tablespoons (30 mL) butter
Salt and pepper
Lemon juice

For the fish bundles, lay the lettuce leaves in a sauté pan of boiling salted water for a few seconds. Remove, and immediately plunge in an ice bath. Lay flat on tea towels to drain, gently patting them dry. Remove the center rib, so you have wide strips of lettuce. Lay a few leaves on a board, slightly overlapping. Lay a fish fillet on top. Season the fish with salt and pepper, then neatly fold the lettuce leaves over to make a package, with the ends of the fillet visible. Make the other three bundles. If you're not cooking until much later, wrap and refrigerate.

For the sauce, put the dill stalks, shallot, garlic, stock, and wine in a medium saucepan. Boil to reduce by three-quarters. Strain, wipe out the pan, and return the sauce to it. Add the cream, and simmer until the sauce coats a spoon, about 5 minutes. Remove from the heat. Whisk in the butter, a piece at a time. Taste, and season with salt, pepper, and lemon juice. Set aside and keep warm.

In a large saucepan, bring 2 inches (5 cm) water to the boil. Lay the fish bundles in a bamboo steamer, and steam until the fish is just cooked, about 10 minutes. Serve with the sauce.

HALIBUT POACHED IN HERB AND CITRUS OLIVE OIL

This dish is a luxury. It is beautiful, delicious, and . . . expensive. If you feel you can't use this much olive oil and keep a clear conscience, why not poach the fish in bouillon, or steam it, then serve it with a smaller quantity of warm fennel and orange oil spooned over? Hmm, maybe I'll start doing that – for the same reasons I eschew bottled water for anything except emergencies. Turbot would work nicely here as well.

Makes: 2 servings

- **2 skinned halibut fillets, about 5 ounces (140 g) each**
- **About 1½ cups (375 mL) olive oil**
- **Zest of 1 orange**
- **½ teaspoon (2 mL) fennel seeds**
- **2 thyme sprigs**
- **1 garlic clove**
- **Freshly ground black pepper**
- **Fleur de sel, for garnish**

Heat the oven to 250°F (120°C). Lay the fillets in a baking dish just large enough to hold them. Pour over enough oil to cover. Add the orange zest, fennel seeds, thyme, garlic, and pepper. Bake until just tender, about 10 minutes. Remove the fish from the oil. Serve garnished with fleur de sel and with a little of the cooking oil dribbled over.

PAN-FRIED SCALLOPS WITH CHIVE BEURRE BLANC

Beurre blanc is a classic wine-butter sauce for fish or seafood, and it is really worth making because it's delicious, easy, and fast. My cooking friend in Canada, Bridget (she of the Strawberry Galette, p. 263), pulled a stunt on me with this recipe once. She used orange juice in place of wine and added something wild like a whole tablespoon of turmeric to the finished sauce. I thought, "She's out of her mind," but she was right, as usual. This sauce is the most marvelous thing on scallops, especially with some soft sautéed endive underneath. (The sauce part, just so you know, makes about a cup/ 250 mL, in case you want to serve it with other fish.)

Makes: 4 to 6 servings

2 dozen bay scallops
Salt and pepper
⅓ cup (75 mL) white wine vinegar
⅓ cup (75 mL) dry white wine
1 shallot, minced
1 cup (225 g) butter, more for frying

Season the scallops, and set aside while you make the sauce. Boil the vinegar, wine, and shallot down to 3 tablespoons (45 mL). Remove from the heat, and whisk in the butter a big pinch at a time. Season with pepper. Strain, cover to keep warm, and set aside.

In a sauté pan over medium-high heat, melt a little extra butter (with a drop of oil, if you like, to prevent burning), and fry the scallops a few minutes on each side, until golden. Serve immediately on the sauce.

TUNA TAIL WITH POPPY SEED CRUST

I had this in a bistro near the Paris apartment I lived in a few years ago and immediately rushed home to reproduce it. The poppy seeds make a crunchy coat, which is great against the barely cooked tuna, and it looks so chic sliced and fanned out on a plate. Serve it with sautéed spinach or with Gingered Watercress (p. 220).

Makes: 2 servings

1 tablespoon (15 mL) black poppy seeds
1 teaspoon (5 mL) freshly ground black pepper
12 ounces (375 g) tuna tail, halved lengthwise
Salt
1 egg white, lightly beaten
1 tablespoon (15 mL) grapeseed oil or other oil, for frying

Combine the poppy seeds and pepper on a plate. Season the tuna pieces with salt, dip into the egg white, and roll in the poppy seed mixture to give them an even black coat.

Heat the oil in a sauté pan over high heat. Add the tuna, and fry about 30 seconds per side, just enough to cook the outside edges. The middle should remain raw-ish. Serve sliced or unsliced.

ANISE FISH STEW WITH ROUILLE

Classic recipes are always victims of endless debate, with connoisseurs getting all up in arms about which ingredients and steps are authentic and which are not. I value authenticity more than most, but only if taste matches reputation and only if authentic ingredients are possible to get. If they're not, I adapt. All this is to explain why I did not call this stew "bouillabaisse," which is essentially what it is: I am simply keeping out of the line of fire. Please don't feel restricted by the fish I've suggested here. There's no reason not to add shellfish either.

Makes: 8 servings

For the rouille

1 egg yolk
2 to 3 garlic cloves, crushed
1 small hot red pepper, minced, or paprika
1 cup (250 mL) grapeseed oil
1 tablespoon (15 mL) tomato paste or puréed roasted red pepper (optional)
Salt and pepper
Lemon juice

For the soup

2 pounds (900 g) trimmed and gutted rich, firm-fleshed fish (such as rascasse, bass, halibut)
2 pounds (900 g) trimmed and gutted delicate fish (such as haddock, flounder, red mullet, snapper)
2 pounds (900 g) fish heads and bones, rinsed (roughly 1 large fish carcass)
About ½ cup (125 mL) olive oil
2 onions, diced
2 large leeks, trimmed, washed, and sliced
1 fennel bulb, peeled, cored, and chopped, with green fronds reserved
6 tomatoes, peeled, seeded, and diced
4 garlic cloves, minced
1 bouquet garni (1 bay leaf, 1 thyme sprig, a few parsley stems, tied in a bundle)
1½ teaspoons (7 mL) fennel seeds
2 large slices orange peel, pith removed, preferably dried
2 pinches saffron threads, crushed
Salt and pepper
A splash of Pernod or white wine
Chopped fresh parsley, for garnish
8 slices baguette

For the rouille, whisk the yolk with the garlic and hot pepper. Slowly whisk in the oil, adding it drop by drop. Whisk in the tomato paste if you want a rust-colored mayonnaise. Season with salt, pepper, and lemon juice. Refrigerate until ready to use.

For the soup, chop the firm-fleshed and delicate fish into bite-sized pieces. Refrigerate in separate bowls. Put the fish heads and bones in a large soup pot, pour over 4 cups (1 L) of water, bring to the boil, then reduce heat and simmer 20 minutes. Strain, reserving the liquid.

Heat the oil in the same pot over medium heat, and fry the onions, leeks, and fennel until soft, about 10 minutes. Add the tomatoes, garlic, bouquet garni, fennel seeds, orange peel, and saffron. Season with salt and pepper. Pour over the fish stock, and simmer for half an hour. Remove the bouquet garni and the orange peel.

Bring the liquid to a rolling boil. Add the firm fish, and cook 5 minutes. Add the delicate fish and the splash of Pernod, and continue cooking until all the fish is tender, about 5 minutes longer.

Meanwhile, toast the bread, and smear the slices with rouille. Ladle the soup into warm soup plates, sprinkle with parsley, and top with a croûte.

LOBSTER STEW

Because lobster is rich in its own right, it can sometimes be overkill to serve it with a creamy sauce. What I love about this "stew," therefore, is the purity of it. In fact, "stew" is misleading because what it really is, is poached lobster with light spring vegetables surrounded by a pool of the most exquisitely light and natural broth you can imagine. It's so healthful, flavorful, and unfussed-with, in a *nouvelle cuisine* kind of way, it makes me want to hop on a plane with it and fly off to a spa for a week.

Makes: 4 servings

2 live lobsters, about 1½ pounds (675 g) each
3 tablespoons (45 mL) butter
1 onion, chopped
1 tablespoon (15 mL) tomato paste
2 tablespoons (30 mL) Cognac
12 asparagus tips
12 slices yellow zucchini
6 radishes, halved
2 handfuls of freshly shelled or frozen peas
Salt and pepper
Lemon juice
A small handful of chopped fresh chervil, for garnish

Pour enough water into a large pot to come up about a finger deep. Bring to the boil, put the lobsters in head first, cover, and steam 5 minutes. Drain, and rinse under cold water until cool enough to work with. Shell the lobsters (see p. 85), reserving 12 of the meatiest legs and the shells; discard the body. You should have four intact claws and two tails that you can halve lengthwise. Wrap the meat and refrigerate it until ready to use. Chop the shells to pieces with a mallet or in the food processor.

Melt half the butter in a large sauté pan over medium heat, and cook the onion until soft. Stir in the tomato paste, and add the lobster shells. (If you think this is crazy, just have patience: the shells go in for their wonderful flavor, but they're later strained out.) Pour over the Cognac and carefully light it. When the flames have died down, pour over 3 cups (750 mL) water, and boil until the liquid is reduced to 1½ cups (375 mL). Strain, pressing down on the shells to extract all the juices. Return the lobster stock to the sauté pan. Discard the shells.

While the sauce is reducing, cook the vegetables, separately, in a pot of boiling salted water until al dente, 30 seconds to 2 minutes, depending on the vegetable. When each is done, lift to a strainer with a slotted spoon, and immediately plunge into an ice bath to preserve the color. Drain.

Bring the lobster stock in the sauté pan to a simmer, uncovered. Add the lobster, and poach gently for 3 minutes. Add the vegetables, and continue to cook for 2 minutes. Arrange half a tail and a whole claw in each of four soup plates. Using a slotted spoon, divide the vegetables evenly around the meat. You should have about 1 cup (250 mL) sauce left in the pan; if you have too much, quickly boil it down. Whisk in the remaining butter. Taste, and season with salt, pepper, and lemon juice. Ladle the broth over the lobster and vegetables, scatter over the chervil, and serve.

DINOSAUR EGG

This is chicken in a salt crust, but I call it "dinosaur egg" because before you cut it, the white-domed shape really does look like something you might stumble upon in the back garden (in a good way, I mean). You don't eat the crust, but I like to bring the whole thing to the table intact anyway, because it's spectacular, especially when you surround it with a nest of fresh herbs and fistfuls of wheat or lavender spears. (Not that you have such props ever at the ready, but sometimes it's worth rummaging them up for effect.) I know it's a strange baking method, but the salt crust really does drive the herb flavor right to the bone and keep the meat ultra moist. It's extraordinary (not *just* weird).

If you find the crust tearing when you roll it, just mix in a little more flour and it will stay together fine. If you find the mixture dry, add a splash of water to achieve the texture of dough.

Makes: 4 servings

For the chicken

1 (3-pound/1.3 kg) chicken

Loads of fresh herb sprigs (such as parsley, thyme, rosemary, tarragon, bay . . .)

4 to 5 garlic cloves, crushed with the back of a knife

Pepper

A drizzle of olive oil

For the crust

6 egg whites

4 cups (500 g) flour

2 cups (540 g) coarse salt

For the egg wash

1 egg yolk

Heat the oven to 325°F (160°C). Slide plenty of herbs under the chicken skin, saving some for inside. Put garlic in the cavity, along with the rest of the herbs. Rub the chicken with pepper and olive oil.

For the crust, mix the egg whites, flour, and salt well, then add enough water to make a dough with the consistency of play-dough. On a lightly floured surface, roll out one-quarter of the dough into an oval a few inches larger than the chicken, to make a base for the chicken to sit on. (If it rips, it's probably because it needs a little more flour.) Set the dough base on a baking sheet. Lay the chicken on top. Roll out the remaining dough into an oval large enough to cover the chicken and the edges, drape it over the chicken, and press the edges to seal hermetically. No holes or rips allowed, so patch them if necessary. Whisk a splash of water into the egg yolk, and paint the pastry case all over.

Bake for 1½ hours. Let the bird sit out of the oven about 10 minutes before serving. Cut off the crust and discard it. Carve the meat and serve.

CHICKEN TAGINE WITH OLIVES AND CITRON CONFIT

When a recipe is exotic sounding, we often assume it will be difficult to make. I felt that way about tagine until a Moroccan woman made it before my eyes in a flash and proved that, in fact, it's easier than a sauté! If you want to make this more French (but why bother?), leave the skin on the chicken and brown it well in oil in a sauté pan before you add the other ingredients and carry on with cooking. I serve this with a bowl of Minty Couscous (p. 190) on the side, which is very un-Moroccan of me (for Moroccans, couscous is a wholly separate dish involving vegetables and often meat), but it's good!

Makes: 4 servings

4 chicken legs, split at the joint and skinned
Salt and pepper
2 onions, grated or sliced
3 garlic cloves, minced
Skins of 2 preserved lemons (see p. 141), chopped
2 tablespoons (30 mL) olive oil
1 teaspoon (5 mL) ground ginger
2 teaspoons (10 mL) ground cumin
2 teaspoons (10 mL) ground coriander
2 pinches saffron
Pinch turmeric
1 cup (165 g) green olives with pits
A generous handful or two of fresh coriander leaves, roughly chopped

Put everything except the olives and fresh coriander in a pot, add a couple of glasses of water, cover, and simmer until the chicken is done, 40 minutes to an hour, removing the lid if there is too much liquid so that some can evaporate. (The dish should be quite liquid, but it's not a stew.) At the end of cooking, add the olives and fresh coriander. Serve.

POULE AU POT

Chicken and vegetables poached together in a pot is about as basic as you can get, and yet the end result is so soothing and attractive it seems special. This is a dish that makes you rise from the table feeling warmed and satisfied, but pure and virtuous at the same time.

Makes: 4 servings

1 (3-pound/1.3 kg) chicken
About 8 cups (2 L) chicken stock
1 bay leaf
1 thyme sprig
1 tarragon sprig
6 garlic cloves, peeled
2 large or 4 small leeks, trimmed, washed, and thickly sliced
Salt and pepper
12 pearl onions, peeled
4 carrots, peeled and cut into chunks
3 celery stalks, cut into finger lengths
½ small turnip, sliced
3 parsnips, peeled and sliced

Lay a large piece of cheesecloth on a work surface and put the chicken on it breast side down. Gather up the edges and tie them with kitchen string. Put the chicken into a big pot, breast side up, and pour over the chicken stock. Bring to the boil. Skim off the foam that rises until no more forms, about half an hour. Add the bay leaf, thyme, tarragon, garlic, leeks, and salt. Turn the chicken breast side down. Cover, and simmer gently about 20 minutes more. Add the pearl onions, carrots, celery, and turnip. Continue cooking until the juices in the chicken run clear and the vegetables are tender, about 20 minutes longer. The chicken will pull apart easily when it's done. Fish out the bay leaf and herb sprigs. Remove the cheesecloth. Carve the chicken, removing the skin if you like, and arrange on a platter with the vegetables and with some broth pooled around.

COQ AU RIESLING

This is a classic chicken sauté with mushrooms and cream which everyone always likes. I make it when I have a Riesling in the house that's not 100 per cent dry, because I'm not a fan of the sweeter varieties for drinking. They do make a fabulous sauce, however, to which you can add a squeeze of lemon at the end if you think it needs a lift. If you want to be really authentic, use goose fat for all the frying instead of butter and oil.

Makes: 4 servings

6 chicken legs, split at the joint
Salt and pepper
2 tablespoons (30 mL) butter
1 tablespoon (15 mL) olive oil
4 shallots, minced
1 garlic clove, minced
2 tablespoons (30 mL) Cognac
1 cup (250 mL) dry or off-dry Riesling
½ cup (125 mL) chicken stock
½ pound (225 g) mushrooms, quartered
½ cup (125 mL) crème fraîche or sour cream
A squeeze of lemon juice (optional)
Chopped fresh parsley or tarragon, for garnish

Season the chicken legs with salt and pepper. Melt half the butter with the oil in a sauté pan over medium-high heat, and brown the chicken on all sides, working in batches. As the chicken is browned, remove it to a plate. Add the shallots and garlic to the pan, and sauté for 1 minute. Pour over the Cognac to deglaze. Put the chicken back in. Pour over the wine and stock, cover, and simmer until the chicken is tender, about 20 minutes, turning once.

Meanwhile, melt the remaining butter in a frying pan over medium heat, and cook the mushrooms until golden. When the chicken is cooked, remove it to a serving platter, and cover with foil to keep warm. Boil the cooking liquid down to sauce consistency. Stir in the crème fraîche and the mushrooms. When hot, taste, and correct the seasonings, adding a squeeze of lemon if you think it needs it. Pour the sauce over the chicken, scatter over the parsley, and serve.

POULET AU PAPRIKA

A Hungarian classic, you say! Well, I guess so, but it's the spitting image of a classic French sauté, too, and, whatever its origins, it is certainly considered part of the French repertoire now. Not to get defensive or anything, I should be saving that for my next point: according to all the classic tomes, hot paprika is a big no-no. What a pity, because that's exactly how I like this dish best.

Makes: 4 servings

4 chicken legs, split at the joint
Salt and pepper
1 tablespoon (15 mL) bacon drippings or oil
1 red pepper, cut into roughly 2-inch (5 cm) julienne
1 onion, sliced
½ small fennel bulb, finely chopped (optional)
1 tablespoon (15 mL) high-quality hot or sweet Hungarian paprika
1 garlic clove, minced
½ cup (125 mL) white wine
2 tomatoes, roughly chopped
1 bay leaf
2 tablespoons (30 mL) sour cream or crème fraîche
A squeeze of lemon juice (optional)

Season the chicken with salt and pepper. Heat the fat in a sauté pan over medium-high heat, and, working in batches, brown the meat on all sides. Remove. Drain off all but a tablespoon of fat from the pan.

Lower the heat to medium-low, and add the julienned pepper, onion, fennel (if using), and paprika. Cook until the vegetables are soft but not colored, about 12 minutes; add the garlic for the last minute. Deglaze the pan with the wine. Add the tomatoes and bay leaf. Season with salt and pepper. Put the chicken back in. Cover the pan and cook, turning the meat occasionally, until tender, about 30 minutes.

Remove the chicken to a serving platter, and cover with foil to keep warm. Turn up the heat and boil down to sauce consistency. Turn off the heat, stir in the sour cream, check the seasonings (including the paprika, adding more if you like, and a squeeze of lemon if needed), and remove the bay leaf. Pour over the chicken, and serve.

TURKEY PAUPIETTES WITH CHESTNUTS AND BRUSSELS SPROUTS

Confession time: I have never put on a Thanksgiving or Christmas dinner all by myself. I don't know how I've managed to squeak through to this age without inheriting the task (I'm sure my mother would like an explanation, too), but there you go. A full-blown holiday dinner remains a goal for my future. In the meantime, here is a one-pan version, ideal for small apartment kitchens and just right for an intimate get-together of loved ones. No need to gather ye chestnuts while ye may. You can buy them vacuum-packed or in jars, all ready to go. Serve this dish with a squash or pumpkin purée to complete the feast.

Makes: 6 servings

6 turkey cutlets, about 5 ounces (140 g) each
Salt and pepper
1 tablespoon (15 mL) butter, or pork or duck fat
1 large onion, finely chopped
5 ounces (140 g) ground pork or turkey leg
¼ cup (20 g) fresh bread crumbs
A generous handful of chopped fresh parsley
About 6 large sage leaves, shredded
4 slices bacon, cut into lardons
¼ cup (60 mL) Cognac or Madeira
1 cup (250 mL) chicken stock
1 pound (450 g) Brussels sprouts, blanched
½ pound (225 g) cooked chestnuts

Pound the turkey cutlets between two pieces of plastic wrap until very thin, but be careful not to tear them. Season with salt and pepper, and set aside. Melt the butter in a sauté pan over medium heat, and gently fry the onion until soft but not browned. Meanwhile, combine the ground pork, bread crumbs, and herbs in a bowl. Add the onion. Season well with salt and pepper. Fry a tiny piece of stuffing. Taste to check the seasonings. Adjust as necessary. Place a spoonful of the mixture on each cutlet. Wrap them into bundles, and tie each one into a pin-cushion shape with three strings to secure. Wrap in plastic and twist to shape into perfect rounds, then remove the plastic.

In a large sauté pan, fry the bacon until cooked but not crisp, and remove to a plate, leaving the fat behind. Now brown the turkey bundles well on all sides. Deglaze with the Cognac, and reduce to about a tablespoon. Add the stock, cooked bacon, and blanched Brussels sprouts. Cover, and simmer until tender, about 15 minutes. Add the chestnuts, turning the paupiettes over as you do so, and continue cooking for 5 to 7 minutes. Stick a metal skewer in, and touch it to your lip to make sure the center of the stuffing is completely cooked. The skewer should be very hot. Serve.

DUCK À L'ORANGE

I'll sing you a song of duck à l'orange:
it's sour and sweet;
it's always a treat;
it's not just for chefs;
it makes no great mess.
And here is the best part of duck à l'orange:
it tastes like a dream,
and it doesn't take long!
Fa-laaa!

Okay, so that is not exactly poetry, but I can assure you that this recipe is. It is modeled on one I found in a book about chef Alain Ducasse by Linda Dannenberg, an American who has written very good books about French food.

Makes: 3 to 4 servings

4 oranges, washed
2 duck breasts, about ¾ pound (375 g) each
¼ cup (55 g) sugar
1 tablespoon (15 mL) water
3 tablespoons (45 mL) red wine vinegar
⅔ cup (150 mL) duck, chicken, or veal stock
2 tablespoons (30 mL) butter
Salt and pepper
A squirt of lemon juice

Prepare the oranges: Remove the peel from 2 oranges with a vegetable peeler. Set the oranges aside. Cut the white pith off the back of the peel with a very sharp knife. Cut into julienne, put into a small pot, cover with cold water, bring to the boil, and drain. Now do that two more times to get all the bitterness out. Rinse in cold water, drain, and set aside. Squeeze the juice of the 2 peeled oranges into a bowl. Remove and discard the skin and pith from the remaining 2 oranges. Working over the bowl of juice, cut between the membranes to section the oranges; put the sections into another bowl. You now have a dish of blanched julienned orange zest, a bowl of orange juice, and a bowl of orange sections.

Prepare the duck breasts: Score the fat side of the breasts with a knife. Set them fat side down in a sauté pan over low heat. Render the fat, about 10 minutes. Remove the duck, and pour off the fat. Increase the heat to medium-high, and put the breasts back in the pan, skin side down. Sauté until done to your liking, or about 7 minutes on the fat side, then another 3 on the other. Remove to a carving board to rest, covering with foil to keep warm.

Make the sauce: Put the sugar and water in a small saucepan. Bring to the boil, swirling the pan but not stirring, until the caramel is golden, about 5 minutes. Stir in the vinegar and reserved orange juice. Reduce slightly. Now add the stock and the reserved zest. Boil down until the sauce coats a spoon. (The sauce can be prepared in advance up to this point, then reheated once the duck is cooked.) Remove from the heat, and whisk in the butter a piece at a time. Check and adjust the seasonings, adding a little lemon if needed. Add the reserved orange sections.

Carve the duck breasts, and arrange on a serving platter. Spoon over the sauce, and serve.

DUCK BREASTS WITH GREEN PEPPERCORN SAUCE

It's not that I'm avoiding whole duck (or is it?), but I find that the legs and breasts cook so differently that they're better cooked separately. I like legs for duck confit, but if it's breasts, I sauté because they are quick, attractive, and easy to carve. This is a classic sauce, for reasons that will be immediately apparent upon tasting.

Makes: 1 or 2 servings

1 duck breast, about ¾ pound (375 g)
1 tablespoon (15 mL) Cognac
2 tablespoons (30 mL) red wine
2 teaspoons (10 mL) green peppercorns in brine, drained
½ cup (125 mL) veal stock
2 teaspoons (10 mL) butter

Heat the oven to 400°F (200°C). Score the fat side of the duck breasts with a knife. Set them fat side down in an ovenproof sauté pan over low heat, and render the fat, about 10 minutes. Pour off the fat, and transfer the pan to the oven to finish cooking the duck, about 10 minutes. Remove the duck, and set aside to rest, loosely covered with foil to keep it warm, while you make the sauce.

Deglaze the sauté pan with the Cognac and wine and boil to reduce by half. Add the peppercorns and veal stock, and reduce by half again. Remove from the heat, and whisk in the butter. Carve the duck breast. Spoon over the sauce, and serve.

ROASTED QUAIL WITH GRAPES

Being celebratory without effort doesn't take much if you have a recipe like this one up your sleeve. My longtime cooking teacher, Anne Willan, served it with Grated Potato Cakes (p. 180), and I loved the crispness of them with the quails, so that's what I do, too. Start with a vegetable first course to keep things balanced, then follow up with a salad and perhaps a wedge of Roquefort.

Makes: 8 servings

8 quail
3 tablespoons (45 mL) grapeseed oil
3 tablespoons (45 mL) Cognac
Salt and pepper
1 cup (250 mL) chicken stock (homemade or low sodium)
1 lb (450 g) seedless green and red grapes, halved

Rinse, pat dry, and truss the quail. Mix the oil with 1 tablespoon (15 mL) of the Cognac, and salt and pepper. Rub well all over the hens in a dish, and set aside half an hour to marinate. Heat the oven to 450°F (230°C).

Heat a roasting pan on the stovetop over medium-high heat, and brown the quail well on all sides, about 10 minutes total. Spoon out any excess oil from the pan, and transfer the quail to the oven to finish cooking, about 25 minutes or until the juices run clear at the leg.

Transfer the quail to a serving platter, and cover with foil to keep warm. Pour the fat off the pan, and discard. Over medium-high heat, add the remaining 2 tablespoons (30 mL) Cognac to the pan and carefully light it. When the flames die out, add the stock and boil to reduce by about half. Reduce the heat to low, add the grapes, and heat for about 3 minutes to warm through and barely soften them. Pour the sauce and the grapes over the quail, and serve.

BRAISED QUAIL WITH MUSHROOMS

Many modern recipes are just assembly, so it is gratifying to make a dish like this one, which makes you actually feel like a real cook. The flavors are deep and melded, and it looks as salivatingly good in the cooking pan as it does on the plate.

Makes: 4 servings

4 quail
Salt and pepper
2 tablespoons (30 mL) butter, more if needed
1 teaspoon (5 mL) olive oil
4 slices bacon, cut into slivers
1 onion, chopped
1 tablespoon (15 mL) flour
1 cup (250 mL) white wine
1 cup (250 mL) veal stock
¾ pound (375 g) mushrooms, halved (one part black trumpet, one part chanterelles, and two parts cremini)
Chopped fresh parsley, to taste

Rinse, pat dry, and truss the quail. Season all over with salt and pepper. Melt half the butter with the oil (or even lard if you want) in a heavy casserole over medium-high heat, and brown the quail on all sides. Remove and set aside. Add the bacon to the pan, brown it, and remove. Finally, fry the onion until golden, adding more fat to the pan beforehand if needed.

Stir the flour into the onions, and cook 1 minute. Deglaze with the wine. Return the bacon and quail to the pot. Pour over the stock, cover, reduce the heat, and simmer until the quail are done (the juices will run clear at the leg), about 20 minutes.

Meanwhile, melt the remaining butter (a little more if you like), and cook each type of mushroom separately, as the various types cook differently, until they are tender. Season with salt and pepper as you go. At the end, toss all the mushrooms together with the chopped parsley.

When the quail are done, remove from the cooking liquid and keep them warm. Boil down the pan juices until reduced to a thin sauce consistency. Add the mushrooms to the sauce, and stir to heat through. Tilt into a serving dish, arrange the quail on top, and serve.

PORK CHOPS
WITH GREEN OLIVES AND PRESERVED LEMON

I make jars of lemons preserved in salt for tagines (you can also buy them in Middle Eastern shops), but I don't make tagines that often, so I have started flinging the lemons into other dishes. Diced preserved lemon (and it's actually the skin of the lemon you eat, not the flesh) is great with fish fried in butter or thrown in with nice fat chops to make a slightly exotic supper in a pan; it also perks up vegetable dishes. A couple of branches of cherry tomatoes, drizzled with olive oil and roasted at 400°F (200°C) until the skins have wrinkled and the fruit is soft, 20 to 30 minutes, look marvelous on the side of the chops.

If you want to make preserved lemons on your own, a 4-cup (1 L) jar will hold about five. Cut small organic lemons into quarters but without going all the way through, so the four quarters are still attached at one end. Put a generous tablespoon of coarse salt inside each lemon, close it up again, and pack into the jar. When they're all in there, press them down, cover, and let sit overnight. Next day, press them down again, and if they have not released enough juice to cover themselves, add enough lemon juice to cover. Seal and refrigerate one month before using (not before). They'll last about six months in the fridge.

Makes: 2 servings

2 pork chops, on the bone
Salt and pepper
A pinch or two of sugar
2 tablespoons (30 mL) olive oil
¾ cup (175 mL) white wine
Skin of 1 preserved lemon, chopped
½ cup (85 g) green olives, with pits
A small handful of chopped fresh rosemary or thyme

Season the chops on both sides with salt, pepper, and a judicious sprinkling of sugar. Heat the oil in a sauté pan over medium-high heat, and brown the chops on both sides. Pour over the wine, and add half the lemon, half the olives, and the rosemary. Cover, and simmer over medium-low heat until tender, about 20 minutes. Remove the chops to warm plates. Boil down the liquid a little if necessary, and toss in the remaining olives and lemon. Serve the chops with the juices spooned over.

PORK CHOPS WITH RED ONION CONFIT

Onion confit is worth knowing about for times when you don't have it in you to go as far as sauce. The sweet tangle of soft red onion threads goes very well with pork, and it helps make dinner a little bit dressy, which is always good for morale.

Makes: 2 servings

For the confit

1 large red onion
1 to 2 tablespoons (15 to 30 mL) butter
Salt and pepper
A splash of balsamic or red wine vinegar

For the chops

2 pork chops, on the bone
Salt and pepper
Pinch sugar

Slice the onion very thinly. Melt the butter in a frying pan over medium heat, add the onion, season with salt and pepper, and cook gently, stirring occasionally, until soft, about 15 minutes. Add the vinegar, and reduce until the liquid evaporates, about a minute. Transfer to a bowl, and keep warm.

Wipe out the pan, and set it over medium-high heat. If the chops are lacking in fat, you may need to add a little oil or butter, or both, to the pan. Season the chops with salt, pepper, and sugar. Fry until golden and cooked through, about 5 minutes per side. Serve with a spoonful of red onion confit on top.

PORK CHOPS AND POTATOES

This recipe sounds so pedestrian: pork chops sandwiched between layers of potatozzzzz . . . But it is, in fact, excellent. The potato slices get wonderfully soft, soaking up all those bacony beer and juniper juices; meanwhile, the chops stay nice and moist, especially when you buy fat ones. The top potatoes get very golden and a bit crisp. Très yummy – and to think it all happens in one dish! Follow with a green salad; it will help make the meal feel virtuous.

Makes: 4 servings

4 fatty pork chops, on the bone
2 garlic cloves, sliced
Salt and pepper
1 tablespoon (15 mL) pork drippings or butter
1½ pounds (675 g) potatoes, peeled and thinly sliced
1 onion, thinly sliced
4 slices bacon, cut into lardons
½ teaspoon (2 mL) juniper berries
½ cup (125 mL) white wine, dry cider, or beer
½ cup (125 mL) beef or chicken stock
A handful of chopped parsley, for garnish

Heat the oven to 325°F (160°C). Cut slits in the chops, and slide in slices of garlic. Season the chops with salt and pepper. Melt the pork fat in a frying pan over medium-high heat, and brown the chops, about 3 minutes per side. In a casserole large enough to hold the chops, layer half the potatoes and onions. Season with salt and pepper, and lay the chops on top. Scatter over the bacon and juniper berries. Cover with the remaining potatoes and onions. Season again. Pour over the wine. Cut a piece of parchment to fit over the potatoes and lay it in on top. Bake, uncovered, for about an hour and a half, pouring in the stock at halftime. Serve garnished with parsley.

SAUSAGES AND LENTILS

French lentils have the advantage of being beady once cooked, so they keep their bite, delicious with juicy slices of sausage on top. A salad of mâche is perfect on the side; or, if you prefer something hot, sauté winter greens such as kale, chard, or spinach.

Makes: 8 servings

1 pound (450 g) du Puy lentils
6 cups (1.5 L) chicken stock
½ onion, peeled
1 bunch thyme
4 to 6 fresh fat sausages from the butcher
1 tablespoon (15 mL) butter
2 shallots, minced
¼ cup (60 mL) walnut oil or olive oil
Salt and pepper

Put the lentils in a saucepan with the stock, onion, and thyme. Bring to the boil, and simmer, uncovered, until cooked al dente, 25 to 35 minutes. If there is still a lot of liquid once the lentils are tender, drain it off. Discard the aromatics.

Bring another pot of water to boil for the sausages. Prick the sausages with a fork to prevent them from bursting, add them to the boiling water, and cook them until they're done, which is to say no longer pink in the center. Timing will depend on the type of sausage.

Meanwhile, melt the butter in a frying pan over medium heat, and gently sauté the shallots until translucent. Add the lentils, and reheat. Moisten with walnut oil, and season with salt and pepper. When the sausages are done, slice them, and serve them fanned atop beds of lentils.

PORK FLORENTINE

Here's a useful recipe for buffet-style entertaining because it's equally good at room temperature as it is hot. I like Celeriac Rémoulade (p. 67) on the side, or if you want something warm, serve Potatoes Boulangère (p. 185).

Makes: 6 servings

1 boneless pork loin, about 2 pounds (900 g)
Salt and pepper
7 ounces (200 g) fresh spinach
2 slices bacon, cut into lardons
1 medium onion, chopped
1 garlic clove, minced
¼ cup (20 g) fresh bread crumbs
1 tablespoon (15 mL) cooking oil
½ cup (125 mL) white wine

Heat the oven to 375°F (190°C). Set the pork on a cutting board, and cut through it lengthwise, three-quarters of the way through. Open out the meat. Now make the same lengthwise cut down the center of the left and right sides. The meat should now lie flat, looking a bit like a plowed field. Lay plastic wrap over it, and pound flat with a mallet. Remove the plastic, season the meat with salt and pepper, and set aside.

Rinse the spinach and spin dry, allowing a little water to remain clinging to the leaves. Put it in a sauté pan over medium heat, cover, and wilt, about 5 minutes. Lay the spinach on a clean tea towel, and squeeze it dry. Chop, and set aside.

Wipe out the pan, and put it back on the stove over medium-high heat. Fry the bacon until cooked but not crisp, and drain on paper towel. Pour off all but a tablespoon or two of the fat, and fry the onion in it until golden. Add the garlic, and cook for 1 minute. Stir through the bread crumbs, spinach, and bacon. Season with salt and pepper.

Pat the stuffing over the meat, leaving a border at the far short end about as thick as your finger. Roll up the loin, and tie to secure. Wipe out the sauté pan, and heat the oil in it over medium-high heat. Brown the meat on all sides, pour in the wine, then transfer to the oven, and roast until tender and the juices run clear, about 45 minutes. Remove from the oven, and let the meat rest 10 minutes. Wrap for later, or slice and serve with the pan juices poured over.

WHOLE STUFFED CABBAGE

Hot or at room temperature, this is good: a *boule*-shaped layering of frilly cabbage leaves and a savory pork stuffing. It looks impressive, but it's very straightforward to make, and if you feel at all intimidated, remember it is very much a peasant dish, one you might stumble upon in central France. I serve wedges in soup plates with a puddle of cooking juices spooned around.

Makes: 6 servings

1 medium or 2 small savoy cabbages (about 1½ pounds/675 g total)
3 ounces (85 g) bread
About ¼ cup (60 mL) milk
1 tablespoon (15 mL) butter
1 tablespoon (15 mL) olive oil
2 onions, chopped
1 shallot, chopped
3 garlic cloves, chopped
¼ pound (110 g) mushrooms, chopped
A few handfuls of chopped fresh thyme
1 teaspoon (5 mL) quatre-épices (p. 152), more to taste (or smoked paprika)
Salt and pepper
About 1 pound (450 g) pork sausage meat

Core the cabbage. Gently peel away the leaves to expose the heart (by heart, I mean the ball of more yellowish leaves at the center that are too tightly packed to bother prying apart). Shred the heart, and set aside to add to the stuffing. Cut the thick ribs out of the outer leaves (they will look like you've stolen a sliver from a pie). Bring a large pot of water to the boil, and salt it generously. Blanch the cabbage leaves for 5 to 7 minutes. Drain, and refresh under ice-cold water. Drain, and pat dry with a towel.

Break the bread into crumbs in a bowl, pour over the milk, and set aside to soften. Heat the butter and olive oil in a frying pan over medium heat, and gently fry the onion and shallot until transparent, about 5 minutes. Add the garlic, mushrooms, shredded cabbage, and thyme. Cook another 5 minutes. Stir in the bread, and cook until the milk has evaporated. Stir through the quatre-épices, and season generously with salt and pepper. Add this mixture to the sausage meat in a large bowl, along with the reserved shredded cabbage, and mix thoroughly with a fork. Make a small ball and fry it in the frying pan. Taste to check the seasonings, and adjust as needed.

Lay a tea towel on the counter, and on top of that lay a piece of cheesecloth or muslin large enough to wrap the original cabbage in. You're going to reconstruct the cabbage, only with layers of stuffing between the leaves. So, first lay down the large outer leaves, slightly overlapping, and with the prettiest side facing down. Spread over a layer of stuffing about ½ inch (1 cm) thick. Arrange another layer of leaves on top and repeat the action. Continue until you have run out of leaves and stuffing. Pull up the edges of the cheesecloth and towel, like a bag, and twist, as if making the head of a puppet, to shape the cabbage into a round. Remove the towel, leaving the cheesecloth. Tie the cheesecloth with string to secure the package. (The cabbage can be prepared to this stage several hours in advance of cooking.)

To cook, set the cabbage in a steaming basket over about 2 cups (500 mL) of simmering water or good chicken stock. Flavor from the cabbage will drip into the water and give it a rich, savory taste. When the cabbage is done, boil down the cooking juices, and serve a spoonful around each wedge of cabbage in a soup bowl.

MILK PORK

For some reason, the only place you ever see this dish in France is in the southwest – the rest of the country apparently missed the boat (although Italy seems to be all over it). It's a good braising trick if you don't have a bottle of wine at hand. With milk, you get moist, tender pork in a sauce that's pale and creamy. All you need is some sautéed spinach or roasted squash (p. 218) on the side and dinner's ready.

Makes: 6 servings

1 boneless pork roast, about 3 pounds (1.3 kg)
4 to 6 garlic cloves, cut into slivers
Salt and pepper
2 tablespoons (30 mL) butter
1 onion, peeled and cut in half
1 carrot, peeled and cut in half
2 large rosemary branches
2 bay leaves
4 cups (1 L) whole milk
A generous handful of chopped fresh chives and/or parsley, for garnish

Make small slits all over the meat with a sharp knife, inserting a sliver of garlic into each as you go. (If you can do this several hours or the night before cooking, all the better.) Rub the meat all over with salt and pepper. Heat the oven to 325°F (160°C).

Melt the butter in a deep, lidded casserole (*cocotte*) over medium-high heat, and brown the meat well on all sides. Add the onion, carrot, rosemary, and bay leaves. Pour over the milk, and bring to a simmer. Cover the dish, and transfer to the oven. Braise until the pork is tender, about 2 hours, turning the meat at least once.

Remove the meat from the pot, and wrap in foil to keep it warm. Discard the herbs, carrot, and onion. The cooking juices will be curdled and ugly, but this is how they're meant to be. Boil them down to about a cup (250 mL), then purée with an immersion blender until smooth. Taste, and adjust the seasonings.

Carve the meat and arrange in a serving dish. Pour over the sauce, sprinkle with the chives and/or parsley, and serve.

PORK BELLY WITH LENTILS

When my friend Camille was temporarily living in Normandy, I used to go spend weekends there, and we'd cook up storms like we did in the good old days at our Paris apartment. She lived not far from a famous *charcutier,* which is where we got inspired to try our hands at pork belly. We were so proud of ourselves the first time we made this recipe that we made it again and this time invited our friend Ivan, who is an amazing cook. He loved it, too, so I think it's safe to print.

Makes: 6 servings

For the belly

1 pork belly (not cured), skinless but with the fat layer attached, about 3 pounds (1.3 kg)
Salt and pepper
4 large carrots, peeled and cut diagonally into large chunks
3 onions, quartered
A few thyme sprigs
2 bay leaves
6 black peppercorns
1 cup (250 mL) dry cider
¼ cup (60 mL) honey
2 tablespoons (30 mL) Dijon mustard
1 tablespoon (15 mL) cider vinegar

For the lentils

1 cup (225 g) du Puy lentils
1 shallot
1 bay leaf
1 thyme sprig
Salt and pepper

Heat the oven to 450°F (230°C). Score the fat on the belly, and season both sides with salt and pepper. Make a bed in a small roasting pan with the carrots, onions, thyme sprigs, bay leaves, and peppercorns. Lay the belly on top, skin side up. Pour over the cider and a cup (250 mL) of water. Roast for 30 minutes to get the fat running. Stir together the honey, Dijon, and a spoonful of water. Brush onto the fat and lower the heat to 325°F (160°C). Continue cooking, basting occasionally with the pan juices, until the meat is very tender, about 3 hours. Remove from the oven, but do not turn off the oven. Increase the heat to 450°F (230°C).

An hour before the belly is done, start the lentils: Rinse them in cold water, drain, and put in a saucepan with 1½ cups (375 mL) water, the shallot, the bay leaf, and the thyme. Bring to the boil, cover, and simmer gently until tender, 30 to 40 minutes, checking occasionally to make sure no more water is needed. Drain, discarding the shallot and herbs. Return to the saucepan, season with salt and pepper, and set aside.

Transfer the belly to a baking sheet. Return it to the oven for 15 minutes to crisp the skin.

Meanwhile, strain the juices from the roasting pan into a measuring cup, reserving the vegetables and keeping them warm. Pour the fat off the juices, using some to moisten the lentils and saving the rest for another use. Reheat the lentils gently.

Deglaze the roasting pan with the vinegar, and reduce to a glaze, then add the cooking juices and reduce for a minute or two.

Slice the belly, and serve with the vegetables and pork-fat-moistened lentils.

ROAST PORK WITH ROSEMARY, QUATRE-ÉPICES, AND HONEY

This is remarkably quick but tastes like a dish that took all afternoon, and it makes the kitchen smell like a dream. The moment when the sauce drapes over the slices of meat, just before you serve, is particularly satisfying. Quatre-épices is a classic French spice mix used by *charcutiers.* If you can't find it in shops, stir together 1 tablespoon (15 mL) white pepper, 1 teaspoon (5 mL) ground ginger, 1 teaspoon (5 mL) nutmeg, and ¼ tsp (1 mL) ground cloves; this makes 2 tablespoons (30 mL), which is, coincidentally, what you need for this recipe.

Makes: 8 servings

1 boned pork roast, about 3 pounds (1.3 kg)
Salt and pepper
1 tablespoon (15 mL) olive oil
2 handfuls of chopped fresh rosemary
2 tablespoons (30 mL) quatre-épices (see above)
⅓ cup (75 mL) honey, warmed until runny if necessary
½ cup (125 mL) water or dry cider

Heat the oven to 400°F (200°C). Season the meat well all over with salt and pepper. Rub with the olive oil. Mix together the rosemary and quatre-épices on a sheet of wax paper, and roll the meat in them to coat evenly. Set the meat in a roasting pan, fat side up. Drizzle over the honey. Pour about ¼ cup (60 mL) water into the pan, and roast the pork for 20 minutes. Reduce the heat to 350°F (180°C), and continue roasting until the juices run clear, about 40 minutes more, adding another ¼ cup (60 mL) water during cooking if the pan has gone completely dry.

Keep the juices warm while you carve the roast. Fan the meat onto a platter. Taste the juices, and correct the seasonings. Pour over the meat, and serve.

BEEF AU BLEU

Blue cheese sauce is so fast and easy, it's great to pull out for weeknight dinners. I eat pasta tossed in it all the time, but the tanginess of it is also wonderful dribbled over sliced beef. Either watercress salad or Endives with Oranges (p. 221) is ideal on the side.

Makes: 6 servings

1 sirloin steak, about 2 pounds (900 g) and 2 inches (5 cm) thick
Salt and pepper
A little olive oil
½ pound (225 g) blue cheese
½ cup (125 mL) heavy cream

Move the oven rack to the top rungs, and heat the oven to broil for a good 10 minutes. Season the steak on both sides with salt and pepper, and rub all over with a little olive oil. Set the meat in a cast-iron pan, and broil 4 to 6 minutes per side or until done to your liking. Remove to a carving board, cover with foil, and let rest 10 minutes. Set aside the pan with the cooking juices.

Meanwhile, crumble the cheese into a saucepan, pour over the cream, and gently heat to melt, stirring occasionally. Carve the meat, and arrange on a serving platter. Spoon over a little of the sauce, and pour the rest into a sauce jug for passing around at the table.

PEPPER STEAK

I used to have a pepper steak recipe I liked, but I haven't made it since I was taught this version by a friend's mom, Martine Labro, one of the best home cooks I know in France. It is so fast and simple that it's almost embarrassing, but, trust me, this is the ultimate in pepper steak. Martine doesn't bother with the beef stock herself, but I like the depth of flavor it gives.

Makes: 4 servings

2 to 4 tenderloin or eye of round steaks (estimate 5 ounces/140 g per person)
1 to 2 tablespoons (15 to 30 mL) green peppercorns in brine, rinsed and drained
About ¼ cup (60 mL) red wine or strong black tea
Salt
½ cup (125 mL) beef stock
½ cup (125 mL) crème fraîche

Bring the meat to room temperature before cooking, about 20 minutes. Soak the peppercorns in the wine in a bowl. Heat a large frying pan to high, and season the meat with salt. When the pan is very hot, fry the steaks on both sides to your liking.

Let the meat rest on a board while you make the sauce. Drain the peppercorns. Deglaze the pan with the stock, and boil it down to a generous tablespoon, about 2 minutes. Lower the heat, and add the peppercorns and cream to heat through. Put the meat back in the pan, turning once to coat. Serve.

STUFFED TOMATOES

Nothing against meat loaf, but when you fill tomatoes with meat stuffing, it really is nicer to look at, and it seems lighter. With Aubergine Ruffles (p. 207) on the side, this makes a chic weeknight supper or a small main course in a more expanded dinner. It is difficult to say how many tomatoes you'll need for the filling because it depends on their size, but for the record, you'll get about 1½ cups (375 mL) meat filling here. I recommend large tomatoes, because what you mostly want in every bite is the meat, with the tomato as an accompaniment. Speaking of which, feel free to experiment with a combination of beef, veal, and pork, or with lamb. Also, remember this general concept when you have leftover stew meat or duck confit.

Makes: 4 to 6 light servings

4 to 6 large tomatoes
Salt and pepper
Olive oil, for frying
1 onion, minced
2 to 3 garlic cloves, minced
2 teaspoons (10 mL) herbes de Provence, more to taste
1 pound (450 g) ground beef
1 thick slice of bread, turned into crumbs
1 tablespoon (15 mL) Dijon mustard
1 or 2 pinches paprika, more to taste (optional)

Slice a sliver off the bottom of the tomatoes so they sit flat without wobbling. Slice the tops off the tomatoes. Hollow out the insides, being careful not to break the sides, and reserve the pulp and the tops for another use (such as chopping up to throw in pasta sauce). Pat the tomatoes dry inside with paper towel, season with salt, and leave upside down on paper towel to drain for about 20 minutes. Heat the oven to 350°F (180°C).

Heat the oil in a frying pan over medium heat. Gently sauté the onions until soft, about 10 minutes, adding the garlic and herbes de Provence for the last minute. Add the beef. Pour over ⅓ cup (75 mL) water. Season with salt and pepper, and cook until the meat is no longer pink and the liquid has evaporated.

Remove from the heat and stir in the bread crumbs, mustard, and paprika (if using). Taste, and check the seasonings. Spoon the meat filling into the tomatoes. Set the tomatoes on a small baking sheet, and bake until they're soft and hot, about 30 minutes.

BEEF TENDERLOIN WITH RÉMOULADE SAUCE

Sometimes it's just too much to coordinate a piping-hot meal for a crowd. So here's a brilliant solution: don't. This roast beef is perfect at room temperature, and indeed it shouldn't be hot if you're going to dollop on a perky mayonnaise sauce full of chopped pickles and herbs. Boiled new potatoes tossed in olive oil and fleur de sel (p. 179) are all you need on the side, then a green salad afterward, and why not cake for dessert? There, a whole easy menu, already planned!

Makes: 4 to 6 servings

For the roast

1 beef tenderloin, about 2 pounds (900 g), at room temperature
1 tablespoon (15 mL) olive oil
Salt and pepper

For the sauce

1 egg yolk
2 teaspoons (10 mL) Dijon mustard, more to taste
1 teaspoon (5 mL) anchovy paste
½ teaspoon (2 mL) tarragon vinegar
¼ cup (60 mL) olive oil
¾ cup (175 mL) peanut or safflower oil
2 to 3 handfuls chopped cornichons
2 tablespoons (30 mL) capers
2 tablespoons (30 mL) chopped fresh tarragon
1 tablespoon (15 mL) chopped fresh parsley
1 tablespoon (15 mL) chopped fresh chervil
Freshly ground black pepper
Salt
Lemon juice

Heat the oven to 400°F (200°C). Weigh the meat, rub with olive oil and season with salt and pepper, then roast it 12 minutes for the first pound (450 g) and 10 minutes for each additional pound. (For 2 pounds/900 g, about 22 minutes for medium-rare.) Let rest at least 10 minutes before carving.

While the beef roasts, make the sauce. Whisk together the egg yolk, mustard, anchovy paste, and vinegar. Add the olive oil drop by drop, whisking constantly, then dribble in the peanut oil, whisking constantly. The mayonnaise should be very thick. Stir in the cornichons, capers, and herbs, adjusting the quantities of any of these to suit your taste. Grind in some pepper. Taste, and adjust the seasonings with salt and squirts of lemon. Cover, and refrigerate until ready to serve with the sliced roast.

BEEF AND CARROT STEW

Nostalgia settles over me whenever I make this wintery stew. The first time I had it was in the middle of France in a mountain restaurant with someone I adored. I remember the way the cool air smelled that night, how high up we felt, how big the world seemed, and how adventurous we thought we were. This is best made a day ahead.

Makes: 6 to 8 servings

About 4 pounds (1.8 kg) stewing beef, cut into chunks (bones left on if there are bones)
Salt and pepper
7 ounces (200 g) thick bacon, cut into lardons
2 tablespoons (30 mL) olive or grapeseed oil, more if needed
2 onions, sliced
2 garlic cloves, crushed
2 tablespoons (30 mL) sherry vinegar or red wine vinegar
3 cups (750 mL) dry red or white wine
3 cups (750 mL) beef stock
1 bay leaf
1 celery stick, cut into 2
1 bouquet parsley
1 bouquet thyme
4 black peppercorns
2 tablespoons (30 mL) cornstarch
3 pounds (1.3 kg) large carrots, peeled and thickly sliced

Season the meat on both sides with salt and pepper. Fry the bacon in a large casserole over medium heat until cooked but not crisp, about 7 minutes. Remove to a medium bowl, and set aside. Add half the oil and fry the onions until soft, about 10 minutes, adding the garlic toward the end. Add to the bacon. Increase the heat to medium-high, and add the remaining oil to the pot. Working in batches, brown the meat well on all sides. Add to the onions as browned.

Deglaze the pan with the vinegar, scraping up the good bits from the bottom. When the vinegar has almost disappeared, add the wine. Now, put the meat, bacon, onions, and garlic back in the pot. Pour over the stock, adding more water if needed to cover. Tie the bay leaf, celery, parsley, thyme, and peppercorns together in a cheesecloth bundle. Add it to the pot. Season with salt. Bring to the boil, cover, reduce the heat, and simmer for 2 hours.

At this point, dissolve the cornstarch in some of the cooking liquid, and stir it into the pot. Cook, uncovered, for half an hour. Add the carrots and continue cooking for half an hour, until the meat and carrots are tender and the sauce is reduced to gravy consistency. Serve.

BEEF IN BEER

In northern France, this is known as *carbonnade de boeuf,* and with the beer and brown sugar you can certainly detect the Flemish influence. Good boy-food. (Or is that sexist?) Serve with potatoes or with egg noodles tossed in butter and chopped parsley.

Makes: 6 servings

2 tablespoons (30 mL) butter or beef drippings, more as needed
1 tablespoon (15 mL) olive oil
3 pounds (1.3 kg) sirloin tip, cut into fat strips
3 large onions, sliced
4 garlic cloves, chopped
2 tablespoons (30 mL) flour
1 tablespoon (15 mL) brown sugar
1½ cups (375 mL) beef stock
2 cups (500 mL) dark or amber beer
1 tablespoon (15 mL) red wine vinegar
Salt and pepper
1 bouquet garni (bay leaf, thyme sprig, a few parsley stems)

Heat the oven to 325°F (160°C). Melt the butter with the oil in a sauté pan over medium-high heat, and, working in batches, brown the beef strips on both sides. Remove from the pan. In the same pan, fry the onions until soft, about 15 minutes, then add the garlic and cook for 1 minute. Remove from the pan. (Check if there is fat in the pan. If not, add a good tablespoon of butter and let it melt.) Add the flour and sugar to the pan, and cook, stirring, for 1 minute to make a roux. Gradually whisk in the stock, and bring to the boil, stirring. Add the beer and the vinegar, and bring back to the boil, cooking until thickened, about 10 minutes. Remove from the heat.

In a large casserole, layer the onion mixture alternately with the beef strips, seasoning each layer as you go with salt and pepper. Tuck in the bouquet garni, and pour the liquid over. Cover, and bake for 2½ hours. If you can wait a day before eating, cool the dish completely when it's out of the oven, and refrigerate overnight. The flavor will be even better when you reheat.

VEAL BLANQUETTE

This white veal stew is a French classic that I always avoided because I assumed it would be bland and stodgy. I'd never have bothered to try it, if it hadn't been the special at a Paris bistro where a friend and I lunched one day on the way home from our exercise class. (What? Doesn't everyone eat stew on the way home from working out?) Well, it was so delicious I could have pinched myself, and I was immediately determined to track down a recipe for myself. It took a few rounds of testing to get it just right, but I finally did it. I was calling it "beige-ette de veau" initially, because mine never seemed to turn out truly white, but now it does, even though the recipe hasn't changed. Hmm . . . a mystery. Anyway, beige or *blanc*, it stands out as one of the best things I have ever eaten in my life. I recommend Vichy Carrots (p. 216) on the side, for color.

Makes: 6 servings

10 ounces (280 g) pearl onions
4 pounds (1.8 kg) veal shoulder, cut into chunks
8 cups (2 L) chicken stock
1 bouquet garni (bay leaf, thyme sprig, and a few parsley sprigs)
1 carrot
1 onion, poked with 2 cloves
Salt and pepper
5 tablespoons (75 g) butter
12 ounces (375 g) small cremini or button mushrooms
3 tablespoons (45 mL) flour
½ cup (125 mL) crème fraîche or half sour cream, half heavy cream
A few handfuls of finely chopped fresh parsley, for garnish

Bring a large pot of water to the boil. Salt it, and blanch the onions 1 minute. Remove, and set aside. In the same pot, blanch the meat for 4 minutes. Drain, and rinse under cold water.

Return the veal to the pot, and cover with all but 1 cup (250 mL) of the chicken stock. (If you need more liquid to cover, add water.) Drop in the bouquet garni, carrot, and clove-studded onion. Bring to the boil, reduce the heat, and simmer very gently, uncovered, 1 to 1½ hours, until the meat is very tender but not falling apart. Remove from the heat.

While the meat cooks, peel the blanched onions. Melt 2 tablespoons (30 mL) of the butter in a sauté pan over medium-high heat, and fry the pearl onions with the mushrooms until golden, about 5 minutes. Pour over the remaining cup (250 mL) of stock, reduce the heat, and cook until the vegetables are tender and all the liquid has evaporated, about 10 minutes. Set aside and keep warm.

Strain the liquid from the veal stew into a saucepan, and discard the carrot, onion, and bouquet garni. You should have about 2 cups (500 mL) of cooking liquid. If you have more, simply boil to reduce. Add the meat to the mushrooms in the sauté pan. Keep warm.

Melt the remaining butter in a medium saucepan. Whisk in the flour and cook, whisking, for 1 minute. Pour over the cooking liquid, and simmer, stirring, to thicken, about 10 minutes, skimming off any film that rises to the surface. Add the crème fraîche, season with salt and pepper, and pour over the meat and vegetables. Gently reheat, transfer to a serving dish, scatter over the parsley, and serve.

BEEF BOURGUIGNON

I learned all the classic French stews in the old-fashioned way, which meant overnight marinating and quite a lot of to-do. This version is certainly simplified, but rest assured, none of the taste is lost. To me it's as rich and comforting as ever, and I love that it reminds me of my years in the Burgundian countryside.

Makes: 8 to 10 servings

For the stew

2 tablespoons (30 mL) olive oil
4 pounds (1.8 kg) boneless stewing beef, such as chuck or sirloin tip, cut into large chunks
4 garlic cloves, lightly crushed
¼ cup (30 g) flour
1 bottle red wine
4 cups (1 L) beef stock
1 bouquet garni (bay leaf, parsley stems, and thyme)
2 carrots, peeled and halved
2 onions, peeled and halved

For the garnish

1 tablespoon (15 mL) olive oil, more if needed
6 to 8 slices bacon, cut into lardons
40 pearl onions, peeled
1 pound (450 g) button mushrooms, halved or quartered if large

Heat the oven to 325°F (160°F). Heat the oil in a large casserole over medium-high heat. Working in batches, brown the meat well on all sides, removing it to a bowl as it's browned. When the meat is done, sauté the garlic for 1 minute. Reduce the heat to medium-low. Add the flour, and cook, stirring, for 2 minutes. Stirring constantly, pour over the wine and the stock. Add the bouquet garni, carrots, and onions. Return the meat to the pot, cover, and bake in the oven until the meat is very tender, about 2 hours.

For the garnish, heat the oil in a frying pan over medium heat. Fry the bacon until cooked but not crisp. Remove to a bowl. Add the onions, and sauté until browned all over; add to the bacon. Finally, brown the mushrooms, and add to the bowl. Deglaze the pan with ½ cup (125 mL) water, reduce to a spoonful, then pour over the garnish. Set aside.

When the meat is done, remove it from the pot. Strain the stock, discarding the vegetables. Pour the liquid back into the pot, and boil until thick enough to coat a spoon. Return the meat to the pan with the garnish. Cover, and simmer until the onions are tender and the flavors have blended, about 10 minutes. Adjust the seasonings. Serve.

TOURTIÈRE WITH A TWIST

The Québécois are very proud of their Christmas tourtières (or pâtés, as the Acadians call their versions of the meat pie). A friend of mine made miniature tartlets last Christmas for a cocktail party, so I thought I'd try a variation of my own, inspired by what I once saw a home cook in Montréal do on a weeknight: wrap seasoned ground beef in a fancy pastry log like this. It's all incredibly simple, but it tastes fabulously savory and meaty-moist. Part of it is the texture you get by cooking the ground meat in liquid, rather than frying it in oil. Note that the summer savory is *de rigueur,* which you'll understand as soon as you taste this dish. Now, just in case you plan to get creative with pastry shapes, this recipe makes 4 cups (1 L) meat filling, which is enough for two regular pies or many tartlets.

Makes: 2 tourtière "logs"

1 pound (450 g) ground pork
½ pound (225 g) ground veal, hare, or beef
1 large onion, minced
2 garlic cloves, chopped
1 teaspoon (5 mL) dried summer savory, more to taste
Pinch ground cloves (optional)
Salt and pepper
6 tablespoons (50 g) fresh bread crumbs
1 recipe galette or savory tart dough (pp. 9 or 10), divided into 2 disks
Milk, for brushing

Put ½ cup (125 mL) water in a large sauté pan, and bring to the boil. In a large bowl, combine the ground pork, ground veal, onion, garlic, savory, cloves (if using), and salt and pepper. Stir into the water. Cover, and simmer until the meat is tender, about 20 minutes. Stir in the bread crumbs, and continue cooking, uncovered, until the liquid has evaporated. Check the seasonings, and cool completely.

Heat the oven to 450°F (230°C). On a lightly floured surface, roll out one disk of pastry into a rectangle about ⅛ inch (3 mm) thick. Spoon half of the meat mixture lengthwise down the center of it, leaving a 1-inch (2.5 cm) margin at each end. Fold the short ends in over the meat. Now, fold over the long ends to cover the filling, but trim away any excess pastry at the corners so you don't have four layers of pastry overlapping anywhere.

Carefully transfer the sealed log to a baking sheet, seam side down. Make 2 or 3 slits in the top to let steam escape. Repeat with the other pastry disk and the remaining filling. Brush the tops with milk for a golden crust. Bake until the pastry is crisp and golden, about 25 minutes. Slice and serve warm or at room temperature.

BOEUF EN CROÛTE

A proper beef Wellington is meant to have foie gras in it, but not everyone appreciates the extra richness, nor is it always an easy ingredient to find. This recipe is a simplified version, therefore, but equally grand in presentation.

Makes: 6 servings

1 beef tenderloin, about 1½ pounds (675 g)
Salt and pepper
3 tablespoons (45 mL) butter
A drizzle of olive oil
2 shallots, minced
1 pound (450 g) mushrooms, very finely chopped
Leaves from 1 thyme sprig
1 bay leaf
½ cup (125 mL) Madeira
2 tablespoons (30 mL) crème fraîche
A handful of chopped fresh parsley
2 (7-ounce/200 g) squares puff pastry
1 egg, lightly beaten with a tablespoon of water, for egg wash

Season the beef with salt and pepper. Melt 1 tablespoon (15 mL) of the butter with a drizzle of olive oil in a sauté pan over medium-high heat until hot, then sear the beef on all sides. Remove to a board, and let cool completely, then wrap and refrigerate.

Prepare the mushroom duxelles in the same pan as the beef: Melt the remaining butter, and fry the shallots until translucent. Add the mushrooms, thyme, and bay leaf, and cook, stirring occasionally, until the mushrooms are very tender. Pour over the Madeira, bring to the boil, and cook until all the liquid has evaporated. Add the crème fraîche, and cook down to a very thick paste. Remove from the heat, season with salt and pepper, and stir through the parsley. Discard the bay leaf.

On a lightly floured surface, roll out one piece of pastry to a rectangle ⅛ inch (3 mm) thick; it should be large enough to accommodate the meat with a roomy border around it. Lay on a baking sheet. Spoon the mushroom mixture over the center of the pastry, and set the tenderloin on top. Roll out the second block of pastry to fit over the whole tenderloin generously. Brush the margins of the bottom pastry with egg wash, then drape the second pastry sheet over, pressing the edges to seal well. Trim the edges to a 1-inch (2.5 cm) border. Crimp the edges with your fingers. Refrigerate until ready to bake.

Heat the oven to 425°F (220°C). Brush the whole surface of the pastry with the egg wash and make two slits in the top with a knife to allow steam to escape. Bake 15 minutes. Reduce the oven temperature to 400°F (200°C), and continue baking 20 minutes for medium-rare, or longer, depending on how well you like your meat done. Let stand about 10 minutes before serving in slices.

HERB-CRUSTED LAMB LEG WITH POTATOES

This roasted leg with an herbes de Provence crust gives you lovely slices of meat, and because it's cooked right on the rack in the oven, the drippings conveniently rain down on the potatoes. Baked tomato halves (p. 224) are good on the side; in fact, you can always just tuck them in alongside the lamb to roast.

Makes: 8 servings

1 (5-pound/2.2 kg) bone-in leg of lamb
About 3 garlic cloves, sliced
¼ cup (60 mL) olive oil, plus a little more for the potatoes
2 tablespoons (30 mL) lemon juice
1 teaspoon (5 mL) each salt and pepper
Several handfuls of herbes de Provence
2 pounds (900 g) potatoes, sliced about the width of your little finger
½ cup (125 mL) veal or beef stock

Several hours before cooking the lamb, make slits all over it with the tip of a sharp knife and slide a sliver of garlic into each slit as you go. Stir together the olive oil, lemon juice, salt, and pepper, and rub all over the lamb to coat. Now, pat the herbs all over the meat to cover completely. Put the lamb on a plate, cover, and leave to marinate for several hours in the refrigerator. Let the meat come to room temperature about an hour before roasting.

Heat the oven to 450°F (230°C) with the top cooking rack in the middle and another rack beneath it two notches. Toss the potatoes on a baking sheet or in a shallow roasting pan with a little olive oil, and season with salt and pepper. Pour over the stock. Put the potatoes on the lower oven rack, and put the lamb roast directly on the rack above it, so that drippings from the lamb fall onto the potatoes.

Roast for 20 minutes. Lower the heat to 400°F (200°C), and continue roasting 40 minutes to an hour for medium-rare, longer if you prefer your meat well done. Pour a little more stock or water over the potatoes if they look dry at halftime. They are done when they are soft and nicely caramelized, glossy, and sticky. Let the meat rest for 10 minutes before carving. Serve with the potatoes.

SLOW SHOULDER

Seven-hour leg of lamb, which involves a lot of wine, is the slow lamb recipe you hear of most often. I have tried it several times, but I have to say I'm not as fond of it as I am this one, which barely uses any cooking liquid at all. With very little effort, the lamb emerges incredibly moist and juicy. I use shoulder instead of leg, too, because it's a tougher cut and it fits more easily into a *cocotte.* Use leg if you like, though. Baked tomatoes (p. 224) and/or potato purée (p. 177) are good accompaniments.

Makes: 4 to 6 servings

1 lamb shoulder or leg on the bone, about 2 pounds (900 g)
Salt and pepper
3 tablespoons (45 mL) olive oil
1 cup (250 mL) white wine
1 head garlic, broken into unpeeled cloves
3 bay leaves
4 short rosemary sprigs
1 large bouquet fresh thyme

Heat the oven to 325°F (160°C). Season the lamb generously with salt and pepper, and rub with some of the olive oil. In an ovenproof casserole just large enough to hold the lamb, brown the meat on all sides over medium-high heat. Deglaze with the wine. Lay the garlic and herbs on and around the lamb. Drizzle over the remaining oil. Cover and bake for 4 hours, turning once at halftime. Remove from the oven, and serve from the casserole with the juices spooned over.

PROVENÇAL RACK OF LAMB

This is fast and fabulous. Serve it to someone you love.

Makes: 2 servings

1 rack of lamb (about 8 ribs), frenched by your butcher
Salt and pepper
3 to 4 tablespoons (45 to 60 mL) olive oil
3 to 4 tablespoons (45 to 60 mL) Dijon mustard
½ cup (40 g) fresh bread crumbs
¼ cup (30 g) grated Parmesan cheese
2 handfuls of chopped fresh herbs, such as parsley, thyme, and rosemary

Heat the oven to 425°F (220°C). Season the meat with salt and pepper. Mix together the oil and mustard, then slather all over the rack to coat well. Mix together the bread crumbs, cheese, and herbs, then pack the mixture onto the lamb rack.

Set the lamb, bones arching upwards, in a roasting pan just large enough to hold it. Roast until the meat is done to your liking, knowing that roughly 20 minutes will give you medium-rare meat. Let the meat rest for 10 minutes before carving.

HOW TO FEED

Our chief responsibility as hosts, I've worked out, is to do everything in our power to ensure our own happiness. That may sound selfish, but, on the contrary, it's vital to the success of a party. We can have happy and relaxed people around us only if we're feeling serene and cheerful ourselves. We can entertain well only if we, ourselves, are feeling entertained.

Our own "entertainment" starts from the moment we're sitting with a cup of tea at the kitchen table trying to figure out a menu for the stellar combination of guests we've invited. A solution I always find foolproof is to serve whatever I'm personally hungry for. We all cook better when we're making something we're going to like, so if we're just croaking for a pot of soup, then we should make one, call everyone up, and say, "Hey, there's soup here. Who wants some?" If we have already invited people and the evening is meant to be a bit more swish, then we should still operate on the basis of what we ourselves feel like eating. If that happens to be steak and mashed potatoes, well, there are ways of making them look their Sunday best, and that's all we have to do: let fly on presentation, but keep the food simple.

One cardinal rule for dinner party hosts, supposedly, is never to risk making a new dish, but always to rely on the tried and true. Well, if we're too tired for anything else, fine, but otherwise I say, "How boring is that?" Personally, if I have six guinea pigs coming for dinner, I am hardly going to waste the opportunity for adventure. If I am in the mood and I have time, I'll use people coming over as an excuse to dive into an exciting challenge, such as a terrine or a fancy cake. I've found that as long as I make everyone feel like a participant in the adventure, they're happy whether it turns out or not, and so am I. In fact (tip!), you can always tell people that you're "testing a recipe." That way, if it bombs, you simply agree with them, blame the recipe, and you're off the hook. (Not that I've ever done that . . . *cough.*)

The most important thing, whatever happens and whatever we cook, is never to apologize for our cooking. (I confess that I'm preaching something here that I don't always practice, but that doesn't make me any less convinced of the message.) Nothing kills fun faster than having the cook fall into a slump over something as foolish as, say, overdone carrots. Part of why a host must absolutely have a good time is to keep the spirits of the evening high for everyone. We shouldn't blow it by getting a sour look on our face and being sorry. Instead, we should make a joke, have a big bite of our carrot disaster, smile, and pass the serving platter along. In fact, because it's always so easy to find fault with anything in life, a good practice is to force ourselves to say something positive. Example: "My, what a lovely change to have mushy carrots! It reminds me so much of the early days of my youth."

If it's any consolation, sometimes not being a perfect cook is actually a relief to guests, especially those who thought they weren't good enough cooks to invite you to dinner themselves. (It's amazing what a lopsided soufflé can do for your social life.)

I do think it's wise to manage expectations somewhat by setting a precedent we're comfortable with and sticking to it. I only ever entertain informally, because that's my lifestyle and that's my personality. Also, I'm a fairly democratic feeder: when I throw dinner parties, apart from the fact that I add dessert, my food is essentially the same as I make every other night of the week (excluding, obviously, those evenings when I treat myself to a tin of kippers and a boiled potato). Perhaps I could be accused of erring on the side of simplicity, but for the moment that's my way. We all have our own style, and I think the more honestly we stick to it and entertain in a manner that reveals who we really are to people, the more grateful they'll be to sit at our table. It goes back to what I was saying about our own happiness. We're at our best when we can relax and be ourselves, and we're most appealing when we radiate good energy. Any form of entertaining that works in favor of that doesn't just make a good party, it makes the world a better place.

LE VIN

The first thing I love about French wine is the way the French drink it, which is with confidence, in moderation, and with a refreshing lack of pretense. I know the latter isn't a characteristic that immediately springs to mind, because for some reason as soon as something's French it's automatically accused of being fancy, but in my experience there is far less wine snobbery in the Old World than in the New. For example, where I lived in Burgundy, despite the grandness of so many of the wines, the grapes were treated like any other beloved farm crop, and you could find yourself buying exquisite bottles out of an old barn. I have rarely encountered wine-tasting classes for amateurs in France; only sommeliers take lessons in that, and everyone else simply befriends wine by osmosis over time. I have never been to a French dinner party where wine was made into the main topic of conversation. In fact, here is about as much dinner chitchat as even an excellent wine will take up: *"Ooo là! Alors ça . . . C'est pas mauvais ça! Hien? Ce n'est vraiment pas mauvais."* Then you're back to politics, scandal in your friends' lives, travel stories, and so on. Because of their familiarity with good wine, you see, the French have no need to make a fuss about it. Of course, they appreciate quality when they taste it as much as anyone, but, generally speaking, they place wine on the table as casually as they do bread and salt, and they drink it with the nonchalance with which the rest of us drink tap water.

Something else I love about French wines – and this time I mean the actual wines themselves – is the subtlety and intrigue inherent in so many. Unfortunately, it is often precisely these wines that are dismissed in North America as being "weak." Our palates have become so accustomed to the robust and forward New World styles that we tend not to give the quiet talkers a chance to get a word in. But these wines are styled this way on purpose. Generally speaking, in Europe wines are meant to be drunk with food in the context of a meal. (For example, the French don't sit around knocking back glasses of Riesling like whisky on the rocks; they sip at it between bites of chicken.) New World wines, on the other hand, are usually designed to stand on their own (which probably explains why some, like beer, are like a meal in a glass). In North America, we enjoy drinking wine not only with food but also outside mealtimes, without necessarily any accompaniment at all. Anyone who has never really appreciated French wines might find them worth trying again with this in mind (and with a plate of food in front of them), because food enriches the experience. It's food that makes French wines make sense, if I may be so bold.

This brings me around to the rather elusive term *terroir,* a word that sums up what the French believe matters above all when it comes to wine – and to food, for that matter. *Terroir* is a combination of soil, climate, and weather conditions (some believe that culture and people belong in the definition, too), all of which we can taste in a wine when it has been sufficiently left alone to be able to express itself. I remember a farmer in Burgundy once telling me, "Here, we make wine in the vineyards, not in the cellar." He was taking a shot at the kind of new-style wines that are made, more or less, by following a recipe in order to produce exactly the same boring, anonymous wine year after year. Traditional methods, on the other hand, mean allowing well-tended grapes to become what they will on the vine and ultimately express the authentic character of their place and time in the bottle. Overall, Europe tends to place more value on this than other wine-growing zones, but it has no monopoly on the approach. Plenty of vintners in the New World create wines in this way, too, and are valiantly trying to promote them. This approach is so important. When we let wines (or any food) remain attached to their roots – whatever their roots – we win. We win in quality of the end product and we win in authenticity. I'd even argue that we win a piece of ourselves, too, because what makes a wine great is not just how well it goes with our steak *béarnaise* but the story it has to tell.

For fear of being accused of offering no practical advice at all (again!), I might add a word about wineglasses. I once attended a tasting organized by a wineglass company whose line boasts a different glass for every living wine known to man. The taste tests indeed proved that the shape of a glass affects the taste of what's in it. Here's the catch: the effect is not always an improvement. I left holding nothing against the line of glassware (it was all very handsome and elegant, and the rims were desirably thin), but I did decide that I neither needed nor wanted so much paraphernalia in my life just for a glass of wine at home. I'm not a three-star restaurant. I'm not a wine bar. I'm but Maison de la Casa House Laura (and I do the dishes), so I figure it's entirely possible to get through life with a set of roomy wineglasses for reds and a set of more average-sized glasses for whites. I do hate any glass that has an opening the awkward size of a quarter. (I'm afraid I do hold this against Champagne flutes. I'm dying to bring back the *coupe!*) Otherwise, motivation to own glasses beyond the basics, for me, boils down purely to aesthetics, and to my general greed for tableware. I'd never buy a glass because I felt my Côtes du Rhône wouldn't taste right without it. I'd buy it only because it was so beautiful I was sure my next dinner-party table would be begging for it.

Side Dishes

FRENCH POTATO PURÉE

Unlike mashed potatoes, which are comparatively stiff and thick, this puréed French variation is smooth, thin, and elegant. It is also loaded, not surprisingly, with butter and milk. Perhaps it's not the kind of thing you feel you should eat every night of the week, but we all need treats now and again, and I see no reason to feel guilty about it.

Makes: 6 servings

2 pounds (900 g) floury potatoes, such as Yukon Gold or russets, scrubbed but not peeled
Salt and pepper
1 garlic clove, peeled
1 bay leaf
1 thyme sprig
1 cup (250 mL) milk
½ cup (110 g) cold butter

Put the potatoes, whole, in a large pot and cover with cold water. Salt the water. Bring to the boil, then simmer until the potatoes are very tender, about half an hour, depending on size.

Meanwhile, drop the garlic, bay leaf, and thyme in a saucepan with the milk, and bring to the boil. Turn off the heat, cover, and set aside to infuse for 10 minutes. Discard the garlic and herbs.

When the potatoes are done, drain them and peel them while still hot. Wipe the pot dry. Working over the pot, run the potatoes through the fine disk of a food mill. Beat in the butter a piece at a time, then beat in the warm milk. You are looking for a very soft, fine purée, not unlike baby food. Check the seasonings, and serve.

BOILED PARSLIED POTATOES

How I love a big bowl of these pale, smooth-complexioned potatoes tossed in warm butter and parsley with the steam rising off them! (Besides, they are so French.) No matter how badly a week has gone, a generous helping of these at a Sunday lunch makes me feel like the world's going to be okay. You want waxy potatoes here, the kind that hold together when cooked, rather than the floury kind that fall apart.

Makes: 4 servings

2 pounds (900 g) medium-small waxy potatoes, such as red potatoes, unpeeled
3 tablespoons (45 mL) butter
A handful or two of chopped fresh parsley
Salt and pepper

Bring a large pot of water to the boil. Salt it and add the whole potatoes. Boil until tender, about 25 minutes. Drain, and peel. Toss with the butter and parsley to coat. Season with salt and pepper. Serve.

BOILED NEW POTATOES WITH OLIVE OIL AND FLEUR DE SEL

Tiny new potatoes are so delicious in their own right that olive oil, salt, and pepper can be the best way to show them off. These are an especially good option if you think you may not get to them when they're hot, because olive oil doesn't mind cooling off the way butter does.

Makes: 6 servings

2 pounds (900 g) new potatoes
Olive oil
Fleur de sel and freshly ground pepper

Bring a large pot of water to the boil. Salt it (not with fleur de sel, just with regular salt). Add the potatoes, and cook until tender when you test them with a fork, about 20 minutes. Drain. Toss in olive oil to lightly coat. Season with fleur de sel and pepper. Serve.

GRATED POTATO CAKES

Cream and potatoes combined is no great revelation, but when the cream's role is to replace butter and hold everything together in a less oily way, that's news (at least, it was to me). These potato cakes get wonderfully crisp, and because they are baked in the oven, they're miles neater than when they're fried in a pan. Anne Willan used to serve them under Roasted Quail with Grapes (p. 139). I also like them as a crisp contrast to baked fish.

Makes: about 8 potato cakes

1 pound (450 g) potatoes, such as Yukon Gold or russets, peeled and grated

¼ cup (60 mL) heavy cream

Salt and pepper

Heat the oven to 400°F (200°C). Generously oil or butter a baking sheet. Squeeze the water out of the grated potatoes in a tea towel, and spill the potatoes into a bowl. Toss in the cream, and season with salt and pepper. Spoon the potatoes into about 8 small pancakes on the baking sheet.

Bake for 15 minutes. Flip and bake 15 minutes longer, or until cooked through, crisp-edged, and golden. Keep warm on a serving platter until serving.

POMMES ANNA

In this recipe, the cream is used to "soak" the potatoes, so you don't actually use all of it (calm down). It's a little trick that makes the potatoes meld together into a soft, herb-marbled brick that's a little less greasy than the traditional buttery recipe.

Makes: 6 to 8 servings

3 pounds (1.3 kg) potatoes, such as Yukon Gold
2 cups (500 mL) heavy cream
Salt and pepper
A handful or two of chopped fresh thyme and rosemary
Melted butter, for brushing

Heat the oven to 400°F (200°C). Cut two sheets of parchment paper to fit an 8-inch (20 cm) baking pan. Line the bottom of the pan with one parchment sheet, and brush the parchment and the sides with butter. Peel and thinly slice the potatoes, then toss in a bowl with the cream to saturate. Let sit 10 minutes.

Pull the potatoes from the cream, and arrange them in overlapping layers on the baking pan, seasoning each layer with salt and pepper, and scattering over the herbs as you go. Brush the other sheet of parchment with butter, and place it butter side down on the potatoes. Set a heavy dish on top to weigh down the potatoes. Bake until tender, 1 to 1½ hours. You can scoop out the potato, or, if you want to cut it into squares or wedges, let it cool a bit first so it holds together.

ACCORDION POTATOES

A woman I once cooked with in the south of France taught me this method for potatoes, and I still love to make them when I'm in the mood for a little fun. All you do is slice potatoes, without cutting through all the way, so that the slices remain hinged at the bottom. When the potatoes bake, the slices get crisp and golden, fanning out slightly like leaves in a book, like a jewelry box for rings, like the folds of a gypsy's accordion . . . However you want to think of them, they're awfully cute.

Makes: 4 servings

2 pounds (900 g) medium-small potatoes, such as Yukon Gold or red potatoes
Bay leaves and thyme sprigs
Salt and pepper
2 tablespoons (30 mL) olive oil
2 tablespoons (30 mL) melted butter

Heat the oven to 375°F (190°C). Cut the potatoes crosswise, as for hard-cooked eggs, into slices no thicker than your finger, but cut only about three-quarters of the way through. Lay the herbs between a few of the folds. Arrange the potatoes on a baking sheet, and season with salt and pepper. Drizzle with oil and melted butter, and bake until golden and crisp on the outside and soft inside, 45 minutes to an hour.

DUCK FAT POTATOES

Duck fat does make the most deliciously crisp potato wedges, but I also prepare potatoes like this using half butter and half olive oil (a few tablespoons of each). Sometimes, instead of parsley at the end, I add chili powder or herbes de Provence up front. Cooking time varies depending on the size of the potato pieces. My only advice is not to take them out too soon because they are at their best when they're wonderfully crisp on the outside and soft in the middle.

This recipe is done in the oven, but you can also do duck fat potatoes in a sauté pan on the stovetop. In that event, slice or dice the potatoes and fry them in probably a little less fat to start off with, until they're completely golden on all sides and crisp, but still soft in the center. This takes a good half-hour. Season during cooking, and toss with the parsley at the end.

Makes: 4 servings

2 pounds (900 g) potatoes, such as Yukon Gold, peeled if you prefer and cut into wedges or medium-thick slices
½ cup (125 mL) duck fat, melted
Fleur de sel and freshly ground pepper
A generous handful of chopped fresh parsley

Heat the oven to 425°F (220°C). Toss the potatoes with the duck fat on a baking sheet. Scatter over the salt and pepper. Bake, stirring occasionally, until the potatoes are well browned and crisp, 30 to 40 minutes. Toss with the parsley, and serve.

POMMES DE TERRE À LA BOULANGÈRE

Here's a potato gratin, but with stock instead of milk. It's named for the baker's wife because it's a dish meant to cook for a long time in a slow oven until the potatoes have completely absorbed the liquid and melded together. Lovely with roasts.

Makes: 6 servings

3 tablespoons (45 mL) butter
1 tablespoon (15 mL) olive oil
4 onions, sliced
2 pounds (900 g) potatoes, such as Yukon Gold, thinly sliced
Salt and pepper
A handful of chopped fresh thyme
2 cups (500 mL) beef stock

Heat the oven to 300°F (150°C). Melt half the butter with the olive oil in a sauté pan over medium heat, and gently fry the onions until soft and lightly golden, about 15 minutes. Spread half in the bottom of a medium shallow casserole. Layer half of the sliced potatoes on top, season with salt and pepper, and scatter over the thyme. Build another layer of onions, then a final one of potatoes, and finally pour over stock. Dot with the remaining butter. Cover with foil, and bake until all the liquid has been completely absorbed, 2 to 3 hours, removing the foil for the last hour.

THIS IS NOT RICE PILAF

I was positively desperate to call this "Edith Pilaf," and the only thing that stopped me is that it is not rice pilaf at all – it's only rice, cooked in the strange way I've seen French people do it (i.e., like pasta) and then tossed with strands of soft, golden onion. Oh well. I guess it's not the name that matters, it's character – and this is one very congenial dish.

Makes: 6 servings

¼ cup (55 g) butter
2 onions, sliced
2 garlic cloves, crushed
A handful of chopped fresh thyme
Salt and pepper
1½ cups (325 g) rice

Heat the butter in a large sauté pan over medium heat. Gently fry the onions until soft and slightly golden. Add the garlic and thyme, and cook for 1 minute. Season with salt and pepper, and set aside.

While the onions are cooking, bring a large pot of water to the boil. Salt it, as for pasta, then simmer the rice until tender, about 15 minutes. Drain well. Toss with the onion mixture, and heat through before serving.

CRUSHED CHICKPEAS WITH OLIVES AND LEMON

Chef friends are constantly telling me how to prepare their dishes, and I always rush straight home to try out their suggestions. The trouble with chefs, however, is that they often leave out vital steps (presumably because they take them for granted). That's what happened when I got this recipe, which explains why I massacred it about three times before I finally figured out how it was meant to be and why it was imparted to me with such raves. Chickpeas have never been so delicious!

I use dried chickpeas to start, but if you're in a rush and need to use tinned, you need a 19-ounce (540 mL) tin, rinsed and drained. If you have cooked chickpeas in the freezer, you need about 2 cups (350 g). Since the peas get crushed, I don't see much point trying to discard the skins, but in case you leave them whole, put the cooked chickpeas in a bowl and cover them well with cold water. Rub them between your hands, and the skins will come off and float to the top. Scoop them out and discard. It may also interest you to know that 1 cup (150 g) of dried chickpeas will yield about 2½ cups (or 375 g) cooked.

Makes: 4 servings

1 cup (150 g) dried chickpeas, soaked overnight in cold water, rinsed, and drained
1 onion, peeled
1 bay leaf
About 3 tablespoons (45 mL) olive oil
2 garlic cloves, minced
Salt and pepper
½ cup (85 g) sliced green olives
A handful of chopped fresh parsley
Zest and juice of 1 lemon

Put the drained chickpeas in a saucepan with the onion and bay leaf. Cover with cold water. Bring to a simmer, and cook, covered, until very tender, about 45 minutes. Drain, discarding the onion and bay leaf.

Heat the oil in a sauté pan over medium heat, and gently fry the garlic for 30 seconds. Add the chickpeas and salt and pepper. As they heat through, crush them a bit here and there with a potato masher, leaving some chickpeas whole. Remove from the heat and stir through the olives, parsley, and lemon zest. Add lemon juice to taste. Drizzle with extra virgin olive oil, and serve as a base for fish or chicken.

WHITE BEANS WITH CRÈME FRAÎCHE

I always start with dried beans, unless I'm in a mad rush, in which case I cave in and use tinned (well rinsed and drained). On a winter's night, these make a lovely side dish for roasted pork. They're substantial, but somehow they don't seem heavy, what with their pale countenance swathed in a creamy veil. Innocence, beanified.

Makes: about 6 servings

About 1½ cups (350 g) dried white beans, soaked overnight in cold water, rinsed, and drained
1 sprig thyme
1 bay leaf
1 garlic clove, peeled
½ onion, peeled
A generous spoonful of crème fraîche
Salt and pepper

Put the beans in a large saucepan. Poke in the thyme, bay leaf, garlic, and onion. Cover generously with water, slap on a lid, bring to a simmer, and cook gently until tender, about 40 minutes. Drain the beans, discarding the aromatics. Stir in just enough crème fraîche to hold them together, season with salt and pepper, and serve.

LENTILS WITH WALNUT OIL

Shake your fear of lentils, if you have one, because French lentils are special. When cooked, they don't turn to mush like the fat brown lentils of my 1970s childhood; instead, they remain wonderfully intact tender beads with a nutty bite. When I cook them, I like to leave just a little liquid around them so they're not completely dry. Then I serve them with sausages, chops, grilled fish, or shrimp. I also love them with toasted walnuts and pinches of goat cheese scattered over top.

Makes: 6 servings

1 cup (200 g) du Puy lentils
1 bay leaf
1 thyme sprig
2 tablespoons (30 mL) olive oil
1 large red onion, diced
2 garlic cloves, minced
A splash balsamic vinegar (optional)
Walnut oil
Salt and pepper

Put the lentils in a saucepan with the bay leaf and thyme. Pour over 1½ cups (375 mL) water, bring to the boil, reduce the heat, and simmer, uncovered, until tender, 30 to 40 minutes. All the liquid should be absorbed by the time they're done; if not, drain off any excess. Discard the bay leaf and thyme sprig.

Meanwhile, heat the olive oil in a sauté pan over medium-high heat, and fry the onion until soft. Add the garlic, and cook for 1 minute, then deglaze the pan with a splash of balsamic vinegar, if you wish. Add the lentils, toss with the onion, splash in some walnut oil, season with salt and pepper, and serve.

MINTY COUSCOUS

Real couscous, which I have had made for me in Morocco, is a marvel, not to mention a lengthy labor of love involving a lot of rubbing between the palms. This precooked business doesn't hold a candle to it. Still, it's good, especially with mint swirled through, and it takes just 5 minutes. Who am I to argue with that?

Makes: 8 servings

3½ cups (875 mL) water
½ teaspoon (2 mL) salt
3 cups (450 g) quick-cooking couscous
1 tablespoon (15 mL) olive oil, more if desired
Leaves from two large bunches of mint, chopped

Bring the water to the boil in a large saucepan, and add the salt. Pour in the couscous and the olive oil, give a quick stir, cover, and turn off the heat. Let sit about 5 minutes. Fluff with a fork to break up any lumps. Check the seasonings, stir though the chopped mint, and serve.

LAZY RATATOUILLE

There are those who mightn't consider ratatouille a lazy dish because there is quite a lot of cooking involved, but you must recognize that this is *mindless* cooking. Basically, you can launch into this recipe and let your brain go to Mexico until the dish is done. Besides, ratatouille is the most practical thing: good warm or cold, today or tomorrow or the next day, and it goes with meat, fish, or chicken. Spoon the very end of the leftovers into a tart shell, pour over a cup (250 mL) of milk beaten with 3 eggs, salt, and pepper, and bake at 375°F (190°C) until the custard is set, and you have a wonderful lunch, too.

Makes: 8 servings

2 big eggplants
2 red peppers
2 yellow peppers
About ½ cup (125 mL) olive oil
4 small zucchini, cut into thick rounds
2 onions, sliced
2 garlic cloves, minced
2 peperoncini, crushed
1 bay leaf
1 rosemary sprig
Salt and pepper
8 tomatoes, seeded and roughly chopped
A handful or two of chopped fresh basil

Heat the oven to broil. Thickly slice the eggplants crosswise, and lay the rounds on cake racks that you've set in the sink. Salt very generously, and leave 30 minutes for the excess water to drain off. When they are ready, you'll need to rinse them well under the tap and pat them dry with a towel.

While the eggplant drains, put the red and yellow peppers in the oven and broil, turning them now and again, until the skins are blackened on all sides, about 20 minutes total. Remove to a bowl, cover with plastic wrap, and let sit 5 minutes. The skin will now peel off easily. Peel and seed, then slice the flesh into julienne, and put it in a large bowl. Turn the oven down to 450°F (230°C).

Put a little oil on a baking sheet, and toss the zucchini slices in it. Roast, turning once, about 10 minutes. Add to the peppers. Finally, cut the rinsed and dried eggplant into large chunks, toss in some oil, spread on the baking sheet, and roast until tender and golden, about 15 minutes. Add them to the bowl.

At some point during all the preceding, heat a spoonful of olive oil in a sauté pan over medium-high heat, and fry the onion until soft. Add the garlic, peperoncino, bay leaf, and rosemary, and fry for 1 minute. Stir in the tomatoes. Cook until the tomatoes are very soft and the whole mixture thickly soupy, about 15 minutes. Remove the bay leaf and rosemary.

Pour the tomato sauce over the vegetables and toss. Check the seasonings. Serve at room temperature with the basil scattered over.

TIAN OF PROVENÇAL VEGETABLES

I ate this marvelous side dish in the south of France, scribbled down my friend's recipe, then went home and made a disaster of it over and over again until I wanted to tear my eyes out. I couldn't understand what I was doing wrong: I layered everything, remembering to put the oily sautéed onions on the bottom to prevent burning and to keep the tomato slices on top so their juices would drip down through and keep everything else moist, but still the dish refused to meld together in the "confit" way I had experienced at my friend's place. Finally, after about a year, I cornered her in a restaurant and demanded the secret (I was the one buying lunch). It's not much of a secret, actually, but it makes all the difference in the world: the oven has to be blazing hot. The result is a dish of eggplant, zucchini, peppers, onion, and tomato, cooked until the flavors have concentrated and the whole thing has melded together like something preserved.

Makes: as much as your baking dish can hold

Onions
Olive oil
Eggplant
Zucchini
Sweet peppers
Tomatoes
Salt and pepper

Sauté a couple of thinly sliced onions in olive oil. Chop up equal amounts of eggplant, zucchini, and colored sweet peppers. Spread the sautéed onions over the bottom of a roasting pan or gratin dish. Layer in the vegetables, seasoning with salt and pepper as you go. Lay a proportional quantity of sliced tomato on top. Drizzle over olive oil.

Bake in a 450°F (230°C) oven until the liquid has evaporated and the vegetables have sunk into a deep-colored confit, about 2 hours. Check the tian at about halftime. If you find the top browning too quickly, lay on a piece of foil and continue cooking.

CHARD GRATIN

Chard makes a fabulous gratin, because it's almost two vegetables in one: white stems that have some bite, and iron-rich deep green leaves. A trick I have learned with gratin is to make the béchamel sauce extra thick, because the vegetables will always give off some water, which thins it out. This makes a hearty side dish, or, if you add chopped ham to the mix, a simple supper. Add a touch of paprika to the béchamel if you're a fan.

Makes: 4 servings

For the béchamel

1½ cups (375 mL) milk
¼ onion, peeled
1 bay leaf
1 garlic clove, peeled and halved
2 tablespoons (30 mL) butter
2 tablespoons (30 mL) flour
¼ cup (60 mL) crème fraîche
Salt and pepper

For the gratin

A large bunch chard, washed (about 2 pounds/900 g)
1 tablespoon (15 mL) olive oil
1 onion, sliced
Salt and pepper
4 ounces (110 g) high-quality Gruyère or Emmental cheese, grated (about 1 cup/250 mL)
A handful of finely grated Parmesan cheese

For the béchamel, heat the milk with the onion, bay leaf, and garlic to the boiling point. Remove from the heat, cover, and set aside to infuse for 10 minutes. Remove the onion, bay leaf, and garlic.

Melt the butter in a saucepan over medium-low heat. Whisk in the flour, and cook, stirring, for a minute. Gradually whisk in the milk. Cook, stirring constantly, until very thick, a matter of minutes. Stir through the crème fraîche. Season with salt and pepper. Set aside.

For the gratin, bring a pot of water to the boil, and salt it. Cut the stems and thick center ribs from the chard. Slice the leaves, and set aside. Cut the ribs into 1-inch (2.5 cm) lengths, and toss into the boiling water. Cook until just tender, drain, and rinse under cold water. Set aside. In the same pot, heat the olive oil over medium heat, and cook the onion until soft. Add the chard leaves, and cook until tender, a matter of minutes. Season.

Heat the oven to 400°F (200°C). Butter a gratin dish, and cover the bottom with the chard stems. (If you're adding chopped ham, it can go in now). Scatter over half the Gruyère, and grind over some pepper. Top with the cooked chard leaves. Spoon over the béchamel. Sprinkle with the remaining Gruyère along with the Parmesan. Bake until piping hot and golden on top, about 15 minutes.

CAULIFLOWER GRATIN

I know this is not the most exciting thing on earth to look at, but who's looking? I make this for myself when I'm alone or for very intimate suppers when I'm with another hungry person or two who, like me, are craving the comfort of something warm and tasty yet utterly unchallenging to the palate. This is the main dish in that context, really. The slice of ham you serve with it is the side.

Makes: 4 to 6 servings

For the sauce

1½ cups (375 mL) milk
1 bay leaf
1 garlic clove, peeled and halved
3 tablespoons (45 mL) butter
3 tablespoons (45 mL) flour
½ cup (50 g) grated Gruyère cheese
Salt and pepper
Pinch paprika
Pinch cayenne pepper (optional)

For the gratin

1 medium cauliflower, cut into florets
Salt and pepper
¼ cup (20 g) fresh or dry bread crumbs
1 tablespoon (15 mL) melted butter
A few handfuls of grated Parmesan cheese

For the sauce, bring the milk to a simmer in a saucepan with the bay leaf and garlic. Cover, turn off the heat, and let infuse, about 10 minutes. Remove the bay leaf and garlic.

Melt the butter in a saucepan over medium-low heat. Whisk in the flour, and cook for a minute to remove the raw flour taste. Gradually whisk in the milk. Cook, stirring, until thick, a matter of minutes. Stir in the cheese, season with salt and pepper, and flavor with paprika and cayenne (if using). Set aside.

Heat the oven to broil. Bring a shallow pot of water to the boil. Set a steaming contraption in it, add the cauliflower, and steam until tender, about 5 minutes. Season with salt and pepper. Toss with the sauce, and turn into a gratin dish. Scatter over the bread crumbs, drizzle over the butter, sprinkle with Parmesan, and bake until bubbling and light golden on top, about 5 minutes. Serve.

PETITS POIS À LA FRANÇAISE

This is one of the most classic French vegetable dishes. Gorgeous to look at and utterly delightful to eat: fresh and substantial at once. I have a friend who can eat this whole dish all on her own and call it dinner. Or is that me . . . ?

Makes: 4 servings

2 tablespoons (30 mL) butter
16 pearl onions, peeled and halved
4 slices bacon, cut into lardons
2 cups (250 g) frozen or shelled fresh peas
½ cup (125 mL) chicken stock
Salt and pepper
1 Bibb lettuce, cored and sliced

Melt the butter in a sauté pan over medium-high heat. Add the onions and cook for 2 minutes, then add the bacon and continue cooking until done but not crisp. Add the peas and stock. Season with salt and pepper. Cover, and cook until the peas are almost tender, about 5 minutes. Stir in the lettuce, cover, and cook for 1 minute to wilt. Check the seasonings, and serve.

SPRING VEGETABLE TUMBLE

Don't be limited by the vegetables I suggest here; you can change the combination depending on what you have in the fridge. It's a method more than a recipe, anyway: vegetables cooked until they're just shy of being tender, then tossed in butter and herbs to finish. Simple, but stunning.

Makes: 4 servings

8 baby carrots, halved lengthwise
4 ounces (110 g) snow peas
4 ounces (110 g) asparagus, cut into thirds
6 radishes, halved
4 ounces (110 g) yellow beans, cut into thirds
4 ounces (110 g) baby turnips, quartered
1 cup (125 g) frozen or shelled fresh peas
2 tablespoons (30 mL) butter
Salt and pepper
A few handfuls of chopped fresh herbs (chives, tarragon, parsley, chervil . . .)

Bring a large pot of water to the boil. Salt it, and blanch all the vegetables separately. Exact time will depend on the vegetable, but count on a few minutes each and be near by to taste-test for al dente. As the vegetables are done, fish them out with a hand-held strainer, and refresh each in ice water. Drain.

In a large frying pan over medium heat, melt the butter. Toss the vegetables together to finish cooking and warm through. Season with salt and pepper. Toss with the herbs, and serve.

GREEN VEGETABLE TUMBLE

"Tumble" is my word for very French mixed-vegetable dishes like this one. I love how organic everything looks, jumbled together and spilled onto a serving platter. The bacon gives depth, and the mixed fresh herbs add the high notes. It's nice when vegetable dishes are allowed to have some complexity, rather than being just boiled afterthoughts.

Makes: 4 servings

1 pink shallot, minced
3 tablespoons (45 mL) white wine vinegar
10 ounces (280 g) asparagus, cut into 2-inch (5 cm) pieces
6 ounces (170 g) shelled fava beans
2 slices bacon, cut into lardons
6 ounces (170 g) frozen or shelled fresh peas
½ cup (125 mL) chicken stock
3 tablespoons (45 mL) olive oil, plus a drizzle for frying
2 teaspoons (10 mL) balsamic vinegar
Juice of ½ lemon
Salt and pepper
A generous handful of chopped fresh tarragon
A generous handful of chopped fresh mint
A scattering of chopped fresh chives

Put the shallot in a ramekin with the vinegar. Set aside. Cook the asparagus in a pot of boiling salted water until tender. Lift them out with a strainer, immediately plunge into ice water to cool completely, and drain. Blanch the fava beans 1 minute in the same water, drain, plunge into ice water, drain, and peel.

Heat a thread of olive oil in a frying pan over medium heat, and cook the bacon until crisp. Add the peas and favas, pour over the stock, bring to the boil, and cook until just tender, about 2 minutes. Add the asparagus to warm through. Drain the shallot, and add it, discarding the vinegar. Add the 3 tablespoons (45 mL) of olive oil, balsamic vinegar, lemon juice to taste, and salt and pepper. Stir through the herbs, and serve.

ROASTED VEGETABLES

You don't really need a recipe, but since I ate a baking sheet full of these for dinner three nights a week last winter, I figured the idea was worth passing on. The important thing is the high oven heat and leaving the vegetables in the oven long enough, so they get a bit candied.

Makes: 6 servings

6 small potatoes, peeled and cut into medium wedges
4 carrots, cut in half crosswise, then halved lengthwise
3 leeks, trimmed and cut into logs
2 handfuls of cherry tomatoes
3 tablespoons (45 mL) olive oil
Coarse sea salt and pepper
2 tablespoons (30 mL) butter
2 bay leaves
1 branch of rosemary, cut in three

Heat the oven to 400°F (200°C). Toss the vegetables with the olive oil, salt, and pepper. Spread over a baking sheet. Cut the butter into little pieces, and scatter over top. Tuck in the herbs. Bake until tender and slightly caramelized, about an hour, tossing occasionally.

SAUTÉED SLIVERED ARTICHOKES

In France, small Mediterranean artichokes, called *poivrades*, have virtually no choke and are so tender you can eat them raw when they're thinly sliced. My friend Camille always fries them until the edges caramelize, which is what's happening here. North American baby globe artichokes are also choke-free.

Makes: 4 to 6 servings

Juice of 1 lemon, more for serving
12 baby artichokes (about 2 ounces/55 g each)
¼ cup (60 mL) olive oil
2 garlic cloves, minced
Fleur de sel and ground pepper
Parmigiano-Reggiano cheese, for garnish (optional)

Fill a large bowl with cold water, and add the lemon juice. Cut the stems off the artichokes, trim about ¼ inch (5 mm) off the tops, and peel away a few layers of outer leaves to expose the tender, yellowish leaves inside. Slice very thinly lengthwise, and drop into the bowl of lemon water to prevent discoloring.

Heat the oil in a sauté pan over high heat. Drain the artichokes. Toss them in the hot oil, and fry until cooked through and crisp-edged, about 5 minutes. Toward the end, scatter over the garlic. Season with salt and pepper to taste. Tip into a serving dish, squeeze over a little more lemon juice, garnish with shavings of Parmigiano-Reggiano (if using), and serve.

WARM FENNEL SALAD WITH OLIVES, PINE NUTS, AND ORANGE

I eat fennel raw quite a lot, and usually when I cook it, I cook the daylights out of it, because I love when it gets all soft and tangled. For me, then, this recipe was a refreshing change. The fennel is tender and caramelized but still quite firm, and the resulting mellow anise flavor is excellent with the kaleidoscope of orange, onion, olives, and nuts for garnish.

Makes: 4 servings

1 large fennel bulb
Olive oil
Fleur de sel and freshly ground pepper
1 organic orange
½ small red onion
A handful of small black olives
A handful of toasted pine nuts
1 organic lemon

Trim the stalks from the fennel, reserving a handful of green fronds. Cut the bulb in half lengthwise, then cut into lengthwise slices about ¼ inch (5 mm) thick. Heat a little olive oil in a sauté pan over high heat, and, working in batches and seasoning with salt and pepper as you go, fry the fennel on both sides until golden and tender, about 3 minutes per side. As the fennel is done, arrange it on a serving platter.

Zest the orange over the fennel. Cut the skin from the orange with a sharp knife, taking care to remove all the white pith from the fruit. Cut between the membranes to section the orange, and arrange the sections over the fennel. Squeeze the juice from the membranes over the whole salad.

Slice the onion into paper-thin rings, and arrange over the salad. Scatter over the olives and pine nuts. Zest the lemon over the salad, and squeeze over lemon juice to taste. Drizzle over a little more olive oil. Finally, scatter over the reserved fennel fronds, and serve.

SAUTÉED ASPARAGUS

I'm not particularly proud to admit it, but I don't know anything about grills or barbecues. In fact, I am quite sure that I would blow myself up if I ever tried to light one. (Besides, aren't barbecues why God invented men?) Despite this deficiency, I can do rather a lot with a sauté pan, including getting a grippingly good "grilled" look on asparagus. I have converted scores of asparagus-boilers with this recipe.

Makes: 6 servings

2 bunches asparagus, about 1 pound (450 g) each
Olive oil
Fleur de sel
Freshly ground pepper

Trim the tough ends from the asparagus, and discard. Heat a few tablespoons of oil in a sauté pan over medium-high heat. When very hot, add the asparagus in batches, not overlapping. Sauté, turning occasionally with tongs, until slightly golden and tender, but still maintaining a bit of bite, about 5 minutes, depending on how thick the asparagus is. Season with salt and pepper. Arrange on a platter, and serve.

PAN-FRIED FENNEL

A fashionable Frenchwoman once gave me a recipe for steamed fennel: you halved the bulb and put it in one of those bamboo steamer basket contraptions, steamed it tender, drizzled over a thread of olive oil, and allowed yourself a little salt and toasted sesame seeds on top. That was meant to be a good recipe for slimming. I am grateful to know about it, but I am ever so much *more* grateful to know that fennel is better (I think) when cooked to golden brown in olive oil, as in this recipe, to accompany fish or chicken. (Leftovers are good tossed in pasta or strewn over pizza.)

Makes: 4 servings

1 large fennel bulb
Salt and pepper
2 tablespoons (30 mL) olive oil

Trim the stalks from the fennel bulb, cut the bulb in half lengthwise, and cut into lengthwise slices about ¼ inch (5 mm) thick. Season with salt and pepper. Heat the oil in a heavy sauté pan over medium-high heat, and fry the fennel on both sides until tender and slightly golden. Some pieces will fall apart, but don't worry about it. They will be cooked in about 10 minutes, but I often leave them up to 20 so they get very soft, golden, and more intensely sweet. Serve.

AUBERGINE RUFFLES

Way back when, I was the queen of zucchini ruffles. I loved how slicing courgettes super thin and sautéing them made them curl into delicate emerald-edged flounces. The idea works with eggplant, too, and they're so pretty: pale creamy ruffs, this time with purple-black edges. They do wonders to dress up Stuffed Tomatoes (p. 156).

Makes: 4 servings

2 pounds (900 g) eggplant
Olive oil
Salt and pepper
Finely chopped fresh parsley

Thinly slice the eggplants crosswise. Brush both sides with olive oil, then season both sides with salt and pepper. Either lay them in a single layer on a baking sheet and bake in a 500°F (260°C) oven until they are soft and golden, about 15 minutes per side, or fry them in batches in a sauté pan over medium-high heat until they are soft and golden. Toss with salt, pepper, olive oil, and chopped parsley. Serve warm or at room temperature.

SAUTÉED CUCUMBER WITH MINT

I'd never seen cooked cucumber until I went to France, and until I tried it I thought it sounded *très bizarre.* As it turns out, it is lovely, warm, pale, and soft. Try it tossed with fresh mint or dill and served with fish.

Makes: 4 servings

1 English cucumber
A spoonful of olive oil
Salt and pepper
A handful of chopped fresh mint or dill

Peel, halve lengthwise, and seed the cucumber. Cut into chunks the size of large croutons. (Or slice into thin half-moons. It depends on whether you want al dente chunks or soft, silkier petals. Both have their merits, depending on what you're serving them with.) Heat the olive oil in a sauté pan over high heat. Sauté the cucumber until hot and softened to your liking, about 5 minutes, depending on size. Taste, and add salt and pepper. Toss in a handful of mint. Serve warm or at room temperature.

GLAZED RADISHES CHÂTEAU DU FEŸ

Radishes are peppery when raw, but cooking mellows out their flavor considerably, and they taste as innocent as baby turnips. These look fabulous on a festive table, like a bowl of jewels.

Makes: 6 servings

1 pound (450 g) radishes
Salt and pepper
A knob of butter
1 or 2 sugar cubes

Put the radishes in a sauté pan just large enough to hold them. Add enough water just to cover, and season with salt and pepper. Boil until tender, 7 to 10 minutes, by which time the water should be nearly gone. Add a knob of butter and a cube or two of sugar. Cook a minute or two, stirring often, until the sugar melts and the radishes become glazed.

RADISHES AND PEAS

This is pink and green and oh so pretty. I serve it with lettuce-wrapped fish (p. 119), but it would also be gorgeous with any chicken-in-cream sort of concoction.

Makes: 6 servings

2 to 3 tablespoons (30 to 45 mL) butter
2 bunches radishes (about 1¼ pounds/ 525 g), quartered or sliced
2 cups (250 g) frozen or shelled fresh peas
Salt and pepper
2 green onions, thinly sliced
A generous handful of chopped fresh dill

Melt the butter in a sauté pan over medium heat, and gently cook the radishes until half cooked, about 5 minutes. Add the peas with ¼ cup (60 mL) water. Continue cooking until the peas and radishes are tender, another 5 minutes. Season with salt and pepper, scatter over the green onions and dill, and serve.

GREEN BEAN LACES WITH OLIVES AND PINE NUTS

The lacing idea came when I had rather fat green beans that I wanted to make look more like slender haricots verts. So, I just pulled them apart down the middle. They look very elegant and make great picnic fare – a sort of salad, but one that won't wilt away like lettuce. You can serve thesre just warm, or at room temperature.

Makes: 4 to 6 servings

1 pound (450 g) green beans, topped and tailed
Salt and pepper
2 tablespoons (30 mL) olive oil
1 to 2 small shallots, minced
¼ cup (50 g) pine nuts, toasted
⅔ cup (110 g) sliced black olives
Lemon zest
Lemon juice (optional)

Blanch the beans in boiling salted water until tender, drain, and refresh them in ice-cold water. Drain well. Tear the beans down the middle into "shoestrings."

Heat the oil in a sauté pan. Add the shallots along with the bean laces and toss to heat through. Finally, toss inwith the toasted pine nuts, sliced olives, and lemon zest. Check the seasonings (if you feel you want a squirt of lemon juice, too, go ahead). Spill the beans (no pun intended) onto to a plate, and serve . . . or serve later at room temperature.

GREEN BEANS WITH HAZELNUTS AND CRÈME FRAÎCHE

The idea of anything creamed or in cream used to make me hide under the table. I don't know why I thought I wouldn't like it. I must have been brainwashed in adolescence by the diet brigade. Then one fine day, a dish of creamed corn changed my whole attitude: it was served at a dinner party, and I couldn't get enough of it. So, this is to say that if you can't get green beans and crème fraîche to make sense in your head, just try this recipe, because it more than makes sense in your mouth.

Makes: 4 servings

½ cup (55 g) hazelnuts
1 pound (450 g) green beans
1 tablespoon (15 mL) olive oil
1 pink shallot, minced
Salt and pepper
Lemon juice
2 tablespoons (30 mL) crème fraîche
A small handful of chopped fresh tarragon
A small handful of chopped fresh parsley

Heat the oven to 350°F (180°C). Spread the nuts on a baking sheet, and toast in the oven, stirring once, until slightly darkened and fragrant, about 8 minutes. Remove, chop, and set aside.

Top and tail the green beans, and cook them in a large pot of boiling salted water until tender, about 7 minutes. Drain, and rinse under cold running water to set the color.

Heat the oil in a frying pan over medium-high. Add the shallot, and cook for 1 minute, then add the beans, and toss to heat through. Season with salt and pepper. Add a squirt of lemon juice. Remove from the heat, and stir in the crème fraîche to coat. Toss in the hazelnuts and chopped herbs. Arrange on a platter, and serve.

BROCCOLI PURÉE

Broccoli is a tricky vegetable, and I can't say it's one of my favorites. I don't mind the bouquets raw, but somehow those frizzy heads cooked on the end of their long stems make me feel like I'm eating a pot scrubber. Recently, however, a friend got me onto puréeing broccoli, and what an eye-opener that was: when stem and bouquet become one with a bit of lemon to dress them up, you get a very vibrant and versatile side dish, great with fish. Just one tip: peel the stems; otherwise they are too fibrous to purée.

Makes: 3 or 4 servings

1 head broccoli, about 14 ounces (400 g)
1 leek, trimmed
Salt and pepper
1 tablespoon (15 mL) butter, more to taste
Lemon zest and juice to taste

Bring a big pot of water to the boil. Cut the florets off the broccoli stem in even sizes. Peel the stem, and slice thinly. Slice the leek into rings, and rinse well.

Salt the boiling water, as for pasta, and add the broccoli and leek. Cook until the broccoli is very tender, about 10 minutes. Drain, and return to the pot. Drop in the butter, and purée with an immersion blender. Taste, and adjust the salt. Add pepper, lemon zest, and juice. Serve hot while it still has its bright color.

CELERIAC PURÉE

The brown coconut-sized root that celeriac is doesn't exactly jump off grocery store shelves yelling, "Taste me!" so I am speaking out on its behalf. Celeriac has a very mild celery taste, which you almost can't recognize in this smooth, pale form. It is excellent in place of potato purée when you want something a bit different, and it's wonderful with game.

Makes: 4 to 6 servings

1 large celeriac, about 2 pounds (900 g)
Juice of ½ lemon
¼ cup (60 mL) milk
1 bay leaf
1 teaspoon (5 mL) salt
3 tablespoons (45 mL) butter
¼ cup (60 mL) heavy cream
Pepper

Peel the celeriac, and cut it into roughly 1-inch (2.5 cm) pieces. Put the celeriac, lemon juice, milk, and bay leaf in a large pot. Add 8 cups (2 L) water and the salt, bring to the boil, and simmer until the celeriac is very tender.

Drain, reserving a cup (250 mL) of the liquid. Remove the bay leaf. Stir the butter and cream into the celeriac. Working in batches, purée until very smooth in a blender, adding as much of the reserved cooking liquid as needed to achieve a soft, smooth consistency. Season with pepper and salt, and serve.

ROASTED CUMIN CARROTS

Roasting carrots intensifies their sweetness, and if you leave them long enough, they get wonderful golden edges, slightly crisp. Cumin is a classic "perfume" for them. No wonder.

Makes: 4 servings

8 slender medium carrots
Olive oil, for drizzling
2 teaspoons (10 mL) cumin seeds, lightly crushed
Salt and pepper

Heat the oven to 400°F (200°C). Halve the carrots lengthwise, leaving a bit of green top attached for looks. Toss on a baking sheet with the olive oil, cumin seeds, and salt and pepper. Roast, stirring once at halftime, until tender, golden-edged, and slightly crinkly, about 30 minutes, depending on their size. Serve.

VICHY CARROTS

The town of Vichy has a special place in my heart because I spent quite a lot of time there during one of my nine lives. It looks like a mini Paris, with elegant white buildings and fabulous parks for walking – features that hint at the grand place it was until it disgraced itself during the war. I like to imagine it as it was back in earlier times, when the upper crust of Europe flocked there to take the medicinal waters. Vichy water has a bicarbonate taste, and that's the water these carrots are meant to be cooked in. If you wanted to come a little closer than tap water, you could add a pinch of baking soda for a hint of that taste, but frankly I don't bother. Along with roasted and raw, this is my favorite way to have carrots. They're also good when you substitute orange juice for the water, although I'm not sure what Vichy would think of that.

Makes: 6 to 8 servings

2 pounds (900 g) carrots
¼ cup (55 g) butter
1 to 2 teaspoons (5 to 10 mL) sugar
Pinch salt
A handful of chopped fresh parsley

Slice the carrots into coins. Put them in a sauté pan with the butter, sugar, salt, and 1 cup (250 mL) water. Simmer, tossing occasionally, until the carrots are tender and the liquid has reduced to a glaze. Scatter over the parsley, and serve.

ROASTED BEETS WITH SAUTÉED GREENS

These are pure candy. How considerate of nature to make beets cheap, good for us, *and* gorgeous ruby red at the same time.

Makes: 6 servings

3 large beets with greens, or 6 to 8 small ones, scrubbed clean
Olive oil
Butter
Salt and pepper

Heat the oven to 425°F (220°C). Chop the tops off the beets, leaving about 1 inch (2.5 cm) of stem on the bulb, and set aside. Remove the tail-like root end, and discard. Cut each beet into about eight sections (or halve small beets), as you would cut an apple for pie, leaving a little stem at the top of each wedge.

Put the beets on a baking sheet. Drizzle over the olive oil, and toss the beets to coat well. Dot with butter, and season with salt and pepper. Roast until they are soft and well caramelized, about an hour, depending on the size of the beets (small beets will obviously cook faster).

Just before the beets are done, heat a little more olive oil in a sauté pan over medium-high heat. Coarsely chop the green tops along with their red stems, and sauté until tender, about 5 minutes. Season with salt and pepper. Serve with the roasted beets.

ROASTED SQUASH RINGS

When you bake butternut squash in its shell, it steams inside and stays perfectly soft with no dried edges. That's the way to go for purée. But when you want crisp-edged, golden caramelization, you need to lay out the slices on a baking sheet. This is another case where a vegetable proves it can be better than candy.

Makes: 4 servings

1 butternut squash, about 1 pound (450 g), halved lengthwise and seeded, but not peeled
1 tablespoon (15 mL) olive oil
Salt and pepper
A few fresh thyme sprigs
A few bay leaves
1 to 2 tablespoons (15 to 30 mL) butter

Heat the oven to 400°F (200°C). Slice the squash into half-moons about half as thick as your finger. Toss with the olive oil to coat. Arrange in slightly overlapping rows on a baking sheet. Season with salt and pepper. Scatter over the thyme, and poke in the bay leaves. Dot with the butter. Bake, turning at halftime, until the squash is soft with slightly candied brown edges, 30 to 45 minutes. Serve.

SAVOY CABBAGE RIBBONS

Last winter I got onto a savoy cabbage kick. It's a time of year when I have no use for lettuce but nonetheless crave greens. This light and leafy cabbage is perfect because it slices so easily into rumpled ribbons ranging from yellow to dark green. Lettuce-like, only warm and more substantial.

Makes: 4 servings

½ head savoy cabbage
¼ cup (55 g) butter
Salt and pepper

Core and shred the cabbage. Melt the butter in a large pot or sauté pan over high heat. Add the cabbage, and season with salt and pepper. Cook, tossing, until the ribbons of cabbage soften and shrink down somewhat, about 7 minutes. Serve.

GINGERED WATERCRESS

A Mauritian I knew in Paris showed me how to prepare watercress this way, and I adore it. It's different because, for once, the oil is not olive and because there are such careful amounts of ginger, garlic, and tomato that everything is just a hint, taking nothing away from the delightful pepperiness of the cress. I always had it served to me with curry, but I also like it with braised meats or with fish.

Makes: 6 servings

3 bunches watercress, washed and spun dry (about 1½ pounds/675 g trimmed)
3 tablespoons (45 mL) peanut or grapeseed oil
2 garlic cloves, minced
A 1-inch (2.5 cm) piece of ginger, peeled and minced
1 tomato, seeded and chopped
Salt and pepper

Cut the watercress into manageable lengths. Heat the oil in a wok or skillet over high heat. Add the garlic and ginger, and cook, stirring, 1 minute. Add the tomato, and cook to a paste, a minute or two more. Add the cress, and cook down, turning occasionally with tongs, until soft, again a matter of minutes. Season and serve.

ENDIVES WITH ORANGES

This is unusual and attractive. The slightly bitter endive gets caramelized and therefore a little sweet, but that's set off nicely by the acidity of the vinegar and orange juice. Because the vegetable part is very mellow, the slices of fresh orange are bright and juicy in the mix. I serve this dish with Beef au Bleu (p. 153).

Makes: 4 servings

4 large endives
2 tablespoons (30 mL) butter
2 tablespoons (30 mL) sugar
2 tablespoons (30 mL) red wine vinegar
⅓ cup (75 mL) red wine
Salt and pepper
2 oranges

Halve the endives lengthwise. Put the butter, sugar, and vinegar in a large sauté pan, bring to the boil, and reduce to caramel, about 5 minutes. Add the red wine. Lay in the endive, cut side down. Season with salt and pepper, cover with foil, and cook over medium-low heat, turning a few times, until tender, 20 to 30 minutes.

While the endive cooks, cut around the oranges with a knife to remove the peel, pith, and outer membrane. Working over a bowl to catch the juices, cut between the membranes to section the oranges. Set aside the sections, and add the juices to the endives.

When the endives are soft, uncover the pan, and continue cooking, turning the endives occasionally, to reduce the liquid to a glaze and caramelize the endives. At the last minute, add the orange sections to heat through, and serve.

CARAMELIZED PEPPERS AND TOMATOES

I initially made this raggle-taggle tangle of soft-caramelized peppers and tomatoes to garnish my Brandade Cakes (p. 89), but I quickly realized it would go well with all sorts of other things. A batch hanging around in your fridge for a week would make your weeknight cooking very creative.

Makes: 4 to 6 servings

4 colored sweet peppers
2 generous handfuls of cherry tomatoes
1 whole head garlic cloves, sliced
Salt and pepper
¼ cup (60 mL) olive oil

Heat the oven to 300°F (150°C). Seed the peppers, and cut into thin fingers. In a baking dish or on a baking sheet large enough to hold the peppers in a single layer, toss the peppers with the tomatoes, garlic, and salt and pepper. Pour over the olive oil, and bake until the peppers are very soft and wrinkled, about 3 hours.

THYME CREAMED TOMATOES

One of my cooking buddies in Paris (Chris Mooney of the sardine tartines, if you must know, p. 36) gave me this recipe, which he was remembering by heart from Edouard de Pomiane's classic, *French Cooking in Ten Minutes.* I later looked up the recipe, and the original included putting a chopped onion in the pan before adding the tomatoes (I haven't tried that yet, but I'm sure it's good). Plus, de Pomiane called these "Polish Style" tomatoes (and his parents were from Poland, so I suppose he'd know). Well, fine, so perhaps this dish is Polish. But you can't tell me that anything with this much butter and cream isn't at home on a French table. Serve as a side dish for roasts or savory suppertime crêpes.

Makes: 4 to 6 servings

2 tablespoons (30 mL) butter
4 medium tomatoes, halved horizontally
A generous handful of chopped fresh thyme
Salt and pepper
½ cup (125 mL) heavy cream

Melt the butter in a sauté pan over high heat. Add the tomatoes, cut side down. Poke their backsides a few times with the tip of a knife to prevent the skins from bursting. Cook 10 minutes. Flip, scatter with the thyme, and cook 5 to 10 minutes more on the other side, until soft. Season with salt and pepper. Pour over the cream, and reduce to a thick sauce around the tomatoes, about 5 minutes. It will brown a bit and swirl together with the tomato juice. Serve.

BAKED PROVENÇAL TOMATOES

Baking a tomato intensifies its sweetness, and when it's not a day for raw and sliced, a warm, slumping, fruity tomato half, topped with crunchy garlicky parslied crumbs, is an ideal side dish. These are very easy to throw together as an afterthought. I like them with lamb.

Makes: 4 servings

4 medium tomatoes
Salt and pepper
A handful of fresh bread crumbs
A handful of chopped fresh parsley
1 garlic clove, minced
Olive oil, for drizzling

Heat the oven to 400°F (200°C). Cut the tomatoes in half at the waist. Lay them cut side up in a baking dish. Season with salt and pepper. Mix the bread crumbs, parsley, and garlic in a small bowl, and sprinkle evenly over the tops of the tomatoes. Drizzle over a little olive oil. Bake until hot and slumping, about 20 minutes. Serve.

HOW TO MAKE A GLASS OF WATER

"Fruit tepid, water cold in the glass. This is the way that things taste best." So wrote the 20th-century novelist Colette, and although at first glance she seems to state the obvious, anyone who has had the misfortune of biting into a cold tomato or drinking stale water from a sun-warmed plastic bottle knows exactly where she was coming from. It is amazing how often we punish ourselves by exerting exactly the same effort to do something badly as it would take to do it well.

Colette's glass of water is a fine example of how a little care put into the ordinary can make our day. Imagine you're just in from an hour of deadheading roses or mixing concrete under the scorching sun. You reach for a tall glass with a thin rim, drop in the thinnest slice of lemon, fill it with cold spring water from the tap, lean against the counter, and take a long, slow, satisfying sip. My, but the perfect glass of water is a beautiful thing! If you think I'm exaggerating, consider the alternatives: water from a fat porcelain mug (slithery), water from a nipple-topped plastic bottle (tastes like plastic and has undesirable Freudian implications), warm water (tastes like it's for washing up), water fighting for space in a glass of ice cubes (stings), water from metal or stoneware (feels like there might be a toad at the bottom) . . .

Just as water tastes best cool and from a thin-rimmed glass, so is all food better when it's served right. Besides, good food deserves to be shown off to its best advantage. When it is, think how much more grateful we are for the experience of eating! So, stand back and consider the details. Ask yourself, "Am I serving this food as beautifully as I can?" (picture milk in its carton, then imagine it in a pale blue jug); "Are my dishes and utensils going to make the food taste even better than it already is?" (warmed bowls for hot soup, the right-sized spoon); "Have I presented this food so it's comfortable to eat?" (unshelled seafood in stew may be pretty, but it's impossible to get at without disgracing yourself; salad in a martini glass is just absurd).

As cooks whose aim it is to please, we must pay attention to these niceties – consider the end user, as the bad poets of industry say, and make our food user-friendly. Presentation really comes down to respecting food as well as the people we're feeding. Seen another way, it's about bringing out the best in food, and by extension bringing out the best in those on the receiving end of it. Here's the point: you get what you give. And it *is* worth caring, because sometimes the smallest gesture can be the spoonful of sugar that makes a day go down.

A few suggestions:

- Avoid individually plated food at home, unless it makes sense. In most cases it's fussy and pretentious, and it works against conviviality, not least because it takes you away from the table for eons between courses. (There are exceptions.)

- Serve dishes so that the flavors you want experienced together end up in the mouth at the same time. It's no good having fish perched on a tower of grains and vegetables if the sauce is way down below on the plate. In fact, I am against skyscrapers on plates altogether. What's the point if the first bite sends your precious structure crashing to a heap anyway?
- To press the point further, let food be natural, not contrived.
- Give food room on a plate so that it's nicely framed; too much heaped right out to the edges is unappetizing. (A good way to keep in check is to consider the "margins" of a plate off limits.)
- Visually speaking, garnishing food or putting it on a plate is just like accessorizing an outfit. There are shoes that work with that smart black sweater and there are shoes that don't. Likewise, parsley sprigs aren't for everything. (Making these decisions isn't work, by the way, it's fun.)
- Go easy with garnishes. Less is more.
- It's a general rule that one ought to refrain from putting inedible garnishes on a plate (for instance, whole stars of anise afloat in soup, as I was once served, with disastrous results, in a chic Provençal restaurant, or a flaming pinecone, which I also had arrive on a plate one time beside a lamb chop).
- There are always exceptions, but it's generally recommended not to garnish a dish with an ingredient it doesn't contain because it's considered misleading. Example: topping a chocolate mousse with a twist of orange zest indicates there is orange flavor in it.
- Warm plates for hot food, if you can.
- Invest in natural-fiber cloth napkins, large enough to cover a lap, not so small that they sit there like a patch about to be sewn on your skirt.
- Plastic cutlery and paper napkins have no positive effect on the human spirit.
- It's nice to have salt in a cellar and pepper in a grinder. That way you can better control how much you're putting on. Shakers always make me nervous because they can so easily get out of hand. I know salt cellars are supposed to have spoons in them, but I just love using my fingers, especially for fleur de sel.
- The smell of scented candles competes with the smell and taste of food (and the cheap kind are positively eye-watering). Use unscented candles in the dining room, at least while you're eating.

LA SALADE

The relationship between the French and their salads can be tricky to understand. I think that's because they don't have one relationship with salads; they have different relationships with different types of salads.

One category is what they call *salades composées*, which are hearty affairs, usually more toppings than greens, intended for substantial lunches. You find them on the menu in cafés and simple bistros. For example, there's *salade landaise*, which has duck gizzards in it; *salade norvégienne*, which has smoked salmon; *salade Parmentier*, which is loaded with potatoes . . . you get the idea. (See *Salade Niçoise*, p. 228, if you'd like to take one for a spin.)

When salad appears on a dinner menu, it will be much lighter. In fact, it usually amounts to no more than a bowl of leafy greens with a light dressing (for example, Mixed Greens with Walnut Vinaigrette, p. 230). Interestingly, unlike in North America, a green salad such as this is almost never served as a first course. Instead, it comes after the main course, with or before the cheese. Virtually the only green salads served as first courses, for whatever mysterious reason, are Chèvre Salad (p. 65) and Bacon and Egg Salad (p. 66). Don't ask me why; that's just the way it is. In fact, a sure way to spot a tourist in a French restaurant is if you hear someone ask for "just a green salad" as a starter. (To tell the truth, requests like that drive chefs in any restaurant of stature right out of their minds because they feel they have better things to do than toss greens in vinaigrette. I sympathize, but I suppose it's par for the course.) Any other starter salads, apart from the mysteriously sanctified two I've mentioned, will be vegetable salads with no lettuce in them whatsoever, or "salads" that are, for example, seafood combinations, perhaps with the odd leaf for garnish. You'll find all sorts of these in the first-course chapters (pp. 53-103).

At the end of the day, keep in mind that we're at our own dining tables at home, and we can approach salads however we please, so I wouldn't get too worked up about trying to replicate notions of *salade en France*. I just thought I should set the record straight on the French manner so no one stays up all night wondering why some salad recipes are in one part of this book and others in another.

SALADE NIÇOISE

The most famous of these composed lunch salads is *salade niçoise,* and because it's such a classic, naturally everyone argues over which versions of the recipe are authentic and which aren't. The purists will stand firm on the fact that no self-respecting *salade niçoise* should ever contain cooked vegetables. I am sure they are quite right. Nonetheless (with sincere apologies, ladies and gentlemen of the jury), they are too good in there for me to leave out. Here, then, is my apparently rebellious version of the salad. It is a veritable picnic on a plate and it loves to be washed down with a chilled rosé on a lazy summer's day.

Makes: 2 servings

For the vinaigrette

½ garlic clove, minced
1 teaspoon (5 mL) tarragon vinegar
½ teaspoon (2 mL) Dijon mustard
¼ cup (60 mL) mild olive oil, or half olive oil and half peanut oil
Lemon juice
Salt and pepper

For the salad

About 10 leaves from a head of Bibb lettuce
About 6 fresh basil leaves, shredded
6 cherry tomatoes, halved
6 baby red potatoes, boiled until tender, and sliced
4 ounces (110 g) green beans, blanched in salted water, refreshed, and drained
3 baby artichoke hearts, cooked and quartered
1 very small red onion, sliced very finely and separated into rings
A handful of niçoise olives
2 hard-cooked eggs, quartered
3 or 4 anchovy fillets
Fleur de sel and freshly ground pepper

For the vinaigrette, whisk together the garlic, vinegar, and mustard. Whisk in the oil, adding it in a thin stream. Taste, and add some lemon if the dressing isn't sharp enough. Season with salt and pepper.

Toss the lettuce leaves with a very little bit of the vinaigrette and the shredded basil, and arrange on a platter. Separately toss the tomatoes, potato slices, green beans, and artichoke hearts in a bit of vinaigrette, and arrange on the platter. Scatter over the onion and olives. Arrange the eggs and anchovies on top. Season with salt and pepper, and eat.

MY HOUSE VINAIGRETTE

Everyone seems to have a salad-dressing standard that they fall back on and could make blindfolded. This is mine, and I love it because it is a light vinaigrette, and yet it has real depth and complexity of flavor thanks to the secret ingredients of stock powder and soy sauce (*shhh*). You don't need much of them, as a little goes a long way, but I find them indispensable for drawing the oil and vinegar together and rounding out the dressing. (A dressing of just oil and vinegar alone often tastes like exactly that: sharpness + oiliness.) The basic ratio for vinaigrette is one part vinegar to two parts oil, but because the sharpness of vinegars varies so much, it's really safest to operate on the basis of taste. I find generally that if I use a tablespoon (15 mL) of red wine vinegar, I need at least ¼ cup (60 mL) of oil to tame it, but it depends on the oils and vinegars, so taste and adjust as necessary.

Makes: about ⅓ cup (75 mL)

½ teaspoon (2 mL) Dijon mustard
1 garlic clove, minced (optional)
2 teaspoons (10 mL) red wine vinegar
A drop or two of balsamic vinegar
A drop or two of soy sauce
A pinch of beef stock powder
3 to 4 tablespoons (45 to 60 mL) olive oil, to taste
Salt and pepper

Mix together the mustard, garlic (if using), red wine vinegar, balsamic vinegar, soy sauce, and stock powder. Gradually whisk in the oil. Season with salt and pepper. Taste, and adjust as needed.

MIXED GREENS WITH WALNUT VINAIGRETTE

It never ceases to amaze me how recipes that sound almost overly simple often turn out to be the best. A salad with walnuts doesn't sound all that earth shattering, but made with love it is one of the most fabulous bowls of greens I can imagine eating. This is a good green salad to follow, say, Beef Bourguignon (p. 162) or another hearty sort of stew.

Makes: 6 servings

Vinaigrette

1 teaspoon (5 mL) red wine vinegar
½ teaspoon (2 mL) Dijon mustard
¼ cup (60 mL) walnut oil
Salt and pepper
Lemon juice
Olive oil, to finish

Salad

6 large handfuls of mixed greens (butter lettuce, frisée, arugula, radicchio, endive, romaine, mâche . . .)
2 handfuls of toasted walnuts, finely chopped
A generous handful of barely chopped fresh dill

Whisk together the vinegar and mustard. Whisk in the walnut oil, drop by drop. Season with salt and pepper. If acid is needed, add lemon juice. If more oil is needed, add olive oil.

Tear the greens into large bite-sized pieces in a flat bowl. Add the nuts and dill. Just before serving, add only enough dressing to coat lightly when tossed. Toss and serve.

So, without wanting to give a cheese class here, there are a few practical pointers I can pass on if it helps steer novices away from what one might call "cheese crimes."

- It is a "cheese crime" to "steal the nose." This means that when you slice cheese, you should always cut it in such a way as to respect its original shape. In other words, if there is a nice wedge of Brie on the table with bulging love handles, you don't dive in with your knife and whack off the tip, leaving your neighbor with mostly rind. It's only fair, after all.
- To ensure maximum eating pleasure, serve cheese at room temperature, rather than straight from the fridge. There is nothing worse than sinking into a lovely Livarot, only to feel like you're having your teeth molded in cold putty for a set of dentures.
- Never cut or grate cheese until you are ready to use it, because the more the surface is exposed to air, the faster it loses aroma and flavor.
- Don't wrap cheese in plastic, if you can avoid it. Waxed paper lets it breathe better.
- Finally, keep cheese in a separate compartment or box in the fridge because it is fatty stuff and so easily absorbs odors from other foods (such as fish). That said, keeping cheese separate is just as much for the purpose of protecting the rest of what's in your fridge. Take it from me: I once put a particularly ripe Mont d'Or in the fridge beside a packet of butter. The next morning, the Mont d'Or was as fabulous as ever, but the butter was inedible.

On to the best part: eating all those French cheeses! In English-speaking cultures, there is a great tradition of wine and cheese outside normal mealtimes, usually in some form of drinks soirée. The French do not eat cheese this way. Sometimes they have it for a snack, but mostly it comes during dinner. In fact, in a French meal, cheese is a course in its own right. It lands on the table after the main course (right when you think you couldn't possibly eat another bite of anything for the rest of your life, and yet nibble, nibble – it's not so hard after all, is it?). There is always bread to go with cheese. And because of where the cheese course falls in the meal, there is virtually always red wine as an accompaniment (red simply because you'll usually have moved on to red at the meat course).

Just as an aside, it is very tricky to pair wine and cheese. They *sound* great together, but they often don't *taste* great together. Try a big bite of Roquefort washed down with a mouthful of Bordeaux sometime and you'll see what I mean (*shriek*). Oh well, sometimes atmosphere, nostalgia, or flights of fancy win out over actual taste in the long run, and perhaps they should. Romance is always way more interesting than rules.

LE FROMAGE

There are at least as many French cheeses as there are days in the year, and the sheer volume of choice can be hair-raising. Keep this in mind, however: French cheese is just cheese. There's no need to make a big deal of it. Having said that, French cheeses are one of the great culinary achievements of mankind, especially when they're well made and well looked after. To get the most out of them, all you really need to know is which styles you like best and the difference between good cheese and bad. This can be a very pleasant, osmotic education. The only homework is to eat lots of cheese!

A number of years ago, I had the good fortune of doing a huge amount of research on French cheeses for a boss of mine. At first, I was overwhelmed and thought I would never get it, but as I went along, cheese by cheese, I realized that, with few exceptions, the endless count of cheeses actually falls into about six general categories: blue cheeses (such as Roquefort and bleu d'Auvergne), goat cheeses (such as the log-shaped Sainte-Maure and pyramid-style Pouligny Saint-Pierre), hard cheeses (such as Comté and Gruyère), semi-hard cheeses (such as Tomme de Savoie), cheeses with a bloom (such as Brie and Camembert), and washed-rind cheeses (such as Époisses and Mont d'Or). That discovery was like suddenly figuring out that the world is round.

The categories simplified things significantly, but, of course, there is enormous range within each. For example, Cantal from the Auvergne and brebis Basque are both cooked cheeses made in similar ways. They are both hard and quite fruity, and both come from the mountains, but one is sheep cheese, the other cow, one tastes floral and nutty, the other slightly sour, one is smooth, the other more textured. Or take goat cheeses: they all start out exactly the same, but depending on the mold they are drained in and how long they're aged, each tastes different and has a distinctive texture. Washed-rind cheeses all tend to be on the runny and stinky side, but to varying degrees, plus the flavor is affected by whether they are washed in alcohol or simply in brine. The diversity goes on . . .

Still, I find most people tend to gravitate toward certain cheese categories more than others. I prefer blue and hard cheeses most of the time, whereas I have a friend who always dives into the runny, stinky varieties. (Hmm . . . perhaps there's a personality test in this somewhere.)

Buying cheese is always a joy in France, and I am quite fussy about where I shop. I stick to my favorite, reliable cheesemongers because it's almost always true that if you go to the best cheese shop near you, you're going to get the best cheese. (Meanwhile, you're never going to get a great Mimolette, that hard, orange cheese from the north, in a French grocery store, because that's not where great cheeses are sold.) Wherever we buy our cheese and whichever we decide we prefer, we all learn by doing – by *eating,* rather. Even the names of French cheeses, which can be initially intimidating, eventually roll off the tongue, at least those we eat regularly. (As for the rest, who really cares? There is only so much one can cram into a brain in a lifetime.)

Desserts

OLIVE OIL AND RED GRAPE CAKE

The top of this cake is a rolling, rustic, sugar-sprayed landscape, and underneath is a fine-textured, mysteriously olive-scented crumb, foiled by the occasional fruity purple squirt of grape. This is one of my top afternoon-tea cakes.

Makes: 8 servings

5 eggs, separated
¾ cup (155 g) sugar, more for sprinkling
¾ cup (175 mL) extra virgin olive oil, more for brushing
Zest and juice of 1 lemon
Zest of 1 orange
1 cup (125 g) cake flour
½ teaspoon (2 mL) salt
9 ounces (250 g) seedless red grapes

Heat the oven to 350°F (180°C). Rub a 9-inch (23 cm) springform pan with a little olive oil, and line the bottom with parchment paper.

Beat the egg yolks and sugar until thick, pale, and ribbony. Mix in the olive oil, lemon juice, and the lemon and orange zests. Add the flour, and stir to combine. Beat the egg whites with the salt to stiff peaks, then gently fold into the batter. Fold in half the grapes.

Pour the batter into the prepared pan, and bake for 45 minutes, opening the oven quickly after about 20 minutes to scatter over the remaining grapes (the other grapes will have sunk to the bottom at this point). When a toothpick comes out of the middle of the cake clean, take it from the oven and set on a wire rack. Brush the top generously with extra virgin olive oil, and scatter over a little more sugar. When the cake is cool, unmold and serve.

ORANGE ALMOND CAKE

There is a significant North African presence in France, which makes Arab culinary influences strong, as you can see in this extraordinary soaked cake with almonds and oranges. This is a stunning dessert, especially when you decorate the top with candied orange zest and serve whipped cream on the side. Whenever I bring it out for a party, there is never a crumb left.

Makes: 6 to 8 servings

For the cake

6 eggs
¾ cup (155 g) sugar
Zest of 3 oranges
1½ cups (200 g) almonds, ground

For the syrup

Juice of 3 oranges
½ cup (95 g) sugar
A spoonful of Grand Marnier (optional)

For the candied zest

2 oranges
1 cup (200 g) sugar

Whipped cream, for garnish

Heat the oven to 350°F (180°C). Grease a 9- or 10-inch (23 or 25 cm) springform pan, and line the bottom with parchment paper.

For the cake, separate the eggs into two large bowls. Beat the yolks with the sugar and zest until very thick, pale, and ribbony, then stir in the almonds. Beat the whites to stiff peaks. Stir a spoonful of the whites into the yolk mixture, then gently fold in the rest. Pour the batter into the pan. Bake until set, about 45 minutes. Let cool slightly, then unmold onto a serving platter.

For the syrup, boil the juice and sugar together in a saucepan for 5 minutes. Remove from the heat, and stir in the liqueur (if using). Spoon slowly over the cake, letting the syrup soak in.

For the candied zest, remove the peel from the oranges with a knife or vegetable peeler. Using a very sharp knife, remove all the bitter white pith from the back and discard. Cut the peels into fine julienne, and put in a medium saucepan with cold water to cover. Bring to the boil, drain, and rinse. Now do that two more times to remove the bitterness from the zests. Put the sugar in the saucepan with 2 tablespoons (30 mL) water and boil, swirling the pan gently but not stirring, until the caramel turns a rich, golden color. Add ½ cup (125 mL) water along with the zests, and boil until the zest is translucent and candy coated, 5 to 10 minutes. The zest will be sweet and chewy with intense orange flavor. Pull from the syrup with a fork, and arrange on top of the cake. Serve with whipped cream.

WALNUT CAKE

I am mad about walnuts, and for years I've been on a mission to find the perfect walnut cake, one that's a dense, damp round of nutty intensity to serve with a ping-pong ball of ice cream. I have discovered that Irish cream liqueur, however un-French, is a marvelous flavoring in this cake, although there are other options. The chocolate is up to you. Sometimes I add it (and if you do, it will have presence, so know that), but when I want to wallow in a fully walnut moment, I don't.

Makes: 8 servings

4 ounces (110 g) shelled walnuts, plus a small handful of halves for garnish
3 tablespoons (45 mL) fine dry bread crumbs
3 large eggs, at room temperature
½ cup (95 g) sugar
1 ounce (28 g) bittersweet chocolate, grated (optional)
¼ cup (55 g) butter, melted until soft enough to pour, but not oily
1 tablespoon (15 mL) espresso coffee, Cognac, Irish cream liqueur, or other liqueur
Icing sugar, for dusting
Whipped cream and chocolate shavings, or coffee ice cream, for serving

Heat the oven to 350°F (180°C). Grease an 8-inch (20 cm) cake pan (a smaller pan with high sides, like a wedding cake top, is also magnificent), and line the bottom with parchment paper.

Grind the walnuts together with the bread crumbs in a food processor. Separate the eggs, putting the whites in a large bowl for whisking and the yolks in a glass or metal bowl. Whisk the yolks and sugar to combine, then set the bowl over a saucepan with an inch of simmering water in it. Continue whisking until the yolks have tripled in volume and become thick, pale, and ribbony, about 8 minutes. Take the mixture off the heat. Scatter over the nut mixture, along with the chocolate (if using), then drizzle over the butter and liqueur. Fold together. Whisk the egg whites to stiff peaks, stir a spoonful into the batter to loosen it, then gently fold in the remaining whites.

Pour the batter into the pan, and bake until a toothpick inserted in the center comes out clean, 35 to 40 minutes. Cool on a wire rack before flipping the cake out onto a serving plate. Decorate with a sifting of icing sugar and a few walnut halves. Some white blossoms look nice, too, if you're feeling fancy. Serve small portions with whipped cream and chocolate shavings or with coffee ice cream.

SAVARIN WITH STRAWBERRIES

Savarin is one of those old-fashioned classics that nobody thinks they have time to make anymore. Well, first make the time, and then make the savarin, because it is so good it will make you dizzy. The syrup-soaked cake is light and spongy, with a seductive, boozy squelch in every bite, and it's not too sweet, with a mysterious hint of yeast taste in the background. My favorite accompaniment is ripe summer strawberries and cream. I heap the berries in the center of the cake, with whipped cream on the side, and the result is smashing, in a romantic, ruffles-and-bows-ish, old-world way: you'll want to wear an enormous white wig and play waltzes when you eat it. Just be aware that when you look at the raw batter you'll never believe it's enough for your pan, but trust me. Also, if you want a really glossy top, you can melt a jelly, such as apricot or red currant, and brush the baked cake with it once all the syrup has been absorbed.

Makes: 8 servings

For the cake

1½ teaspoons (7 mL) active dry yeast
1 tablespoon (15 mL) sugar
½ teaspoon (2 mL) salt
3 tablespoons (45 mL) warm water
2 large eggs, lightly beaten
2 tablespoons (30 mL) milk
Grated zest of 1 lemon
1 cup (125 g) sifted flour
¼ cup (55 g) butter, softened

For the syrup

2 cups (500 mL) water
1¼ cups (250 g) sugar
¼ cup (60 mL) Grand Marnier, Kirsch, rum, or eau-de-vie

For serving

2 cups (500 mL) heavy cream
A few drops of vanilla
1 to 2 tablespoons (15 to 30 mL) sugar
A few generous handfuls of fresh strawberries, hulled and halved or quartered
Mint leaves for garnish, if desired

Butter and flour a 10-inch (25 cm) savarin or other ring mold. Mix the yeast, sugar, salt, and warm water in a large bowl, and let stand 5 minutes until foamy. Add the eggs, milk, lemon zest, and flour. Beat vigorously in a stand mixture with the paddle attachment for a full 10 minutes. (This is necessary to make the dough smooth and elastic, pulling away from the sides of the bowl, which will result in a very light, fine-textured cake.) Cover, and let rise in a warm place until doubled, about an hour.

Punch down the dough. Beat in the softened butter, a piece at a time, until fully incorporated. Spoon the mixture evenly into the mold. Cover, and let rise again until doubled, about 2 hours.

Heat the oven to 350°F (180°C). Bake the savarin until golden brown, about 20 minutes. Unmold onto a wire rack, and let cool slightly, then transfer to a large serving platter.

For the syrup, bring the water and sugar to the boil in a saucepan. Boil for 1 minute. Remove from the heat, stir in the Grand Marnier, and ladle the syrup over the cake until fully absorbed. The cake will expand and become very sponge-like in texture.

To serve, whip the cream with the vanilla and sugar. Then either fold in the strawberries, reserving a few for garnish, and spoon into the hole in the center of the cake, or pass the whipped cream and berries in separate bowls for people to serve themselves.

SQUASH CAKE

Sometimes cakes are nicer in the afternoon with tea, rather than for dessert, because then we have the appetite to enjoy them. This bright yellow cake with an unusual texture, inspired by the traditional pumpkin tortes of southwest France, is substantial enough even for breakfast, actually. To me, it has just the right degree of sweetness to balance the taste of corn flour and squash, with whiffs of orange and rum. (Corn flour is very finely ground cornmeal, by the way.)

Makes: 8 to 10 servings

3 eggs, separated
½ cup (95 g) sugar
⅓ cup (40 g) cornstarch
¼ cup (30 g) corn flour
2 cups (500 mL) squash or pumpkin purée
¼ cup (60 mL) rum
Zest of 1 orange
Cinnamon whipped cream, for garnish

Heat the oven to 350°F (180°C). Grease and line a 9-inch (23 cm) springform pan, and line the bottom with parchment paper. Beat the yolks and sugar until light and pale. Beat in the cornstarch and corn flour until smooth. Beat in the squash, rum, and orange zest. Finally, beat the whites to stiff peaks. Stir some of the whites into the squash mixture to lighten it, then fold in the rest.

Pour the batter into the pan, and bake until a toothpick comes out clean, 45 minutes to an hour. Let the cake cool slightly before running a knife around the edges of the pan and removing the sides. Serve slightly warm (not too warm, or it's impossible to cut) with cinnamon whipped cream.

ANGEL CAKE

Unlike American angel food cake, this French version leaves in the yolks, which makes it slightly denser and perhaps explains its springiness. It's a plain-tasting cake, but there is something about it that reminds my mouth of marshmallows. It's perfect to serve with whipped cream and fresh berries in season or with sweet, ripe peaches, poached in a scented syrup. It's also quite enormous, and so good for a crowd. The mixing method is strange, you'll see, but you have to appreciate anything that needs just one bowl and one whisk.

Makes: 10 servings

6 eggs, separated
1 cup (200 g) sugar
1 teaspoon (5 mL) vanilla
1 cup (125 g) sifted flour

Heat the oven to 400°F (200°C). Grease a 9-inch (23 cm) springform pan, and line the bottom with parchment paper. Beat the whites to stiff peaks. Beat in the yolks, one by one. Continuing to beat, add the sugar and vanilla, and finally the flour. You should have a very high, moussy batter.

Pour the batter into the pan, and bake until risen high, golden on top, and a toothpick inserted in the center comes out clean, about an hour. Be sure it is fully cooked when you take it out – it is a big cake. Let the cake cool 15 minutes. Remove the sides of the pan, and let cool completely. Transfer to a serving platter.

HAZELNUT ROLL

There's something about roly-poly cakes that I find irresistible. Perhaps they remind me of the grocery cakes I craved in my youth but was never allowed to eat. You could easily do an almond version and fill it with jam for a more classic approach. This is a hazelnut rendition simply because it somehow seemed more appealing when I was experimenting one freezing-cold March afternoon. What takes this cake from very good to great is the judicious amount of cinnamon in the whipped cream (it should be very faint) and the cocoa powder sneaked onto the cake before it's rolled up.

Makes: 6 to 8 servings

3 eggs
⅓ cup (70 g) sugar
2 tablespoons (30 mL) flour
½ cup (70 g) ground hazelnuts, more for garnish
⅔ cup (150 mL) heavy cream
A drop of vanilla
Pinch cinnamon
Cocoa power, for dusting
Icing sugar, for dusting

Heat the oven to 400°F (200°C). Butter an 8- x 12-inch (20 x 30 cm) sided baking sheet, line the bottom with parchment, and butter the parchment. Put the eggs and sugar in a glass or metal bowl, set it over a pot with an inch of simmering water in the bottom (do not let the bowl touch the water), and beat until tripled in volume and very thick and ribbony, like cake batter. This will take about 10 minutes. Remove from the heat.

Sift the flour and nuts over the batter, and gently fold together. Pour evenly into the pan. Bake until slightly golden on top, 10 to 12 minutes. Meanwhile, get set up for unmolding the cake: lay a damp tea towel on a cutting board or on the back of another baking sheet. When the cake comes out, flip it onto the towel, carefully peel off the parchment, trim the edges of the cake if you want, and immediately roll it up from the short side, rolling up the towel with the cake. Set aside to cool to room temperature.

Whip the cream to stiff peaks with a hint of vanilla and a pinch of cinnamon. Unroll the cake, sieve over a light dusting of cocoa powder, spread over the cream, and roll up the cake again, this time without the towel. Set on a platter, seam side down. Sift over a little icing sugar and cocoa powder. Decorate with a button-row of hazelnuts. Cover, and refrigerate until serving, which you'll want to do the same day, preferably within a few hours.

CHOCOLATE CREAM CAKE

Julia Child gave this recipe to Anne Willan, who passed it on to me, presumably (in the grand scheme of things) so that I could pass it on to you. I don't know why it isn't more widespread, because it is the most astonishing chocolate cake I have ever eaten. The cake breaks off in sheets as you pierce it with your fork. Serve eroded cliffs of it with whipped cream on the side.

Makes: 10 servings

¼ cup (60 mL) espresso
¼ cup (60 mL) Cognac or rum
1 tablespoon (15 mL) pure vanilla extract
1 pound (450 g) bittersweet chocolate, broken into pieces
6 eggs
½ cup (95 g) sugar, more to taste
1 cup (250 mL) heavy cream, chilled
Sweetened whipped cream, for serving
Gold leaf (optional)

Heat the oven to 350°F (180°C). Grease a 10-inch (25 cm) high-sided cake pan, and line the bottom with parchment paper. Boil a full kettle of water, and set aside. Have at the ready a roasting pan that will accommodate the cake pan comfortably, as well as two saucepans of barely simmering water.

Put the espresso, rum, vanilla, and chocolate into a glass or metal bowl and melt, stirring, over one saucepan of simmering water. Turn off the heat under the water. Break the eggs into a large glass or metal bowl with the sugar. Set over the second saucepan of barely simmering water, and beat until the mixture has tripled in volume and has the consistency of whipped cream. This will take about 10 minutes. In a separate bowl, whip the cream into stiff peaks.

With two or three sweeps of a spatula, partially fold the chocolate into the egg mixture. Add the whipped cream, and continue folding until evenly combined. Pour into the cake pan. Set the pan in the roasting pan, and slide it into the oven. Now, pour the hot water from the kettle into the roasting pan to come halfway up the sides of the cake pan.

Bake until set, about an hour. Turn off the oven, open the door, and let the cake sit for 15 minutes to sink evenly back into the pan. Remove the cake from the oven, and let it sit 30 minutes in the water bath. Remove from the bath, and flip the cake out onto a platter. Let cool. Serve with sweetened whipped cream on the side.

CRAGGY CHOCOLATE CAKE

Flourless chocolate cakes are staples in every French home cook's repertoire. I love this one because it gets a cracked top when it cools. There's something in the inevitable messiness of it that makes it utterly unpretentious to serve, despite its decadence. A garnish of whipped cream flavored with liqueur, vanilla, or orange-flower water is a requirement for a cake this dense.

I have to tell you about a variation in case another time you decide that what you really want is a smooth chilled chocolate slab. Add ½ cup (125 mL) strong coffee to the chocolate when you melt it. Then, instead of separating the eggs, simply beat them whole, then whisk in the melted chocolate and butter mixture. Cut the sugar by ¼ cup (55 g) (for whatever reason), and bake it the same way, only when it's done, cool it, wrap it, and chill it in the fridge overnight. Serve it at room temperature the next day with raspberry coulis, fresh raspberries, and whipped cream. Same cake, in a way, yet not the same cake at all.

Makes: 8 servings

7 ounces (200 g) 70%-cacao bittersweet chocolate, chopped
7 ounces (200 g) butter, softened
4 eggs, separated
1 cup (200 g) sugar
Lightly sweetened whipped cream, for serving

Heat the oven to 375°F (190°C). Line the bottom of an 8-inch (20 cm) springform pan with parchment paper, then grease and flour the pan.

Gently melt the chocolate in a bowl set over a saucepan of barely simmering water, then beat in the butter a piece at a time until smooth. Remove from the heat. In a separate bowl, beat the yolks with half the sugar until thick, pale, and ribbony. In yet another bowl, beat the whites to soft peaks. Scatter over the remaining sugar, and beat to a stiff meringue.

Slowly whisk the chocolate mixture into the yolk mixture. Stir in a spoonful of egg white, then pour the chocolate mixture over the egg whites, and gently fold together with a spatula. Pour the batter into the pan, and bake until the top is set and the cake feels firm, 40 to 50 minutes. Run a knife around the outside edge, then let sit on a wire rack until cool. The cake will sink down, and the top will crack appealingly. Unmold, and serve.

MUDDY MIDDLE CHOCOLATE CAKES

I read an e. e. cummings poem not long ago in which he employed the term "mud-luscious," and I immediately thought of these cakes. They are, of course, the ubiquitous mini molten chocolate cakes, those of the firm sides with runny, fudgy middles. Yes, I know they've been overdone, and perhaps they're almost kitsch at this point, but let's face it: they're still good. If the suggested caramel sauce below doesn't appeal, serve the cake with ice cream. This is yet another recipe from the invincible Ivan of Normandy.

Makes: 6 servings

For the cakes

4 ounces (110 g) bittersweet chocolate
⅔ cup (140 g) butter
4 eggs
⅔ cup (140 g) sugar
½ cup (60 g) flour

For the caramel sauce (optional)

⅔ cup (140 g) sugar
¼ cup (55 g) butter
⅓ cup + 2 tablespoons (100 mL) cream
A squirt of lemon juice

For the cake, butter six ½-cup (125 mL) ramekins, line the bottoms with a disk of parchment, then butter the parchment. Very gently melt the chocolate and butter together, stirring now and then until smooth, in a bowl set over a saucepan of barely simmering water. Beat the eggs and sugar until thick, pale, and ribbony. Beat in the flour, and then beat in the chocolate mixture. Pour into the ramekins, and chill.

For the sauce, add a spoonful of water to the sugar in a saucepan and boil to amber caramel, swirling the pan occasionally but not stirring, about 5 minutes. Remove from the heat, and stir in the butter to melt, then the cream. Finally, add a squirt of lemon juice to taste. The sauce will harden as it sits; gently reheat it before serving.

Just before serving the cakes, heat the oven to 400°F (200°C). Place the ramekins on a baking sheet, and bake until the tops are set, 12 to 14 minutes. Let sit 5 minutes before unmolding onto plates. Serve with caramel sauce on the side.

CHOCOLATE CRÊPES

Fill these with sliced banana or strawberries and serve with cinnamon-flavored whipped cream. To me, they look best folded in half once, then in half again to make a double-decker triangle crêpe. If you want to be extra devilish, drizzle chocolate sauce over top (1 cup/250 mL heavy cream and 8 ounces/225 g chopped bittersweet chocolate heated together until melted and smooth). These freeze well (unfilled) should you suddenly decide you want to save them until next week. Just be sure to put parchment between each crêpe before you put them in a freezer bag.

Makes: 12 crêpes

1 tablespoon (15 mL) butter
1½ ounces (40 g) bittersweet chocolate, chopped
1 cup (250 mL) milk
2 eggs
¼ cup (55 g) sugar
1 teaspoon (5 mL) vanilla
1 cup (125 g) flour

Heat the oven to 150°F (65°C). Put the butter, chocolate, and milk in a saucepan and gently heat, stirring occasionally, until the chocolate is melted. Beat the eggs with the sugar in a bowl. Beat in the vanilla, then the flour. Beat in the chocolate mixture. Strain into a jug, and let sit half an hour. Add more milk or water if necessary to give the consistency of thin cream.

Fry the crêpes in a nonstick or lightly oiled crêpe pan over medium-high heat, keeping the cooked ones warm on a plate in the oven as you go. You need only about a tablespoon (15 mL) of batter per crêpe. Hold the pan in the air as you pour in the batter, and swirl the pan as the batter hits so that it coats the bottom evenly. (Count your first two crêpes as practice.) If there are holes in the crêpe as it cooks, simply fill them with a little batter. When the underside is cooked and slightly golden, in about a minute, flip and finish the crêpe, 30 seconds to a minute more.

LEMON AND SUGAR CRÊPES

You can fill these crêpes with anything, but here is my favorite way to eat them: while they're still hot, sprinkle the tops with sugar and lemon zest, roll them up, and – hoop! – into the mouth they go. Crêpes are meant to be very thin, and the first one you fry, for some reason, will never work out that way. Don't worry. The second crêpe will be fine.

Makes: about 15 crêpes

For the crêpes

1½ cups (185 g) flour
3 eggs
1 cup (250 mL) milk
1 tablespoon (15 mL) sugar, more for sprinkling
½ teaspoon (2 mL) salt
2 tablespoons (30 mL) melted butter
Melted clarified butter or vegetable oil, for brushing
Whole lemons, for zest

For the topping

Whole lemons, for zest
Sugar, for sprinkling

Put the flour in a bowl and make a well. Put the eggs, milk, sugar, and salt in the well. Stir the eggs and milk together, then gradually draw in flour, mixing to get rid of any lumps. Strain the batter, then stir in the butter. Let rest 1 to 2 hours before using.

Heat a crêpe pan over high heat. Thin out the batter with water to the consistency of light cream. Brush melted clarified butter onto the pan (unless it's nonstick, in which case you need none). Ladle 1 to 2 tablespoons (15 to 30 mL) batter onto the pan, and tip it quickly to cover the bottom. If you have too much batter, pour some off. (Crêpes should be paper thin.) When the edges are brown, flip and cook until the other side is a little golden. As soon as each crêpe is out of the pan, sprinkle with sugar, and grate over a little lemon zest. Roll up. Serve immediately, if possible, or keep the finished crêpes warm under foil until you've finished the others.

PLUM TART PAINTED PURPLE

This is a stunning tart: whole prune plums tucked under a blanket of pastry that gets painted glossy purple with the cooked juices once the tart is out of the oven.

Makes: 8 servings

2 disks sweet galette pastry (p. 9)
3 pounds (1.3 kg) prune plums (quetches)
¼ cup (55 g) sugar
1 egg white, lightly beaten
Crème fraîche, for serving

Heat the oven to 400°F (200°C). On a lightly floured surface, roll one of the pastry disks into a long rectangle, about 5 plums wide plus a 1-inch (2.5 cm) margin on each side. Lay on a baking sheet. Lay down a cobblestone alley of whole plums, leaving a 1-inch (2.5 cm) margin all around. Cut the remaining plums to fill any gaps. Sprinkle over the sugar.

Roll out the second disk of dough into a rectangle slightly larger than the base. Lay it over the plums, and press to seal the edges. Trim the edges neatly so your tart looks like a giant ravioli. Cut two slits in the top of the tart. Paint all over with the egg white for gloss.

Bake until the pastry is flaky and golden, about 25 minutes. The plum juices will have spilled out all over the baking sheet. Dip a pastry brush into them, and paint the tart all over a glossy violet. Serve with crème fraîche.

RASPBERRY TART

There is nothing original about this tart, but originality is often overrated anyway. What's great is that a cookie crust and a creamy filling are a wonderful way to showcase fresh, ripe raspberries in season. I remember seeing a French movie (can't recall the name of it, alas) with a dining scene that took place on the stone terrace of a Provençal château, and the way the women were casually lifting their slices of raspberry tart to their mouths (not with forks, but as if they had slices of pizza in their hands) still makes me groan with envy. It was the sexiest thing. Strawberries, blackberries, or blueberries are options instead of raspberries. And if you like a lighter pastry cream, you can fold ¼ cup (60 mL) heavy cream, whipped, into the cooled pastry cream.

Makes: 8 servings

1 cup (250 mL) milk
½ vanilla bean
3 egg yolks
¼ cup (55 g) sugar
2 tablespoons (30 mL) flour
1 tablespoon (15 mL) raspberry liqueur
1 baked 9-inch (23 cm) cookie pastry tart shell (p. 11), removed from the pan
1 pound (450 g) fresh raspberries

Put the milk in a saucepan. Split the vanilla bean, scraping the seeds into the milk, then drop in the pod. Heat to a simmer, remove from the heat, cover, and let infuse for 10 minutes.

Beat the yolks with the sugar until pale. Beat in the flour. Remove the vanilla bean from the milk, and whisk the milk slowly into the egg mixture. Pour back into the saucepan, bring to the boil, stirring constantly, and cook for 1 minute. Remove from the heat, and stir in the raspberry liqueur. Strain into the tart shell. Cool, and arrange the berries neatly over top. Serve.

LEMON TART

The lemon tart recipe I'm about to share has a golden cookie crust and an intensely lemony filling, the texture of which is somewhere (sublimely) between thick cream and lemon curd. It does, I suppose, call for some explanation, because it is very close to The Lemon Tart of My Dreams in my *French Food at Home* (p. 206), only with more egg yolks and very slight variations on the cream and juice ratios. What can I say: dreams evolve.

It wasn't taste I wanted to improve on (the taste of the original is still excellent – and I just made it, so I am reassured on that point), but I felt that the texture was perhaps more creamy than I seem to want now. Lately I've been craving something firmer. The additional egg yolks achieve this, with the added bonus that they make the tart a much brighter yellow, so that it really says "lemon!" before a bite even gets to your mouth. I suppose this depends too, significantly, on the type of eggs you use, and I strongly recommend farm-fresh eggs from a market to get the ultimate in texture and color. (You could even add another yolk or two if you prefer a more lemon-curd-like texture, but then you're talking about a different tart entirely.)

Now, about the cream. I became very attached to crème fraîche in France. It is more complex than heavy cream because it has a slight tang, but it's not as sharply sour as sour cream. When I'm in a place where I can't buy crème fraîche (woe!), I make the tart with heavy cream instead. I have also used a mixture of half sour cream and half heavy cream as a compromise, but I do not feel that this is an improvement in taste. Sour cream is strong and it competes with the lemon, even when used in small amounts. It also leaves an almost cheesy aftertaste. (This is not a bad thing, just different, so if you like that kind of taste, by all means give it a try.) The only loss with using heavy cream seems to be in texture, and it's not a *great* loss, so I wouldn't lose sleep.

I have been told by honest diners in my home that my lemon tart has a tendency to be too tart. Fair enough: it's true that I prefer my desserts not too sweet. So I increased the sugar by just a few spoonfuls, which pleased everyone. However, I continue to waver on the issue of lemon zest: to add or not to add. Zest does increase the lemon flavor, but at the same time it interrupts that perfectly smooth, puckering, slightly jelled, full-on lemon bite that I'm so crazy about. Well, seeing as I can't even decide for myself, I can scarcely decide for you either: I've left the lemon zest optional.

In *French Food at Home*, I suggested sifting icing over the finished tart. I would never do this now. Increasingly, I like things plain and simple, and, anyway, this tart has such a gorgeous glossy, glassy top, it would be a sin to cover it up. I'll shut up now so you can go make it.

Makes: 8 servings

2 whole eggs + 4 egg yolks
¾ cup (155 g) sugar
¾ cup (175 mL) lemon juice (about 3 lemons)
⅔ cup (150 mL) crème fraîche or heavy cream
Zest of 2 lemons (optional)
1 baked 9-inch (23 cm) cookie pastry tart shell (p. 11)

Heat the oven to 350°F (180°C). Beat together the eggs, yolks, and sugar. Whisk in the lemon juice, then whisk in the cream. Strain into a jug, and stir in the lemon zest. Let the mixture sit for a few minutes to let any bubbles subside.

Skim any foam off the top of the lemon filling. Set the tart shell on a baking sheet in the oven, and pour in the filling. Bake the tart until set but still slightly jiggling in the center, about 25 minutes. The tart will set more as it cools. Serve at cool room temperature.

ROUGH APPLE GALETTE

The best apple galette I have ever eaten was made by my father using apples from an arthritic old tree in our neighbor's garden (no, we didn't steal them; we asked!). I cannot emphasize enough the difference it makes to start with good apples, and old varieties seem best if you can get them. Ask a local apple grower what good baking varieties are local. If you must use grocery apples, Granny Smith and Royal Gala hold their shape nicely.

Makes: 4 to 6 servings

1 disk sweet galette pastry (p. 9)
¼ cup (55 g) brown sugar, more to taste
1 tablespoon (15 mL) flour
½ teaspoon (2 mL) cinnamon
About 6 baking apples, peeled, cored, and sliced
1 tablespoon (15 mL) butter (optional)

Heat the oven to 400°F (200°C). On a lightly floured surface, roll the pastry into a round about ⅛ inch (3 mm) thick and lay on a baking sheet. Stir together the sugar, flour, and cinnamon in a large bowl. Add the apples and toss to coat, then turn onto the pastry, piling them in the middle and leaving several inches of margin. Dot with the butter (if using). Fold the edges of the pastry up so they lie, rough-edged, on the apples. They won't cover the apples completely. Bake until the crust is crisp and golden and the apples are caramelized and soft when pricked with a fork, 40 to 45 minutes. Serve warm or at room temperature.

APPLESAUCE APPLE TART

You get two recipes for the price of one here: an excellent applesauce recipe and the tart recipe itself, which has an applesauce bottom and a top of glazed apple slices. It actually tastes exactly like apple pie, but it looks much more chic, especially if you have a square or rectangular tart shell to bake it in. Now, let me tell you about the applesauce part. First of all, it is the easiest imaginable, because you chop and cook the apples (skins, cores, seeds, and all), then simply run them through the food mill at the end. Second, because the pectin from the seeds ends up in the mix, the applesauce gels somewhat as it cools, so it is the perfect texture for the tart to slice beautifully. Third, thanks to the skins, the applesauce will be a gorgeous, blushing pink. Are you in love yet?

Makes: 8 servings

1 baked 9-inch (23 cm) sweet tart shell (p. 10)
6 applesauce apples, such as Braeburn, unpeeled
¼ cup (55 g) brown sugar
¼ teaspoon (1 mL) nutmeg
2 Royal Gala apples (or other variety that keeps its shape during cooking)
2 tablespoons (30 mL) melted butter
Vanilla ice cream or crème fraîche, for serving

Heat the oven to 400°F (200°C). Chop the applesauce apples, and put them in a saucepan with 2 tablespoons (30 mL) of the sugar, the nutmeg, and ¼ cup (60 mL) water. Cook, stirring occasionally, until very soft. Put through a food mill to remove the skins and seeds. You should have, as a result, about 1½ cups (375 mL) applesauce.

Peel, core, and very thinly slice the Royal Gala apples. Toss with the remaining sugar and the melted butter. Spread the applesauce in the baked tart shell, and arrange the sliced apples over top. Brush the apples with any sugary butter remaining in the bottom of the bowl. Bake until the apple slices are very soft and golden, about 20 minutes, depending on their thickness. Let the tart cool slightly before unmolding. Serve warm (or completely cool for a firmer tart) with vanilla ice cream or a spoonful of crème fraîche.

APPLE ALMOND CREAM TART

The summer before my last year of high school, I went to work as an au pair for a family in Québec with the mission of improving my French. When I think back to it, I wonder why I didn't figure out then that food was my calling, because I spent more of my time cooking and examining what the family ate than I did actively entertaining the children. I still have a recipe notebook from that era with things in it like Andrée's *pâté de campagne* and *croquignoles* (a type of cookie). This apple tart recipe was one of the family specialties, and you are going to love me for giving it to you because it will make you look like a professional pastry chef, and yet it is the easiest tart I know. It has a cookie-style pastry that you simply press into the pan, a creamy middle, and an apple and almond top that tastes heavenly. If you've never braved tart making before, this recipe is for you.

Makes: 6 servings

For the crust

½ cup (110 g) butter
⅓ cup (70 g) sugar
½ teaspoon (2 mL) vanilla
1 cup (125 g) flour

For the cream filling

1 egg
8 ounces (225 g) cream cheese, softened
¼ cup (55 g) sugar
½ teaspoon (2 mL) vanilla

For the topping

3 apples, peeled, cored, and thinly sliced
¼ cup (55 g) sugar
½ teaspoon (2 mL) cinnamon
¼ cup (30 g) slivered almonds or chopped walnuts

Heat the oven to 400°F (200°C). For the crust, cream together the butter and sugar until smooth. Stir in the vanilla. Mix in the flour to make a smooth dough. Press into an 8-inch (20 cm) spring-form pan, going about 1 inch (2.5 cm) up the sides. Bake for 15 minutes or until lightly golden. Remove from the oven, but don't turn off the oven.

While the crust bakes, beat all the ingredients for the cream filling together until smooth. In another bowl, toss the apple slices with the sugar and cinnamon.

Spread the cream mixture in the tart shell. Arrange the apple slices on top, and scatter over the nuts. Bake until the apples are tender and golden, about 40 minutes. Serve warm or at room temperature.

CITRUS SQUASH TART

This is an uplifting alternative to pumpkin pie that, as a local twist on tradition, I used to make for Thanksgiving parties in Paris. The squash provides almost more texture than taste, although the flavor is still faintly there, freshened with citrus and the slight tartness of crème fraîche.

Makes: 8 servings

2 cups (500 mL) puréed cooked buttercup squash
1 cup (250 mL) crème fraîche
¾ cup (155 g) sugar
½ cup (125 mL) blood orange juice, or a combination of orange, grapefruit, and lemon juice
2 eggs
1 teaspoon (5 mL) vanilla
Pinch salt
Pinch nutmeg
1 baked 9-inch (23 cm) sweet tart shell (p. 10)

Heat the oven to 350°F (180°C). Beat together the filling ingredients, and strain into the baked shell. Bake until the custard is just set, about 45 minutes. Cool before serving.

CHOCOLATE TART

A puddingy slice of chocolate with the flavor intensity of a good truffle and just the right degree of wobble is another perfect pairing for a cookie crust. This is a sophisticated dessert to end a late-night dinner with friends.

Makes: 8 servings

1 baked 9-inch (23 cm) cookie pastry tart shell (p. 11)

For the filling

4 ounces (110 g) semisweet chocolate, finely chopped
1 cup (250 mL) heavy cream
½ cup (125 mL) milk
¼ cup (55 g) sugar
1 egg + 1 yolk

For the glaze

3 ounces (85 g) bittersweet chocolate, finely chopped
¼ cup (60 mL) heavy cream

Heat the oven to 325°F (160°C). Put the tart shell on a baking sheet. For the filling, put the chocolate in a bowl. Bring the cream, milk, and sugar to the boil in a saucepan, and slowly pour over the chocolate, stirring to melt. Whisk the egg and yolk in a bowl. Gradually add the chocolate mixture, whisking as you go, and strain into the baked tart shell. Bake until set, about 20 minutes. Cool completely, then remove from the tart pan.

For the glaze, put the chocolate in a small bowl. Bring the cream to the boil, and pour over the chocolate. Stir to melt. Pour over the tart so it coats the top evenly, tipping if necessary. Let set at room temperature for about an hour to firm before serving.

CHERRY TART

This cheerful rustic high-sided tart is ideal for a summer lunch outdoors. It features bright squirts of fresh cherries in a crème fraîche custard, all wrapped in a crumbling crust.

Makes: 8 servings

2 cups (500 mL) sweet cherries, pitted
1 baked high-sided 9-inch (23 cm) cookie pastry tart shell (p. 11)
3 eggs
⅓ cup (70 g) sugar
¾ cup (175 mL) crème fraîche or sour cream
½ teaspoon (2 mL) vanilla

Heat the oven to 375°F (190°C). Arrange the cherries in the crust. Beat the eggs with the sugar, then stir in the crème fraîche and vanilla. Pour the custard over the cherries. Bake until just set, about 25 minutes. Cool before serving.

WHOLE GRAIN STRAWBERRY GALETTE

When I am home in Canada, there is one friend I get together with at least once a week to cook with. We rendezvous in the afternoon to chat and flip through cookbooks (never with any idea what we're going to make before we launch in). Then we cook the day away, in the most gleefully haphazard way, pour ourselves a glass of wine when we're done, and wait for our eaters to show up. This fruit galette is a recipe my friend came up with, and I admit that at the time, I thought she was crazy to be putting strawberries in the oven, especially on a whole grain crust, which I was sure would overwhelm them. (She's the same lunatic who brilliantly put the turmeric and orange juice in the Beurre Blanc, p. 122.) Luckily I kept my mouth shut, because it turned out to be exquisite. The wholesome pastry has a nutty taste that's excellent with strawberries, and the berries don't turn to mush as you might expect but simply get slightly soft and more intense in flavor. A very happy accident indeed.

You may not need all the sugar, depending on the sweetness of your strawberries.

Makes: 6 servings

For the whole grain galette pastry

1⅔ cups (210 g) whole wheat flour
2 teaspoons (10 mL) sugar
¾ teaspoon (4 mL) salt
⅔ cup + 1 tablespoon (155 g) cold butter, cut into small pieces
About ¼ cup (60 mL) ice-cold water

For the filling

½ cup (70 g) ground almonds
3 tablespoons (45 mL) flour
¼ to ½ cup (55 to 95 g) sugar
2½ pounds (1.25 kg) strawberries

Whipped cream, for serving

For the pastry, mix together the flour, sugar, and salt. Add the butter, and, with the fingers, work to a mealy texture. Mix the water in quickly until the dough just holds together. Do not over-mix or the pastry will be tough. Pat into a disk, wrap in plastic, and refrigerate half an hour. Heat the oven to 400°F (200°C).

For the filling, mix the almonds, flour, and ¼ cup (55 g) of the sugar. On a lightly floured surface, roll out the chilled dough into a circle about ⅛ inch (3 mm) thick, and set it on a baking sheet. Spread the almond mixture over the dough, leaving a 3-inch (8 cm) margin. Arrange the strawberries on top. Fold the edges of the dough up over the berries (you won't cover all the berries), and sprinkle over the remaining sugar to taste. Bake for 1 hour. Serve warm with whipped cream.

PRUNE AND APPLE CROUSTADE (PASTIS GASCON)

This is a specialty from the southwest of France, where they make their own type of strudel-y pastry for the base. In France I use brik pastry, but elsewhere I use phyllo pastry from the grocery store and find it works great. Croustade is a half tart/half torte that cuts in a deliciously messy way and makes a wonderful autumn dessert that will have you rethinking your position on prunes.

Makes: 8 servings

1 cup (225 g) dried prunes
⅓ cup (75 mL) Armagnac
6 tablespoons (90 g) butter, melted
4 baking apples, such as Granny Smith, peeled, cored, and cut into cubes
6 tablespoons (125 g) sugar
A squirt of lemon juice (optional)
8 sheets phyllo pastry
Vanilla ice cream, for serving (optional)

Soak the prunes in the Armagnac overnight (or use preserved prunes in Armagnac from a shop, which have even more flavor because they'll have macerated longer). Drain, reserving the liquid, and pit and roughly chop the prunes.

Heat 3 tablespoons (45 mL) of the butter in a sauté pan over medium heat, and cook the apples, turning occasionally, until soft, about 5 minutes. Sprinkle over 2 to 3 spoonfuls of the sugar, depending on the sweetness of the apples, and continue cooking, turning occasionally, until caramelized, about 10 minutes more. Pour over about a spoonful of the reserved Armagnac, carefully light it, and boil until the flames die out and the liquid has disappeared. Remove from the heat, and taste. Depending on your apples, the mixture may need more acidity. If it does, add a squirt of lemon to taste. Stir in the chopped prunes.

Heat the oven to 375°F (190°C). Set the ring part of an 8-inch (20 cm) springform pan on a baking sheet. Working with one sheet of phyllo at a time (keep the rest covered with plastic so it doesn't dry out), lay a sheet of phyllo on a clean surface, and cut into three strips crosswise (not lengthwise). Brush one of the strips with melted butter, and sprinkle with a little sugar and a few drops of reserved Armagnac. Lay another strip on top and repeat. Lay the final strip on top, and brush with butter. Your single sheet of phyllo is now a three-layer-thick strip. Lay it in the ring mold like the spoke of a wheel, so that it runs from the middle out, and up and over the edge of the ring. Continue with the remaining strips, laying them in around the ring, slightly overlapping so that there are no openings. (Don't overlap by too much or the tart will have too thick a bottom.)

Spoon the prune and apple filling into the mold. Fold the pastry strips over the top, twisting somewhat as you go so that the top is a rustic landscape of papery peaks and valleys completely covering the top of the tart. Brush quite generously with melted butter, and scatter over a scant handful of sugar. (You may have some butter and sugar left over once you're done. The same goes for the Armagnac, of which you will have a lot left: use it in fruit salad, or let a piece of pound cake drink it up . . . or serve it in tiny glasses with dessert.)

Remove the springform ring, leaving the formed galette on the baking sheet. Bake until the pastry is fully cooked and golden, about 40 minutes. Slide onto a rack and cool to lukewarm. Serve with ice cream on the side or all on its own.

CHOCOLATE FRAMBOISE

I have carried this recipe around with me since I was about fifteen years old, scrawled in one of my notebooks with insufficient instructions. It was served, I remember ever so vividly, at a formal Easter Sunday lunch hosted by one of the great heroines of my youth, Alexis (whom I wanted to grow up to be exactly like). I don't know why I never made it until recently. Perhaps I was afraid that my version might destroy the beautiful memory I had of it. (You know, like meeting a movie star you've always fantasized about and being crestfallen to discover they're really not interesting after all.) Anyway, I finally broke down and tried it, and luckily it only made the good memory stronger! If you're a chocolate lover, this dessert is nirvana . . . Apologies to Alexis for the outrageous decoration I suggest here. What can I say? It seemed like a good idea at the time, although a friend has told me it is unforgivably tacky.

Makes: 8 servings

12 ounces (330 g) semisweet chocolate, chopped
¾ cup (175 mL) strained unsweetened raspberry purée
½ cup (95 g) sugar
1 cup (225 g) unsalted butter, cubed
5 eggs
1 tablespoon (15 mL) raspberry liqueur
½ cup (125 mL) heavy cream
Several handfuls of fresh raspberries, for garnish

Heat the oven to 350°F (180°C), and bring a full kettle of water to the boil, then turn off the heat. Line a 4-cup (1 L) charlotte mold or metal bowl with foil or parchment.

Put the chocolate, raspberry purée, and sugar in a bowl, set the bowl over a saucepan of simmering water, and heat, stirring occasionally, until the chocolate has melted. Bring to the boil to thicken. Whisk in the butter, a piece at a time, until smooth. Remove from the heat, and beat in the eggs, one at a time, and finally the liqueur. Strain into the mold.

Set the mold in a baking pan that will accommodate it, and pour hot water in to come halfway up the sides of the baking pan. Bake until the mixture has risen and set, about 45 minutes. Remove from the bain-marie and let cool. It will shrink. Cover, and chill overnight.

To serve, unmold onto a serving plate. Whip the cream (you could add a spoonful of sugar to it if you wanted), and spread it over the mound. Working in circles from bottom to top, stick raspberries all over the mound to make it look (vaguely, anyway) like a giant raspberry. Serve, without apology.

MOUSSE AU CHOCOLAT DE MEREDITH

"Everyone is very busy over there making *verrines* these days!" my friend Meredith recently shrilled upon a return trip from Paris. *Verrines* are essentially juice-sized glasses that are filled with everything from crab salads to gazpachos, to puddings. The glasses make easy serving vessels, I suppose, and they do show off what's in them, but it does get exasperating when you can't go anywhere anymore without a *verrine* landing in front of you.

M and I were joking about this one day as I was simultaneously bemoaning my inability to find a chocolate mousse that wasn't too stiff. I had tested a week's worth, and it was beginning to do serious damage to my *self*-worth! I announced I was giving up when Meredith said she had the perfect recipe and not to be so foolish. Here it is, to the rescue, scented with orange zest and liqueur. Now, don't tell Meredith, but with the whipped cream, chocolate shavings, and orange zest that I top this with for embellishment, a verrine, actually doesn't seem like a bad way to serve chocolate mousse at all!

Unlike many mousses, this one doesn't contain cream or butter. If you (or your children) don't like orange in your chocolate mousse, leave out the zest, and replace the Cointreau with a teaspoon (5mL) of vanilla.

Makes: 6 to 8 servings

⅓ cup/70 g sugar
8 ounces/225 g bitersweet chocolate, chocolate
5 eggs, separated
1 tablespoon (5mL) Cointreau
1 teaspoon orange zest
Whipped cream, chocolate shavings and orange zest, for garnish

Put the sugar in the top of a double boiler over simmering water. Pour over ¼ cup/60 ml boiling water, and stir to dissolve. Add the chocolate, and stir to melt into a thick, smooth, shiny pudding-like texture. Remove from the heat, and let cool slightly.

Whisk the egg yolks with the Cointreau and orange zest in a bowl. Gradually whisk in the chocolate mixture. Beat the whites to stiff peaks. Stir a big spoonful of the whites into the chocolate mixture to loosen it up a bit, then gently fold in the remaining whites.

Pour the mousse into a large serving bowl, or into individual coupes (or *verrines*!). Cover, and refrigerate at least four hours to firm up. Serve garnished with whipped cream, chocolate shavings, and a dusting of orange zest.

CRÈME CARAMEL

Do you really need another recipe for crème caramel? Well, I did, even though I already had about two dozen. That's the trouble with classics: there are so many variations that they end up driving you into an obsessive search to find *the* recipe. This one may very well be it. My issue, as we say these days, with crème caramel has always been that it looks glorious – like a full moon reflected on water, what with that dark amber spill of caramel across the pale, wobbly, round face of custard – but too often it tastes like nothing. *Pourquoi?* I've made it over and over again in various ways, and I've come to some valuable conclusions.

First of all, if you cut the eggs down to 3 whole plus 3 yolks, as many recipes do, then the texture becomes the equivalent of a weak handshake. The ratio of eggs to milk in my recipe, however, gives a texture that is smooth and soft/firm, which is how I like it. As for the caramel, you can't be a wimp when you make it. Bravely hold out beyond the point of golden caramel until it becomes dark (without letting it burn, obviously). The reason is that golden caramel tastes very sweet, and that provides no contrast against the similarly sweet custard, whereas a dark, slightly bitter caramel will give the dessert much more complexity. Finally, and perhaps the greatest trick of all, you must not wash the saucepan between making the caramel and infusing the milk. Leave the residue of caramel in the pan and it will join forces with the vanilla to give the milk a richer, vaguely *dulce de leche* flavor, so much more exciting than plain vanilla on its own. So, that's what I've learned so far in this life about crème caramel. I still play around with the recipe (sometimes adding orange zest, or using lime zest and toasted coconut along with coconut milk instead of milk milk), but this basic recipe remains my touchstone. One last thing: serve it slightly chilled; it's even better than at room temperature.

Makes: 6 to 8 servings

2 cups (390 g) sugar
2 cups (500 mL) fresh whole milk
1 vanilla bean
6 eggs
Pinch nutmeg (optional)

Heat the oven to 325°F (160°C). Bring a full kettle of water to the boil, and turn off the heat.

For the caramel topping, dissolve 1 cup (200 g) of the sugar in a medium saucepan with ¼ cup (60 mL) water, and boil, swirling the pan occasionally, until the caramel turns golden and fragrant. Pour into a 9-inch (23 cm) flan or cake pan, and swirl to coat the bottom evenly. Set aside.

Pour the milk into the same saucepan, so that it laps up the caramel on the bottom and sides. Split the vanilla bean, scrape the seeds into the milk, and add the pod. Heat to the boiling point, turn off the heat, cover, and set aside to infuse for 10 minutes. Meanwhile, beat the eggs with the remaining sugar. Add the nutmeg (if using). Once the milk has infused, remove the vanilla pod, and gradually whisk the milk into the egg mixture.

Strain the custard over the hardened caramel, and set the pan in a larger dish or roasting pan. Pour in enough boiled water to come halfway up the sides of the flan pan. Transfer to the oven, and bake until set but slightly jiggly in the center, 45 minutes to an hour.

Remove the flan from the water bath. Run a knife around the outside edge to loosen the flan. Cool completely, then chill. To serve, flip the flan onto a plate, and pour over any caramel remaining in the pan. Serve.

CREAMY STOVETOP RICE PUDDING

In winter, creamy rice pudding is comforting warm, with cinnamon and sugar sprinkled over or with chopped candied orange zest stirred through. In warmer weather, I like it with a handful of berries and fruit coulis on top. Raspberry coulis, for example, is quick. Just whiz a few handfuls of berries up in the blender with sugar to taste, and strain the seeds out.

Makes: 6 to 8 servings

½ cup (110 g) short grain rice
¼ cup (55 g) brown sugar
4 cups (1 L) whole milk
1 vanilla bean
½ cup (125 mL) heavy cream (optional)

Put the rice, sugar, and milk in a saucepan. Split the vanilla bean, and scrape the seeds into the milk, then add the pod. Cook over medium-low heat, uncovered, and stir occasionally to prevent sticking, until the rice has absorbed almost all the milk, about 50 minutes. It should be runny-thick, like tapioca. Remove from the heat, and pluck out the vanilla pod. (You can rinse the vanilla pod and use it again or store in sugar to make vanilla sugar.) Lay a piece of plastic wrap onto the surface to prevent a skin from forming, and cool to warm room temperature.

Whip the cream to firm peaks. Fold as much into the rice mixture as you like. Pour the pudding into a serving bowl, cover, and chill thoroughly. Serve, garnished as you like.

WINTER FRUIT COMPOTE WITH COGNAC

Like fruit salads, compotes get a bad name because of the blasphemous renditions one sees on hotel breakfast buffets. Forget about those, because this compote is heavenly, a perfect make-ahead winter dessert, served slightly warm with a scoop of vanilla ice cream melting alongside. Failing ice cream, crème fraîche and toasted almond slivers are also great.

Makes: 8 servings

8 ounces (225 g) dried prunes
8 ounces (225 g) dried figs, stemmed and halved or quartered
8 ounces (225 g) kumquats
Zest of half a lemon
½ cup (95 g) sugar
¼ cup (60 mL) Cognac
2 cups (500 mL) water

Put everything in a saucepan, and bring to the boil. Cook until the fruits are plump and the sauce syrupy. Turn off the heat, and let the fruit macerate for 30 minutes. Pour into a serving dish (a cut-glass bowl looks lovely), and let cool. Serve.

PUMPKIN MOUSSE

I ripped a similar recipe out of a French cooking magazine because I liked the look of it, but when I made it, it was a vast disappointment. It had coffee in it, which overwhelmed the taste of pumpkin, and it was overloaded with gelatin, which resulted in a strangely dry-textured half pudding/half cake. It was an alien. Still, the idea appealed. So I sent that ragamuffin recipe to finishing school, and after several makeovers, it emerged as this: the most beautiful, pale, and delicate pumpkin mousse you could ever imagine, with impeccable manners and a fetching accent – why, princes would line up to marry it! If you happen to be starting off with a pumpkin or squash on your counter (Hubbard and butternut are good, or a small sugar pumpkin) and are wondering how to turn it into purée, here's your answer: heat the oven to 400°F (200°C); cut the pumpkin into chunks, and peel them; toss with 1 tablespoon (15 mL) butter in a baking dish; cover lightly with foil, and roast until very soft, about 30 minutes, depending on the size of the chunks. Purée in a blender.

Makes: 4 servings

For the mousse

1 tablespoon (15 mL) rum
1 teaspoon (5 mL) gelatin
1¼ cups (300 mL) heavy cream
1 teaspoon (5 mL) vanilla
½ cup (95 g) sugar
1¼ cups (250 g) puréed pumpkin or butternut squash

For the chocolate sauce (optional)

¾ cup (175 mL) heavy cream
4 ounces (110 g) bittersweet chocolate, chopped

For the mousse, stir the rum and gelatin together in a cup, and let soften 5 minutes. In a medium saucepan, heat about a third of the cream with the vanilla until hot. Remove from the heat, and add the gelatin and rum; stir until the gelatin is dissolved. Add the sugar, and stir until dissolved. Finally, mix in the pumpkin. Strain, cool, and refrigerate until starting to get thick.

Whip the remaining cream, and fold it into the chilled pumpkin mixture. Spoon into a serving bowl or individual glasses, cover, and chill at least 4 hours before serving.

For the chocolate sauce (if using), put the cream and chocolate in a saucepan, and gently melt, stirring. If too thick, simply thin out with a little more cream. The sauce will harden as it cools, but you can simply melt it down again before serving. Serve the chocolate sauce dribbled over the pumpkin mousse.

FRESH FRUIT IDEAS

Pineapple Boats

Quarter a ripe pineapple lengthwise, leaving some green top on each piece. Slice off the woody core. Score the flesh down to the skin. Then run a knife between skin and flesh. What you want is for the whole thing to look like it's still intact, but in fact to be cut into cubes for easy eating. You can splash it with rum if you like. Or you can pass around a bowl of whipped cream that you've flavored with rum and brown sugar.

Melon with Raspberries

Halve the melon. Remove the seeds. Fill the well with raspberries or sliced strawberries or both. If you want, add a splash of booze, such as framboise or orange liqueur.

Oranges with Cinnamon

Cut the skin off the oranges, going straight to the flesh and leaving behind no bitter white pith or outer membrane. Discard the skins. Slice the oranges into rounds and arrange on a platter. Sprinkle with cinnamon.

Watermelon with Rosewater

Cut fat, childhood-sized slices of watermelon. (Always buy watermelon with seeds, by the way: I find the seedless kind tend to be woolly-textured and tasteless.) Sprinkle judiciously with rosewater.

Figs with Honey and Fromage Blanc

Choose very ripe figs. Slice them in half lengthwise so they open out like a flower. Arrange them on serving plates with a scoop of fromage blanc alongside. Drizzle over a light honey, such as clover, wildflower, or acacia, and lightly sprinkle, if you like, with toasted pine nuts.

Peach and Blueberry Salad

I don't know how many times I've been told in France not to combine too many fruits for fruit salad. In fact, one friend swears by a "two fruits only" rule (she has the same rule for flower arrangements, now that I think of it). That may be taking things a bit far, but I do agree with the general message that less is more. Sliced peaches tossed with blueberries is a perfect combination, requiring no further embellishment, unless you want a little sugar and cream . . .

NOUGAT GLACÉ

Most French bistro menus have nougat glacé among their dessert offerings, and it's usually what I pick whenever I'm on the fence. I love those cold, snowy slices bejeweled with fruit and nuts, and there's not even an ice-cream machine involved in their making. You can experiment with all kinds of variations of fruit and nuts (chopped dried figs and candied orange zest being one of my favorite combinations). The key is not to use too much, as the fruit and nuts are a garnish in the creamy ice, not the other way around.

Makes: 8 servings

1½ cups (375 mL) heavy cream or crème fraîche
4 egg whites
¼ cup (55 g) + 1 tablespoon (15 mL) sugar
2 tablespoons (30 mL) honey or maple syrup
About ¾ cup (100 g) chopped toasted almonds
About ¾ cup (150 g) assorted chopped dried and candied fruits
Raspberry or other fruit coulis, for serving

Line an 8-inch (20 cm) square pan with plastic wrap, and set aside.

Beat the cream to stiff peaks, and refrigerate. Beat the whites to soft peaks, then sprinkle over a spoonful of the sugar, and continue beating to a stiff, glossy meringue. Set aside, keeping your electric mixer at the ready.

Bring the remaining ¼ cup (55 g) of sugar to the boil with 2 tablespoons (30 mL) water. Let it boil until the syrup forms a thread when thrown in cold water, about 4 minutes (225°F/110°C on a candy thermometer). Now stir in the honey, and bring back to the boil. Run toward the egg whites . . .

With the electric mixer running, add in the whites, and slowly pour the syrup down the side of the bowl for the beaters to pick up and incorporate. Continue beating until the meringue has cooled, which you can tell by feeling the bottom of the bowl. This will take about 10 minutes.

Scatter the nuts and fruits over the meringue. Scoop the whipped cream on top, and gently fold everything together until evenly mixed. Pour into the mold, cover with plastic wrap, and freeze.

To unmold, dip the pan in hot water to loosen, uncover, and flip onto a serving dish. Serve with raspberry or other fruit coulis.

BAKED RHUBARB BATONS

This makes pretty pink legs of rhubarb that hold their shape. Eat them plain, or spread a mixture of mascarpone cheese, lemon zest, and sugar in the bottom of a baked cookie pastry shell (p. 11), and top with this rhubarb and some quartered ripe strawberries.

Makes: 4 servings

¾ pound (375 g) thin pink rhubarb

½ cup (95 g) sugar

Heat the oven to 350°F (180°C). Cut the rhubarb into finger lengths, and put them in a single layer in a baking dish. Scatter over the sugar. Moisten with 1 to 2 tablespoons (15 to 30 mL) water. Bake until just tender but not falling apart, about 20 minutes. Remove to a platter with a spatula. Pour the nice pink syrupy juices over so they pool around the rhubarb. Serve with whipped cream or crème fraîche, ice cream, or meringues, or all three.

PINK GRAPEFRUIT AND ORANGE TERRINE

This is an impressive dessert: the pretty layers of pink and orange citrus are as gorgeous as a flaming sunset, but they taste fresh and cooling.

Makes: 6 to 8 servings

3 pink grapefruits
4 oranges
½ cup (125 mL) sweet white wine
½ cup (95 g) sugar
2 envelopes gelatin
Mint sprigs, for garnish

Peel and section the fruit into a bowl, squeezing out all of the juice from the membranes before discarding them. Measure out ¾ cup (175 mL) of juice, and put it in a saucepan with the wine. Add the sugar, and heat to dissolve. Pour ¼ cup (60 mL) off into a bowl, and soften the gelatin in it for 1 minute. Whisk the gelatin into the juice mixture, and boil for 2 minutes. Cool completely.

Line a 4-cup (1 L) terrine or glass loaf pan with plastic wrap, leaving enough overhang to cover the terrine afterward. Arrange the fruit sections crosswise in the terrine, so the slices of terrine will show half-moon shapes rather than stumps. Pour the liquid over.

Cover with the overhanging wrap, and chill until firm, at least 4 hours and up to 2 days. Garnish with mint sprigs to serve.

WINE JELLY WITH GRAPES

This rather surprising number became one of my top desserts one summer. It is little more effort than setting out a bowlful of grapes to dangle above your lips, but it is, believe it or not, better. The wobbling, glassy wine gelatin, just enough to hold the grapes together, adds a seductive slither to each mouthful and cools everything down in the mouth. I love, too, how the whole grapes pop in the mouth. This is gorgeous to look at, very light, and, considering its simplicity, disproportionately delicious.

Makes: 6 servings

1 tablespoon (15 mL) gelatin
1 cup (200 g) sugar
2 cups (500 mL) dry white or sparkling wine
About 15 ounces (420 g) small seedless red and green grapes
Sweetened whipped cream with vanilla, for serving

Stir the gelatin into 2 tablespoons (30 mL) of water, and set aside to soften. Put the sugar and wine in a saucepan, and heat to dissolve the sugar, without boiling. Remove from the heat, and whisk in the gelatin until completely dissolved. Cool.

Fill six ½-cup (125 mL) ramekins or teacups with the grapes. Pour the wine mixture over them. Cover, and chill for several hours to set. To serve, run a knife around the edge of the molds, and dip the bottoms into hot water for a few seconds, then invert onto serving plates. Serve with the whipped cream alongside.

BAKED APPLES WITH CARAMEL SAUCE

For these classic baked apples, my only advice is to buy organic apples in season (be sure to buy baking apples, not the kind that fall apart when cooked) and that you choose apples that aren't too big. If you do that, you'll have the most perfect autumnal family dessert known to the western world.

If tradition is not what you're in the mood for, how about this: halve apples top to bottom and poke the skin sides with a knife so they don't burst. Set them on a baking sheet, cut side up, sprinkle with sugar and dot with butter. Bake until soft, then serve with a scoop of fresh chèvre, a drizzle of honey, and a scattering of toasted pine nuts and raisins. There: baked apples for a warmer climate.

Makes: 6 servings

6 medium baking apples, such as Northern Spy or Royal Gala
4 to 6 dried figs, stemmed and chopped
About ¼ cup (30 g) chopped almonds, toasted
1 cup (200 g) sugar
⅓ cup + 2 tablespoons (100 g) butter
1 tablespoon (15 mL) heavy cream or crème fraîche
Lemon juice
Cinnamon whipped cream or crème fraîche, for serving

Heat the oven to 350°F (180°C). Core the apples. Using a paring knife, score a ring around the midriff of each apple, just cutting through the skin, to prevent bursting during baking. Stuff the apples with the figs and almonds. Set on a baking sheet, and bake until puffed up and soft all the way through, about 30 minutes.

Meanwhile, put the sugar in a saucepan with a spoonful of water, and boil, swirling the pan occasionally but not stirring, until you have a rich, golden caramel, about 5 minutes, depending on how much water you've added. Don't let it get too dark – it can go from caramel to black in a flash, so keep an eye on it. Remove from the heat, and stir in the butter to melt. Stir in the cream, and add lemon juice to taste.

Serve the baked apples warm from the oven with the sauce poured around and with a generous slump of cinnamon whipped cream or crème fraîche on the side.

SLOW-BAKED HONEY WINE PEARS

After several quiet hours in the oven, wood-hard pears emerge from these honey-wine hot springs heavy and limp with flavor, then they relax onto plates like chubby bathers. I recently discovered that the longer the pears sit in their syrup after cooking, the more ruby colored they get all the way through. Gorgeous served with sweetened, Cognac-scented whipped cream.

Makes: 4 servings

4 Bosc pears or 8 small Anjou pears
1 bottle dry red wine
½ cup (125 mL) honey

Heat the oven to 250°F (120°C). Peel the pears, leaving the stems intact, and lay them in a lidded ovenproof dish just large enough to hold them. Bring the wine and honey to the boil, pour over the pears, cover, and transfer to the oven. Bake 4 to 5 hours, turning now and again, until very tender.

With a slotted spoon, gently remove the pears to a serving bowl. Boil the liquid rapidly until reduced to a syrup, about 20 minutes. Pour over the pears and let sit at room temperature for several hours, or cover and refrigerate until about an hour before serving.

PAIN PERDU WITH SAUTÉED CHERRIES

I went through a phase of believing that French toast of the dessert variety was best made with brioche or challah. Now I am going through a phase where I believe it is best made with day-old baguette. I'm not being cheap. Baguette is less rich and sweet, and it makes an absolutely delicious dessert. Try a mixture of cherries and blackberries or sautéed peaches or plums in season, too.

Makes: 4 servings

For the cherries

2 tablespoons (30 mL) butter
2 to 3 tablespoons (30 to 45 mL) sugar, more to taste
2 pounds (900 g) cherries

For the pain perdu

1 cup (250 mL) milk, more if needed
1 teaspoon (5 mL) vanilla
4 thick slices day-old baguette
1 egg
2 tablespoons (30 mL) sugar, more for caramelizing
1 tablespoon (15 mL) unsalted butter

Vanilla ice cream, for serving

For the cherries, melt the butter in a medium sauté pan over medium heat. Add the cherries, turn the heat to high, and cook, stirring occasionally, for about 2 minutes. Scatter over the sugar, and continue cooking until the cherries break down somewhat, about 2 minutes more. Set aside.

For the pain perdu, stir together the milk and vanilla in a shallow dish, and soak the bread slices in it for about 5 minutes, turning once so that they absorb the milk evenly. Beat the egg with the sugar, and pour onto a plate. Heat the butter in a frying pan over medium heat until sizzling. Take the bread from the milk, holding it above the bowl to drain slightly. Dip into the egg mixture to coat both sides, then drop into the sizzling butter, and fry until golden brown, about 5 minutes per side.

At the last minute, sprinkle the tops with a little extra sugar, and "broil" with a kitchen blowtorch (or place them on a baking sheet under the broiler until the sugar melts, bubbles, and turns golden).

Divide the bread among serving plates. Serve hot with a scoop of ice cream and a spoonful of sautéed cherries.

ORANGES WITH CARAMEL AND CANDIED ZEST

This is a proper dessert, not just sliced fruit. You get squirts of fresh orange flesh, a smooth, tongue-coating syrup, chewy candied zest, plus crunchy toasted almonds and whipped cream. It's light, therefore perfect after a big meal, and, however minimalist, it is glorious served in a cut-glass bowl by candlelight.

Makes: 4 servings

4 organic oranges, scrubbed clean
2 cups (390 g) sugar
1 cup (250 mL) water, more as needed
¼ cup (15 g) slivered almonds, lightly toasted
Lightly sweetened whipped cream, for serving

Slice the ends off the oranges and discard. Working from the top to the bottom, slice the peel off in strips to reveal the orange flesh. Cut the white pith from the back of the peel with a sharp knife. Slice the orange peel into fine julienne strips, put in a saucepan, cover with cold water, and bring to the boil. Drain, and rinse under cold running water. Repeat this process three times. Drain a final time, and set aside.

Working over a bowl to catch the juices, cut between the membranes to section the oranges. Put the sections in the bowl, and squeeze any juice from the membranes over them. Set aside.

In a sauté pan or large heavy saucepan over medium-high heat, melt the sugar, swirling the pan occasionally but not stirring, and let it become amber in color without letting it burn. Add the water and the juice that has pooled around the orange sections. Leave on the heat until the caramel dissolves again (it will have seized). Add the drained julienne of zests, and boil until they turn translucent and become candy coated with a dark amber color, 5 to 10 minutes. The zest will be sweet and chewy with a faint hint of bitterness and intense orange flavor.

Add about 4 spoonfuls of this caramel with candied orange to the orange segments, and toss. Cover, and set aside in a cool place until serving. Cool the remaining caramel somewhat. If it's too thick, thin it out with a bit of water to achieve a thick syrup. Store in a jar in the refrigerator for other uses (it will keep for at least six months).

Serve the oranges with their caramel and candied peel, garnished with the lightly toasted almond slivers and whipped cream.

LE CAFÉ

The Italians may make the best coffee, but the French are better at drinking it. In Italy, coffee is usually taken standing up and on the run, and it's hard to get it served hot because most people want it gluggably lukewarm so they can knock it back like cough medicine and fly out again in under ten seconds. Mind you, that beats the North American way, which is to buy coffee by the half-liter in a cardboard cup and sip it through a plastic top while scrambling down the street. France beats us all hands down. There, café culture is much more leisurely: people sit, take their time, chitchat, and make coffee more of a pause. However out of sync it may be with the modern world, the French way, you must admit, is the most civilized.

What I miss most about French cafés when I am out of range is not the coffee (I'm a tea drinker anyway). What I yearn for is old-world service, which includes getting served a glass of water with coffee without having to ask for it, because the waiters know that to be fully restored one must be hydrated as well as caffeinated. I also miss the nice little chocolate they balance on the edge of your saucer of espresso (I always eat it). And, above all, I miss the people-watching and the eavesdropping. I remember having a coffee in the Big Ben Bar at the Gare de Lyon once while waiting for a train. It was before noon, and a couple beside me were having a bottle of Champagne and foie gras, talking and giggling away as if all the clocks in the world had stopped. I watched them out of the corner of my eye, and when their bill came, the waiter asked if they wanted to pay cash or by credit card. The woman gasped, "I pay cash! *Mais, bien sûr!* One always pays cash! One must never leave a trace!"

The liveliness of a French café may not be easily exported, but taking coffee in slow motion is a tradition easily replicated *chez soi.* The most important habit is to set aside a little peaceful time to savor it; making it is nothing. I prepare my home coffee in one of those double-decker metal coffee pots so common in Europe, because I like the ritual of making it "by hand" and because the aesthetics are so appealing. The exact measurements are built right into those pots, so the strength of the coffee is just so, every time. I love the quiet, gurgling sound that the coffee makes as it chugs up though the alembic mechanics, from the bottom vessel, up a central spout, spritzing out and pooling down dark and hot into the top. Coffee from these pots is strong, ideal for after-dinner coffee, which, by the way, in France is served at the very, very end of a meal, after dessert, rather than with it.

Morning coffee, the kind with a frothy, milky top, which the French call *café crème,* is not so different. I prepare the coffee part exactly the same way as short dinner coffee, only in the morning I pour it into a wide-brimmed cup, then top it up with hot, thick, frothed whole milk. It tastes so warm and good – as good as *café crème* in any French café – and I love how the first sip makes a milky mustache above your lip, for licking off as you reach for *Le Monde.*

And then there is afternoon coffee and people dropping by for it the way they would tea where I come from. Here are a few *petits fours* you might want to have along with it.

LEMON MADELEINES

I am not one to own a zillion different types of molds, but I can make space in my cupboard for a few, especially if they have a certain romance about them, which madeleines do. I admit that, given my upbringing, I'm more likely to have a Proustian moment with a plate of baked beans than with these delicate scalloped lemon-scented cakes. All the same, as a tea drinker with a love of literature, I can only adore them.

Makes: about 2 dozen biscuits

1 cup + 2 tablespoons (150 g) flour
½ teaspoon (2 mL) baking powder
Pinch salt
⅔ cup + 1 tablespoon (155 g) butter
½ cup + 2 tablespoons (125 g) granulated sugar
1 tablespoon (15 mL) brown sugar
1 tablespoon (15 mL) honey
4 eggs
Zest of 1 lemon, more to taste

Grease two madeleine tins, and set them in the freezer. Heat the oven to 400°F (200°C).

Sift together the flour, baking powder, and salt. Melt the butter, and stir in the granulated sugar, brown sugar, and honey. Lightly beat the eggs, and gradually whisk the butter mixture over them. Finally, whisk in the flour mixture to make a smooth batter. Pour into the molds, filling them three-quarters of the way. Bake until the cakes are puffed up, golden around the edges, and cooked through, 10 to 12 minutes. Turn out onto a rack, and let cool.

WALNUT FINANCIERS

Here's another French tea-cake specialty, usually made of almonds (so feel free to substitute if that's what you have). The thin, rectangular molds these are baked in, called financiers, result in crisp-edged cakes with moist, chewy middles, quite distinct from cakes baked in other shapes. If you find yourself resorting to muffin tins, just be sure to fill them only halfway.

Makes: about 20 cakes

⅔ cup (140 g) unsalted butter
1½ cups (200 g) icing sugar
1 cup (125 g) ground walnuts
½ cup (60 g) flour
5 egg whites (unbeaten)
2 tablespoons (30 mL) Cognac or 1 teaspoon (5 mL) vanilla

Heat the oven to 450°F (230°C). Melt the butter in a small saucepan, and set aside to cool. Combine the sugar, walnuts, and flour in a bowl. Stir in the egg whites and Cognac. Finally, whisk in the melted butter.

Fill the financier tins three-quarters full only. Put them on a baking sheet, and bake 5 minutes. Reduce the oven temperature to 400°F (200°C), and continue baking until they are golden on top and a toothpick inserted in the center comes out clean, about 10 minutes more. If you're working in batches, don't forget to turn the oven back up to starting temperature before putting the next batch in. Unmold onto racks to cool.

BRANDY SNAPS

You can't really call these cookies, because they are as insubstantial as bridal veils, delicate rounds of brandy-flavored, caramel-colored lace, very feminine and fragile. They are perfect for when you want a little crumbling textural crunch alongside a creamy dessert such as mousse or ice cream. They are also nice with espresso as a dinner finale.

Makes: about a dozen cookies

2 tablespoons (30 mL) sugar
2 tablespoons (30 mL) golden syrup
¼ cup (55 g) butter
2 teaspoons (10 mL) brandy
¼ cup (30 g) flour

Heat the oven to 350°F (180°C). Lightly butter a baking sheet. Melt the sugar, syrup, and butter together in a saucepan. When it starts to bubble, remove from the heat, and beat in the brandy and flour.

Making only 6 cookies at a time, place a teaspoon of the batter for each cookie, spaced well apart, on the baking sheet. Bake until flat and golden, 5 to 7 minutes. Let cool on the sheet a few seconds, just until they are firm enough to move but still pliable. Remove with a spatula and drape over a rolling pin, or simply leave flat on a rack. Carry on with baking the second batch. Store in an airtight container.

CANNELÉS

This is my friend Isabelle's recipe for *cannelés,* the rum-scented, fluted *petits fours* that are famous in Bordeaux. I remember friends trying recipe upon recipe in France trying to imitate what they tasted in the shops and never quite getting it. Isabelle's recipe has it bang on. You need special molds for these, so inquire at your local kitchen shop.

Makes: 18 mini cannelés

1 cup (250 mL) milk
2 tablespoons (30 mL) butter
½ cup (60 g) flour
½ cup + 1 tablespoon (110 g) sugar
1 egg + 1 egg yolk
1½ teaspoons (7 mL) rum
½ teaspoon (2 mL) vanilla extract

Bring the milk and butter to the boil together in a saucepan. Stir the flour and sugar together in a bowl. Beat the egg and yolk together, and stir into the flour. Slowly whisk in the hot milk mixture until the batter is thin and completely smooth. Stir in the rum and vanilla. Cover the batter and let it sit in the refrigerator for several hours or overnight.

Heat the oven to 450°F (230°C). Pour the batter into the molds, set the molds on a baking sheet, and bake 15 minutes. Reduce the oven temperature to 350°F (180°C), and continue baking until dark brown, 45 minutes to an hour more. The cakes are meant to be quite dark on the outside. Unmold and cool before serving.

CRISP CHEWY MERINGUES

These are the best meringues I have ever eaten, and I love how they look: like clouds fallen right out of the sky onto your favorite china plate. I am not a fan of the bedroom-slipper-sized, rock-hard poof meringues sold in French pastry shops. I prefer crunchy-outside, marshmallowy-in-the-middle meringues, like these. You can make one enormous round of meringue (cooking time will change a bit), and top it with cream and fruit for pavlova, or top it with chocolate pudding and cream, or with lemon curd and cream and raspberries . . . Or you can make mini meringues in "kiss" shapes and sandwich them with whipped cream, flavored or not. You can dip plain meringues in chocolate. Or you can leave them plain, like here, to eat with fruit desserts or coffee.

Makes: about 16 cake-of-soap-sized meringues

4 egg whites
Pinch salt
1 teaspoon (5 mL) vanilla (or orange flower water, or maple extract, or, or, or)
Pinch cream of tartar
⅔ cup (140 g) granulated sugar
⅔ cup (85 g) icing sugar
1 tablespoon (15 mL) cornstarch

Heat the oven to 225°F (110°C). Whip the whites with the salt to soft peaks, add the vanilla, and continue beating to stiff peaks. Stir the cream of tartar into the granulated sugar, and whisk into the whites a spoonful at a time, until the sugar has dissolved and the meringue is stiff and glossy. Sift together the icing sugar and cornstarch. Sift over the meringue, and gently fold until fully incorporated.

Pipe or spoon the meringues onto a parchment-lined baking sheet. Bake until cream-colored and crisp on top when tapped, 1 to 1½ hours. Cool on the baking sheets. Store in an airtight container.

LE DIGESTIF

I doubt that the strong after-dinner drinks of the digestif category do anything to help actual food digestion, although one could argue that they help to digest the more social aspects of an evening, say, the finer points of a scandal revealed by D, the overall effect of M's new hairstyle, the success of your first beef Wellington (p. 164), etc. I am not a great consumer of digestifs myself, because by the time they come around I'm usually falling asleep. Still, I like the idea. There's something very cozy about a smooth, strong drink designed for sipping late into the night . . .

It's precisely this intimate quality of digestifs that makes them worthy of contemplation. Dinner in its own right is very *tête-à-tête,* no matter how many *têtes* – two, twelve, or twenty – are at the table. We reveal so much about ourselves over dinner, and, whether we intend to or not, we get close. Food and wine have that power, at best, to draw us together and connect us for a few hours in an atmosphere that keeps hard reality at bay. One way to view digestifs is as a lingering moment in that blissful bubble . . . topped up with a shot of *vieille prune!*

I don't mean to suggest that this is about the alcohol, because it isn't (herbal teas do the same trick). Rather, it's about stretching the beautiful time you're having so you can savor it longer. After-dinner drinks are worth making the most of, because they become the interlude between all the warmth and sharing that was dinner and the moment where you're thrust back into the cold night air to find your way home again. (Sorry, it had to happen eventually . . .) Anyway, I like their message: they're reminders that dinner isn't just body fuel but a tightening of social and spiritual knots.

Before I get too philosophical (how many digestifs has she *had*?!), we'd better get to logistics. What do we need in the cupboard if we want to create one of these lovely, intimate intervals at the end of a dinner party? I am no doubt the last one to ask, since I am *nul,* as the French say, in my knowledge of hard alcohols. Besides, as I said, I have a hard time staying awake after 10 p.m. at the best of times. However, I did once share a house with a Frenchwoman (Isabelle of the *cannelés,* p. 289) who had the most staggering selection of digestifs I have ever seen in my life, and that was quite an education.

The two best known French digestifs are Cognac and Armagnac (both brandies distilled from wine and aged in oak). They're heart-warming (and I mean literally), and call for glasses with a big bowl for swirling and admiring the contents, as well as for cupping in the hand to warm the liquid slightly. To me, they're both very sensuous elixirs: I could hold a glass up to candlelight and swish it around all night just admiring the twinkling color, never mind drinking. Since these are long, slow drinks, they're ideal for sipping with just one or two other people, as you sit up late at night by a flickering fire solving all the problems of the universe.

When my parents visited me in Burgundy a few years ago, they bought me a dozen thimble-like silver cups from an antique shop in Beaune, designed for the purpose of having a nip of *eau-de-vie* after dinner. (I have used them precisely once in five years, and I feel slightly guilty about it. That said, imagine what you'd think of me if I'd said, "I've used them so many times I can't count!") Anyway, *eaux-de-vie* are another option, usually served in small snifters or even in shot glasses of some kind. They are distilled fruit drinks as clear and powerful as vodka, only unlike vodka, they taste of the fruits that they're distilled from. You see them a lot in the French countryside, where people like to bring out bottles of their own homemade versions. Vieille Prune (prune), Mirabelle (plum), and Poire Williams (pear) are probably the best known, although there are many others. Just so you know: *eau-de-vie* translates as "water of life," and this holds true if you allow yourself just a splash after dinner. More than a splash, and *eau-de-vie* quickly becomes "water of death." (That was a warning.)

Another famous French digestif is marc (most often "de Bourgogne"). Like Italian grappa, it's made from pressed and fermented grape seeds and skins; but unlike grappa (and unlike *eau-de-vie*), it is aged in wood and so takes on not only a hint of woodsy flavor but also an attractive tawny color. Then there's calvados, the famous apple brandy from Normandy. It's aged in oak casks, too, and it's golden and blazing as it trickles down your throat. In Normandy, it's often served partway through a meal as a means of clearing a path for the main course. (Whatever happened to sorbet?) It's referred to as a *trou Normand,* or "Norman hole," for that reason.

There are so many more digestifs, and not just French either. Personally, though, I go for quality over quantity, so I never have more than a few in my cupboard: a nice Cognac perhaps, one fruity *eau-de-vie,* and, with a surname like mine, a decent whisky. I also like to have rum in the house for hot toddy when I'm feeling under the weather (rum, honey, and lemon juice, topped up with boiling water). Otherwise, I tend to lean toward herbal teas. They're not digestifs proper, but they can certainly stand in. Chamomile is soothing and helps you get to sleep; mint is good for the stomach; ginger is heaven on a sore throat, and so on. Plus, the greatest advantage of herbal infusions over spirits is that you can keep them coming. That way you can stay up even longer digesting a lovely evening by candlelight.

44

This is a very attractive glug to have in a jar on the pantry shelf for 44 days. The liqueur is quite sweet and pleasantly flavored with coffee and orange. Winter holiday is a great time to bring it out and serve it in pretty liqueur glasses.

Makes: 1 quart (1 L)

1 large organic orange, well scrubbed
44 coffee beans
44 sugar cubes
4 cups (1 L) vodka

Poke the orange with the tip of a knife or knitting needle, and push the coffee beans through the slits and into the orange flesh. Put the orange in a sterilized preserving jar, add the sugar, pour over the vodka, seal, and shake. Store in a cool, dark place, giving the jar a shake every day for 44 days. Filter the liqueur through a coffee filter into a serving bottle.

Index

D

E

H

I

K

L

M

Q

R

S

T

V

W

Z

SPECIAL THANKS TO . . .

- my editor, Kirsten Hanson, at HarperCollins Canada, for persevering to get this book published in the first place, and for editing it with such attention to detail and quality;
- copy editor Shaun Oakey, for his extremely careful and patient work on the manuscript (and also for his sense of humor);
- designer Sharon Kish, for the beautiful book design, which I adore;
- Aaron Milrad, my legal representative on this book, for handling the contract with such care;
- Johanna Eliot, producer of the television series *French Food at Home,* who was very kind to lend me her kitchen for the photography of this book, and without whose collaboration French food may never have returned to television;
- Halifax-based photographer James Ingram, for the beautiful photography in this book;

- food and props stylist Patti Hetherington, for making the food look great for James's lens, and for all her professional advice as food producer on *French Food at Home;*
- my friends fellow food writer Jennifer McLagan and her husband, Haralds Gaikus, who housed me, fed me, lent me their kitchen for recipe testing, shared recipes, doled out endless excellent advice, and generally put up with me (on two continents) more than most friends could stand;
- all my cooking friends, but in particular those who shared recipes with me that appear in this book – Camille Labro, Anne Willan, Chris Mooney, Ivan Simmonds, Deborah Madison, Patti Hetherington, David Tanis, and Bridget Oland;
- to the many friends who supported me not only through the writing of this book but through the ups and downs of my whole food venture this past decade (you know who you are!);
- to all the readers and viewers who have so kindly written to me at www.lauracalder.com with appreciation for my television series and writing;
- and to my family for their never-ending support and encouragement.

A NOTE ON THE TYPE

This book was set in Adobe Garamond™, designed in 1989 by Robert Slimbach. Its roman weights are based on the typeface created by Claude Garamond (ca. 1480–1561) and its italics on those of punchcutter Robert Granjon (1513–1589).